100 THINGS AVALANCHE FANS SHOULD KNOW & DO BEFORE THEY DIE

Adrian Dater

D1053725

TRIUMPH
B O O K S

Library of Congress Cataloging-in-Publication Data

Names: Dater, Adrian, author.
Title: 100 things Avalanche fans should know & do before they die / Adrian Dater.
Other titles: One hundred things Avalanche fans should know and do before they die
Description: Chicago, Illinois : Triumph Books LLC, [2016]
Identifiers: LCCN 2016003186 | ISBN 9781629371719
Subjects: LCSH: Colorado Avalanche (Hockey team)—History. | Colorado Avalanche (Hockey team)—Miscellanea.
Classification: LCC GV848.C65 D376 2016 | DDC 796.962/640978883—dc23 LC record available at http://lccn.loc.gov/2016003186

This book is available in quantity at special discounts for your group or organization. For further information, contact:

Triumph Books LLC
814 North Franklin Street
Chicago, Illinois 60610
(312) 337-0747
www.triumphbooks.com

Printed in U.S.A.
ISBN: 978-1-62937-171-9
Design by Patricia Frey
Photos courtesy of AP Images unless otherwise indicated

100 THINGS AVALANCHE FANS

SHOULD KNOW & DO

BEFORE THEY DIE

For my wife, Heidi, and son, Tommy

Contents

Foreword

In May 1995 I was a 25-year-old hockey player who had spent my life to that point playing in Canada—as a kid in Burnaby, British Columbia; as a junior in Swift Current, Saskatchewan; and as an NHL player in Quebec City. But one day in May 1995, my Nordiques teammates and I got some shocking news: we would all be moving, starting in a few months, to play hockey in the United States, in Denver, Colorado.

Most of us had barely even heard of Denver. The only things most of us knew were that John Elway played quarterback for the Broncos and that it was supposed to have a lot of snow. Little did I know that I would spend the rest of my playing career in Denver, that my children would all be born there, and that my family and I would call it home to this day.

Quebec City will always be a special place for me, as I started my career there and the fans are great hockey fans. But mostly all I knew as a player there was losing. That all changed when the franchise relocated to Denver and became known as the Colorado Avalanche.

I was very fortunate to be the captain of the Avalanche from 1995 until I retired in 2009. We won a lot of games and were fortunate enough to win two Stanley Cups in that time. The fans of Colorado supported us tremendously right from day one, and I can speak for all the players in saying they played a big part in our fast success in Denver.

Winning is what you strive for as a player, and it is the thing you remember and savor the most as a player. That's why so many of my former teammates and I have so many great memories to look back on as players in Denver.

Adrian Dater covered our team for every year I played in Denver, and more after that. He has done a great job telling the stories of what made the Avalanche such a memorable team, and some of the things that make Denver and Colorado such a special place.

This book tells stories of the people and events that made for a great first 20 years of the Avalanche's time in Denver. Hopefully there will be other books someday that recount other memories and success stories for the Avalanche. It was always with tremendous pride that I was able to wear the Avalanche logo on my sweater, a logo that didn't even exist on that May day in 1995.

This book is a must-have for Avalanche fans who want to know how it all happened. To have played a part in many of the fun stories in this book will always be a humbling thing for me.

So thank you, Avalanche fans, for playing such a big part in all of this too. Without the people of Denver and Colorado as a whole, none of this book could ever have been written.

—Joe Sakic

1
May 24, 1995: The NHL Returns to Denver

I still remember the phone call from Paul Jacobson, the media relations director for COMSAT Video Enterprises. It came at about 7:00 PM on May 24, 1995.

"The team is ours," Jacobson told me.

The team was the Quebec Nordiques, and it had just been sold to COMSAT, a company whose main business was the burgeoning advent of movies-on-demand, particularly in hotel rooms. COMSAT also owned the NBA's Denver Nuggets, and now they had another tenant to play at McNichols Sports Arena.

I knew this wouldn't be a pure scoop for my newspaper, the *Denver Post*. While I got the original (front-page!) scoop on February 18 that COMSAT had put in a $75 million offer for the Quebec Nordiques, the actual sale went down on the night of the 24th. With no viable Internet then, you had to hold on to any breaking news until the paper went to press in the wee hours of the morning. Yes, kids, that's how things used to be done.

Jacobson said it was only fair that he also call reporter Curtis Eichelberger of the rival *Rocky Mountain News*, who had been my competitor on the story for the previous few months. I was a stringer for the *Post*, paid by the story (usually no more than $40, which is what I got for that front-page scoop in February), and Eichelberger was a full-time staffer at the *News*, but that was fine. I had a feeling I'd become a full-time staff writer myself soon, and thanks to the *Post*'s sports editor, Mike Connelly, that's exactly what happened on June 6, 1995. Connelly could have hired some experienced NHL beat writer and just told a part-time, no-benefits kid like me "Sorry, but you're not ready yet," but to my everlasting gratitude, he gave me the shot.

For the next 19 years, I would cover the soon-to-be renamed Colorado Avalanche as the regular beat writer. More important, on May 24 the good citizens of Colorado got an NHL team again. The growing economy of Denver, the good geography of the state, and a league that had good momentum in the US all were big factors in the city getting a rare second chance at NHL hockey. From 1976

As fireworks light the arena behind him, Colorado Avalanche goalie Stephane Fiset skates on to the ice as the first member of the new team to be introduced to the home crowd.

to 1982 the city had a team called the Colorado Rockies, but it was a tire fire from day one. Bad trades, bad draft picks, and short-pocketed ownership led to the sale of the team in 1982 to John J. McMullen, and a transfer to the New Jersey Meadowlands, where they were renamed the Devils.

One of the first quotes I got from an anonymous NHL executive (and I don't even remember who it was now) after the sale was, "Denver is going to get itself one hell of a team." That would prove to be an understatement.

The Colorado Avalanche was a juggernaut right away in the Mile High City. They (technically the Colorado Avalanche is an *it*, but this my book and I'm calling them a *they* from here on out, and wow, does that feel good) won the Stanley Cup their first season in town. They would go on to advance to the Western Conference Finals in five of the next six seasons, winning another Cup in 2001. They would win a division title in their first eight years in Denver and, combined with one in 1994 in Quebec, would establish a new NHL record.

The next 10 years didn't go as well. As of 2016 no Avs team had reached the conference finals in 14 years. The great players either retired or left because the team could no longer afford them. Despite several high first-round draft picks, the team missed the playoffs several times and saw steep drops in attendance after setting an NHL record with 487 straight sellouts.

The Avs are likely to have a stronghold on the people of Colorado for a long time, however. They were the first team to give the city and state a major pro sports championship. They had several Hall of Fame players, and there was rarely a hint of public scandal with anyone in the organization. They jump-started the passion for hockey in the state to the point that dozens of new youth leagues were formed and many new rinks built.

The following 99 chapters take a closer look at the people who made the Avalanche a special team, along with what made, and continues to make, the surrounding area a great place to live or visit. A lot of the book is written in the first person, which I hope you'll forgive me for doing. But I was there for it all, and I feel well qualified to tell their story in a more personal way.

I hope whoever tells the next 20 years of the Avs' story has as much fun as I did in the first 20.

2 One Year, One Stanley Cup

The Quebec Nordiques played in the NHL for 23 years, without ever winning a Stanley Cup or even making it to a Cup Final. By the summer of 1996, the newly renamed Colorado Avalanche had played one season in Denver and won one Stanley Cup. Life isn't fair.

Quebec City is an astonishingly pretty place, founded in 1608 by Samuel de Champlain. Fortified walls, called ramparts, surround the city, remnants of the many battles it saw, including those from the American Revolution (the American Revolutionaries lost the battle, which is why the city stayed in the hands of British rule). The St. Lawrence River runs through it, and the city's name was derived from the Algonquin word *Kebec*, which means "Where the river narrows."

The sport of ice hockey was founded in nearby Montreal, with the first organized game being played in 1875. It quickly spread to Quebec City, where for more than a century a deep passion for the game was ingrained in most inhabitants.

By 1995, however, financially supporting an NHL team became a problem in Quebec City. There were plenty of people to fill the Colisee Pepsi arena but not enough fat-cat corporations to spend $100,000 a year or more on the newly created luxury boxes. So the Quebec Nordiques of 1994–95 became the Colorado Avalanche of 1995–96.

Pierre Lacroix, the general manager, remembered when he first stepped foot on Denver soil on June 1, 1995. The team still didn't have a new name, most everything from the Nordiques days was boxed up to the ceiling of the team's new workplace, McNichols Sports Arena, and players with children needed to be moved in by July because of new school registration deadlines.

Despite all the off-ice chaos that surrounds any franchise relocation, the Avalanche won a championship that first season. The team was already blessed with a solid roster, partially built through years of failure that resulted in high draft picks, and astute trades. One of the biggest and best, an incredible blockbuster that sent Eric Lindros to Philadelphia for several players and draft picks and $15 million in cash, would yield a Hall of Famer in a young Swede named Peter Forsberg.

Former Nordiques owner Marcel Aubut, a rotund, flamboyant throwback of a character, actually traded Lindros twice at the same time—once to the New York Rangers and once to the Flyers. An arbitrator named Larry Bertuzzi—the uncle of a kid named Todd who would later play a role in Avs history—had to sort out the mess, eventually deciding in favor of the Flyers.

The crippling economics of modern sport in a small market forced Aubut to sell the team for $75 million, with the final transaction coming in a San Francisco hotel conference room on May 24, 1995. Aubut's hand trembled as he signed the official deal, as he knew he would instantly be cast by many in his home city as as the villain who let the Nordiques leave town.

The Avs were already an excellent team in the early stages of the 1995–96 season, but Lacroix was convinced they wouldn't become a champion until three significant areas were upgraded. The first was in goal, where despite promising young netminders named

Stephane Fiset and Jocelyn Thibault, the team was unproven. On December 6, 1996, Lacroix stunned the hockey world by acquiring two-time Stanley Cup champ and three-time Vezina Trophy winner Patrick Roy.

The team also needed a veteran forward who could add some grit and who had won Cups before to help mentor the young talent up front. That need was addressed with the acquisition of Claude Lemieux for holdout Wendel Clark (technically Lemieux was acquired for Steve Thomas as part of a three-way deal involving the New York Islanders and New Jersey Devils).

The third area to upgrade was an offensive defenseman, someone who could help give the team more of a two-pronged attack. Enter Sandis Ozolinsh, who was acquired within the first month in a straight-up deal for promising forward Owen Nolan.

Despite those three deals, the Avs entered the 1996 playoffs as considerable underdogs to represent the Western Conference in the Championship Finals against the Detroit Red Wings, a mighty team that had amassed 62 wins, including a 7–0 win over Colorado late in the season.

The Avs almost didn't make it out of the first round, but they hung tough to overcome early jitters and beat the Vancouver Canucks in six games. In that series, the Avs got some luck with the absence of Canucks star forward Pavel Bure, who was injured. A multiple 60-goal scorer and future Hall of Famer, Bure no doubt would have made things much more difficult for a team whose defense, as Canucks coach Pat Quinn memorably put it, had "some marshmallows back there."

In the second round, against a very tough Chicago Blackhawks team, the Avs got more good fortune. Top goalie Ed Belfour, along with Murray Craven, missed Game 2 allegedly after getting sick eating lyonnaise potatoes at a Denver Morton's restaurant (Morton's denied it, or that anyone else got sick). Tony Amonte was lost early in the series to a leg injury, and All-Star defenseman Chris Chelios missed a game because of a listed "equipment problem" that was actually his leg being numb from an overinjection of cortisone by the Chicago team doctor. Down 2–1 in the series, the Avs were on the brink of going down 3–1 when Chicago star Jeremy Roenick came in on a breakaway on Roy but never got a shot off after being blatantly hooked from behind by Ozolinsh. Referee Andy Van Hellemond, who had blown a call against the Nordiques to cost a game in a playoff series the year before against the Rangers, swallowed his whistle.

Joe Sakic one-timed Alexei Gusarov's pass past Belfour in triple overtime to even the series, and the Avs would prevail in six games, winning Game 6 on a double-overtime goal by Ozolinsh.

In the Western Conference Finals against the Wings, the Avs quickly fell behind in Game 1 on a Paul Coffey goal, but then good fortune started to smile once again. Playing a puck on net from deep in the left corner, Stephane Yelle's shot would have sailed harmlessly to the other side of the ice if it hadn't been touched. But inexplicably, Coffey shot the puck right into his own net. It was as if he had temporarily thought he played for the Avs and was trying to one-time a pass in from a teammate. The Avs pulled out a 3–2 OT win on a long shot by Mike Keane, and Roy was sensational in a 3–0 Game 2 shutout at Joe Louis Arena.

The Avs won two of the next four games to close out the series, but not before a major rivalry was started between the two teams that would dominate the NHL for most of the next six years.

That left one opponent to conquer for the Cup. It would be a young franchise named the Florida Panthers, an underdog group that relied on a defensive system that had come into vogue in the league called the neutral-zone trap.

In Game 1, at McNichols Arena (where upper-bowl seats cost as little as $16, a ridiculously low amount compared to today's prices), the Panthers were playing the trap to perfection by late in the second period. They had a 1–0 lead on a fluky Tom Fitzgerald goal, which was looking like it might be enough for goalie John Vanbiesbrouck.

But then the Avs struck for three straight goals—by Scott Young, Uwe Krupp, and Mike Ricci—taking a 3–1 win. Despite Florida coach Doug MacLean using a column by the *Denver Post's* Mark Kiszla that made fun of the Panthers' boring style of play as bulletin-board, press-conference material, the Avs crushed Florida 8–1 in Game 2.

Game 3 started out well for the Panthers, who took a 2–1 lead into the second period. But they lost and did not score a goal the rest of the series. Game 4 ended at approximately 1:00 AM Eastern Standard Time, on a Uwe Krupp goal at 4:31 of the third overtime of a scoreless game.

A team that didn't have a name 12 months before now had its name on the Stanley Cup. It is one of sports' more remarkable stories, and the Avs continued to create many more great memories in the years to come.

3 December 6, 1995—Roy Arrives

I had it, and I was too chicken to write it.

That's one of the first memories I have of the morning of December 6, 1995. My phone rang at about 6:00 AM, and Avs media relations man Jean Martineau was on the other line.

"We're going to announce the acquisition of Patrick Roy in a release in a few minutes," Martineau said. "You're the first to know."

Well, not really. Everybody in the hockey world had heard it by that moment. There was no Internet to write for then, so my story on the blockbuster trade of Patrick Roy to the Avalanche, along with Mike Keane, would have to wait 24 hours. I was excited and energized, and kicking myself.

The night before, the Avs had played the San Jose Sharks at McNichols Sports Arena, in a game won by the Avs in a lopsided score. My lead paragraph on the game went like this: "Well, the Colorado Avalanche wouldn't have needed Patrick Roy on this night, at least."

On December 3 the Canadiens had announced that Roy, their two-time Stanley Cup champion and two-time Conn Smythe winner, was suspended from the team following a blowup with his coach, Mario Tremblay, in a blowout loss to the Detroit Red Wings at the Montreal Forum.

By the afternoon of December 5, I was hot on the scent that the Avs were a prime player to land Roy in a potential trade. Still, nobody really believed it would happen. Patrick Roy—Saint Patrick, the kid from Quebec idolized by everyone in the province, a two-time Cup winner and three-time Vezina Trophy winner? Really, the Canadiens might trade him, after just a "one of those things" blowup during a game?

It didn't seem possible. And it sure wouldn't have been possible, if the Avalanche franchise was still based in Quebec City, as it had been just seven months prior. While Roy was actually born in Quebec City, he was hated by the city's hockey faithful, because that's where the Nordiques played, and the hated Canadiens were just two hours down the road. The Nordiques and Canadiens had a serious rivalry, and there would have been zero chance Montreal management ever would have traded Roy to Quebec.

But with the franchise now in Denver, and Roy and Tremblay at odds, Canadiens GM Rejean Houle felt he had no choice but to turn the page and deal Roy. Actually, as revealed in a book written by Roy's father, Michel, titled *Patrick Roy: Winning, Nothing Else*, the Habs were set to deal their superstar goalie to Colorado a couple months before.

Serge Savard was the GM of the Canadiens to start the 1995–96 season, and after a slow start for his team, he decided to trade Roy. According to Michel Roy's book, Savard had a deal worked out with Avs GM Pierre Lacroix in which Roy would go to Colorado and Owen Nolan would go to Montreal. But on October 17, 1995, Savard was fired by the Canadiens, and the Roy deal seemingly fell through with his ouster.

Then came the game against the Red Wings on December 2 at the Forum. The back story on that game is a little more fascinating in hindsight. Tremblay, in his first year as coach of the Canadiens, boasted to the Montreal press after a victory in Detroit earlier that season, indirectly dissing Red Wings coach Scotty Bowman in the process. Bowman had been Tremblay's coach on the Canadiens in the 1970s. Tremblay and Bowman had some issues in their time as player and coach, and when Tremblay and his Canadiens went into Joe Louis Arena and beat Bowman's mighty Wings, the Habs coach did some chirping.

Bowman rarely forgot any slight, and so when Detroit came into Montreal for the early December game, he was ready for revenge. Detroit got out to a quick lead, and kept pouring it on. When Detroit made it a 6–1 game, most everyone—Roy especially—expected Tremblay to call it a night and pull his No. 1 goalie. Hockey tradition holds that once a game is out of reach, the losing No. 1 goalie gets the rest of the night off, much like a pitcher in baseball who gets the hook from the manager.

For whatever reason, Tremblay left Roy in the game. The score became 7–1, then 8–1 and 9–1. That's when Tremblay finally decided to pull Roy. By then, though, Roy was steaming mad. He stomped past Tremblay on the bench and stopped to chat with Canadiens president Ronald Corey, whom he told he had just played his last game with the team. As Roy walked past Tremblay again back to his spot on the end of the bench, Roy and Tremblay glared eye-to-eye. Roy told him in French, *"Et tu compris?"* which means "Do you understand?"

According to his father's book, Roy had also recently had a blowup with Tremblay on the road in Edmonton. Starting in 1993, under then-coach Bob Berry, the Canadiens had a rule for players on the road: nobody could be seen at the bar of the hotel where they were staying. Early in the 1995–96 season, Roy and teammate Pierre Turgeon were spotted by Tremblay having a beer after a win over the Oilers.

Tremblay, according to Michel Roy's account, read Roy and Turgeon the riot act. Roy came back at Tremblay, saying it was no big deal and that he disliked going out to more crowded spots in general. The night ended, in Michel Roy's account, with Roy and Tremblay glaring at each other from across the bar.

After the embarrassing night with the Red Wings, Roy left the Forum quickly, leaving reporters hanging. He spent most of the night at the home of his agent, Bob Sauve, discussing the events of the evening and pondering his next move. Teammate Mike Keane came over later that night, with Roy's son, Jonathan, in tow. By the next day, Rejean Houle proclaimed he would trade Roy. By the night of December 3, it was only a matter of where he was going.

This is when the night of December 5 comes in, the Avs' game against the Sharks. I'd heard from some trusted sources that the Avs were hot after Roy, that it all made sense given that Lacroix was his former agent and everyone knew the No. 1 question mark on his young team was the goaltending position.

The night of the game with San Jose, I spent most of the time not watching the ice but staring through binoculars at the suite in which Lacroix sat. Remember, this was 1995; rare was the cell phone, and even rarer was anyone on a computer with Internet access. Through my binoculars, I could see Lacroix talking on a landline telephone throughout most of the game. Who was he talking to? I had a huge suspicion it was someone from a 514 area code—the one covering Montreal and much of Quebec.

With me in the press box that night was *Denver Post* columnist Mark Kiszla. Just as hungry for a scoop as I was, Kiszla knew the only story that mattered that night wasn't on the ice. So we made the decision to trudge through the upper deck of a section at McNichols Sports Arena, the one right under Lacroix's suite. There was no other way to get to the suite other than through the stands.

Kiszla and I walked up the stands and stopped a couple rows below where Lacroix was seated. He could easily see and hear us, so we decided to do our talking from there.

"Pierre, anything going on with Montreal tonight?" we asked.

"I haven't heard," Lacroix said.

That was always his stock response to any question involving anything sensitive personnel-wise. Thing is, it was always a bit of a tell. Whenever Lacroix said something like that, it was a good indication something we thought was going on was really going on.

That was about the extent of our conversation. Kiszla and I both went back to our computers, highly suspicious that a trade was about to go down. But neither of us had it cold. Nobody from Montreal seemed to know for sure, despite calls to just about everyone I knew there.

So despite my hunch that a deal was already done, I held off writing anything declarative. When Martineau's call came just a few hours later on my home phone, I instantly felt remorse that I hadn't trusted my instincts more.

By later that evening, though, nobody cared anymore about newspaper scoops. Roy and Keane were on their way to Denver on the private jet of COMSAT Video Enterprises. It hardly seemed real when, in the Avs dressing room, Roy and Keane both put on Colorado sweaters and team baseball caps.

It was and remains arguably the most momentous day in the history of the franchise.

4 Joe Sakic—Mr. Avalanche

He is the franchise's all-time leading scorer. He was a longtime team captain. He played his entire 20-year career for the same organization. He later became the team general manager. He is Joe Sakic, Mr. Avalanche.

Sakic, born to Croatian immigrants Marijan and Slavica in 1969, is one of the NHL's top 10 all-time scorers, with 1,641 points in 1,378 games (625 goals). He won a Hart Trophy as the NHL's most valuable player in 2001, he won an Olympic gold medal with Canada in 2002 as the tournament's MVP, and he won a Conn Smythe Trophy as playoff MVP in 1996. There is pretty much nothing Sakic didn't accomplish in his long career.

Sakic did not speak English until around first grade, growing up first in Vancouver and then the city suburb of Burnaby, British Columbia. He had a younger brother, Brian, who had a very good junior hockey career with the same team Joe played for, the Swift Current Broncos.

But serious Avs fans, such as those of you reading this book, probably know all this. This is a book of *insider memories*, so here are some of mine about Sakic, and don't worry: all his great playing moments are detailed later.

- The first time I ever talked to him was a couple days after the Quebec Nordiques were sold, and I probably bored him for about 35 minutes with really dumb questions. The fact is, in 1995 I hadn't paid much attention at all to the NHL for several years, and I truly don't think I had ever heard of him when the team was sold. Yes, there are a lot of punch lines there that can be had at my expense, and I'd probably chuckle at most of them. I didn't know anything about him, but he sat there on the phone with me the whole time and answered every question with grace.

- His nickname was Quoteless Joe, as he had a reputation for giving vanilla answers to the media. But that was somewhat exaggerated. Most hockey players give vanilla quotes. It's just the nature of players *not* to stand out individually, not to call attention to themselves, especially with things they say. But the real Sakic had a dry sense of humor and liked to gossip as much as anyone. And he read the papers and knew what everyone was saying about him.

- He was a needler. He chided Milan Hejduk for his "woman's body" once, which got a bunch of laughs in the dressing room, and he tagged me with the nickname Barney after an unfortunate fashion choice of purple pants on a road trip once—which got even more laughs. He didn't talk any trash to opponents, though. If he didn't know you, he'd stay quiet. If he knew you, you were fair game for a good verbal jab.

- He did a million wrist curls, especially as a kid developing his strength. He wasn't very big (5'11", about 185 pounds), which scared off 14 other teams from taking him in the 1987 draft. So he made up for it with a ridiculous amount of wrist curls that developed Popeye forearms and helped give him one of the best wrist shots of all time.

- He became a dedicated practitioner of Pilates after a back injury in his final season, caused while on the squat rack, and probably could have played another year or two. People forget: he still managed 12 points in 15 games that final season. Today that gets you a contract for $3 million a year.

- He has just a ridiculous trophy room, inside a ridiculous house. His trophy room is like a separate wing of the Hockey Hall of Fame. There is an electronic revolving jersey rack with originals worn by many of the game's greats. There are glassed-in mementos of his career everywhere. The house itself is full of oak paneling and frosted lighting and smells great too.

- He got his work ethic from his parents, especially his father, Marijan, a skilled carpenter who never took a day off.

- I never saw him get mad. Never. Irritated a couple times, yes. He made an awful lot of money in his career, but he didn't like talking about it much, and sometimes he'd flash a bad look when reporters asked him about his salaries. I think he had a complicated relationship with money. He had a real soft spot for the underprivileged, which is why he devoted a lot of time to his favorite charity—the Food Bank of the Rockies. Trust me, he did a lot of things for the underprivileged that people will never know about.

- But he also made sure he got what he was worth as a player. As documented elsewhere in this book, he nearly left the Avs in 1997 because of money. He wasn't greedy, mind you, but he was no fool at the bargaining table. He did take less money than he was worth in his last couple years, though.

- He was known early in his career as a one-way player, the kind who probably wouldn't win a championship. Some called him lazy defensively. He worked on it harder as the years went by, but he was never a lazy player. He just played on some really bad teams in those early years. "We were slugs," was one quote I remember him giving me about those early Quebec teams.

- That wrist shot—it was something else. He got so much torque on the shot that the puck flew seemingly faster than many others' slap shots. He would come down the right side, lean off the wrong foot, and…*whoosh*, the puck was in the net. Watch the first goal of the 2001 Stanley Cup Finals, against Martin Brodeur, for more of what I'm talking about.

- After he retired, he went out on the ice with a newspaper photographer and me and broke down the secrets of his wrist shot for a video presentation. But then the photographer mistakenly deleted it and it never ran.

- He was and is a devoted husband and family man. His wife, Debbie, is as friendly as they come. They met while he played in Saskatchewan, while she was still in high school. He had a great, mid-1980s white Camaro as one of his first cars, but the engine block froze one night in Swift Current, after he'd shrugged off warnings by his billet parents that he should plug in a car warmer. Debbie still kids him about it.

- His Achilles tendon was sliced to the bone in 1997 by the errant skate of Flyers veteran Dale Hawerchuk, and he thought for a minute his career was over. Quick work by doctors made it otherwise.

- He idolized Wayne Gretzky and emulated his skating stride— sort of like an Olympic speed skater's, low to the ice, leaning forward.

- He had a delicious, secret salmon marinade recipe, and if you were lucky, you'd get a prime piece of BC salmon already in the sauce, with a cedar plank, as a gift from him.

Everybody who has ever known Sakic for any amount of time has nothing but good things to say about him. He never had a hint of scandal in his career. He is the only player I've ever asked to join me in a photograph.

I was lucky enough to call him a friend.

Pierre Lacroix—A Winner and a True Original

There were a few times when he screamed obscenities at me. There was at least one time when I did the same to him. There were times I felt true hatred for the man, and I have no doubt he felt the same for me. He made my life very difficult at times, and I probably did the same to him at times too.

But I miss Pierre Lacroix. A lot. He was the first management figure in professional sports whom I dealt with on a regular basis, and it was a great education for me. Pierre was many things, but in the end I realized: just like in the *Godfather* movies, it was always business with Pierre, nothing personal.

Pierre Lacroix. It's a great name. You can't say it without feeling like an actor speaking the line of some highbrow script or something. "PeaairLakwaa!" It flows fast over the tongue, with a bit of dash.

Lacroix was the Avalanche's general manager from 1995 to 2006, and he later served as team president until departing in 2013. His teams (including one year in Quebec) won an NHL record nine consecutive division titles. Two of his teams won Stanley Cups. He engineered some of the biggest blockbuster deals in NHL history, including the one that brought Patrick Roy to Denver in 1995.

I think it is an absolute joke that he has not gotten wider recognition from the hockey world for what he accomplished. Why is he not in the Hockey Hall of Fame as a builder? Not only is his record as a manager packed with success, but he was a very successful agent for many years before that.

In the buddy-buddy, good-old-boys network that used to characterize the upper reaches of hockey, and still does to some extent today, Lacroix was always seen as something of an outsider. It was not his style to backslap with other GMs or tie one on at the bar with them at league meetings. (Lacroix, a teetotaler, only allowed his lips to touch alcohol twice in his Avs tenure, drinking champagne out of the Stanley Cup.)

I also firmly believe some subtle racism prevented Lacroix from being more widely recognized. He was Canadian, but he was French-Canadian. The good-old-boys network of the NHL has always centered more around English-speaking Canadians from the other provinces. For a long time, and still some today, many French-Canadians were called the epithet Frogs. Take a look at many of the Team Canada player and management rosters from past Olympics or Summits, and you'll see few French-Canadians.

A lot of people in the hockey world were jealous of Lacroix too. Some disparaged him for "inheriting" a great team already when he took over the GM job with the Quebec Nordiques in 1994, but that isn't true at all. The team had been a loser for years, and he shook things up right away by making a blockbuster deal that sent Mats Sundin to Toronto for Wendel Clark.

The Avs were becoming a very good, exciting young team upon transplanting to Denver in 1995, but Lacroix made it a great one in heisting Roy out of Montreal without even giving up any of his top young core players.

He changed the former Quebec team culture from one of "We're too small, we can't compete with the bigger markets" into one of no-excuses, on-the-move action. He was never comfortable with sitting still, always mindful of what was around the corner as an organization, not just where things stood at present or in the past. Sometimes he made some bad choices in thinking he always had to be changing, but the hits were far more in number than the misses.

I could spend a few of the following chapters telling Pierre Lacroix stories, but before I tell just a couple instead, let me reiterate: Lacroix was a great person to learn from, especially for a young reporter.

But, oh man, he was so hard to get *any* information from. Without saying it in so many words, Lacroix's basic belief about the media's desire to know anything about his organization was: *It's none of your damn business.* Like Bill Belichick in football, Lacroix believed it was his job to give the media as little information as possible about what was really going on.

Lacroix had a great way of changing the subject on a question before the person who asked it even knew what was happening. I'd ask about the contract status of a certain player, for example, and the next thing I knew, I found myself listening to him going on about the weather or what great fans the team had.

He really made me dig deeper as a reporter, to make the extra calls and pound more of the pavement with the shoe leather to get my story. He wasn't just going to hand it to me. And to his everlasting credit, he never, ever played favorites with media people. He would never punish a reporter, for instance, by giving a scoop to his or her competition as payback for a story he might not have wanted to see out there.

Away from the job, he was a real gentleman, always deferring to women, his elders, and children. He could be very funny and very charming when the tape recorders were off. He loved to tell stories from his agent days, including the one in which his former player client and later partner in the agent business, Bob Sauve, threw up all over the small airplane they were in after it hit heavy turbulence. Or the one about meeting Patrick Roy's father, Michel, trying to woo young Patrick as a client, but with Michel agreeing only on the condition that he sign his older brother, Stephane, too.

When it was time for business with Lacroix, which was most of the time, he was one tough SOB. He was capable of a very sinister glare when he didn't like what you wrote, and it gave me the willies a couple times in the early days. He woke me up several times at

5:00 or 6:00 AM with phone calls right after a story he didn't like hit his driveway. The other end of the line would get very loud, and any attempt to engage with him on the matter was useless; he'd just keep right on yelling until he was done, and then hang up.

He really seemed to want to believe that the media should be a partnership with the team of sorts, that it should print only the good and not the bad. No matter how many times I tried to explain to him that it didn't work that way, especially in the US sports media, he'd still act as if betrayed by some previous mythical agreement when stuff he didn't like came out.

Anyway, Pierre and I had an at-times testy relationship but one that I hope, in the end, was based on mutual respect. It was from my end, anyway. I would so rather deal with a guy like Lacroix than today's breed of sports management people, most of whom have no personality at all and just give snoozing corporate double-speak all the time. Lacroix had a personality, and even if it wasn't always sunshine and rainbows, it was rarely dull around him.

Here's a good example of my relationship with Lacroix, what it was really like: As the years progressed, it became something of a parlor game for Lacroix to mention me by name in press conferences, always with some kind of punch line attached. Something always along the lines of, "We had to clear this deal with Adrian first before we could sign off on it, so we knew if it was the right thing or not for the organization."

One time, he really let me have it at a press conference, the one that included owner Stan Kroenke after the Avs signed Roy, Joe Sakic, and Rob Blake all on the same day in 2001. I had a story in the previous day's paper saying how things were still up in the air whether they'd all be back or not, and all three could become unrestricted free agents that next day, July 1.

I didn't get the scoop, in other words. Lacroix took great glee in having kept it from me and other media outlets. I actually had staked out the Pepsi Center parking lot much of the night before, hoping to ambush one of the players or Lacroix himself if they came out of the building, where I knew there were some negotiations going on. But I never saw anyone.

Lacroix made several jokes at my expense during the televised press conference, so much so that one of the local TV stations actually did a segment on it. One of the jokes had something to do with me deserving a million-dollar commission or something for "being the agent" of the players (I had lobbied hard in print, obviously, to get all three signed).

I took it all in stride but, yeah, was probably reeling just a bit coming home from that one. I knew he was just kidding around, but there were a couple moments when the jokes seemed just a bit on the edge of getting personal.

Later that night, there was a knock at my door. A courier was standing on the stoop, with a certified letter addressed to me. I signed for it, opened it up, and found an oversized million-dollar bill. On it was a note that said, "I was a little bit tough on you today. All in good fun, Pierre."

I still have that million-dollar bill. I'll always treasure it, actually. That was the man I'll always remember: tough on you but fair in the end. It was never personal, just business.

6 Charlie Lyons—The First Owner

Without a former ski bum from the Colorado mountains, the NHL might never have returned to Denver as it did in 1995.

Young Avalanche fans today probably never have heard of Charlie Lyons, but he was the team's first majority owner, and he was quite a character.

At first glance, Lyons could easily have been mistaken for just another corporate suit. As CEO of COMSAT Video Enterprises and its successive namesake, Ascent Entertainment, Lyons dressed in nice, tailored suits, had an expensive haircut, and had no problem speaking in the latest buzzwords of business.

But the real Charlie Lyons was something of a throwback, a real riverboat gambler who had a fun-loving, wild streak. After receiving a degree in economics from Washington University in the 1970s, Lyons really had no idea what to do with his life. He spent part of his postgraduate years working odd jobs at Colorado ski resorts and having a good time, skiing during the day and partying at night.

But Lyons decided to get serious about his life. He always had a love for politics, and he managed to get a job as an aide to New York senator and US vice president Nelson D. Rockefeller. Lyons even helped with the drafting of the Panama Canal Treaty that transferred sovereignty of the canal to Panamanian hands.

When Jimmy Carter unseated Gerald Ford in 1976, Lyons' job under Rockefeller ended and he again set out to remake himself. He soon landed a job at the Marriott Corp., where he worked his way up the ladder to become a top executive.

Then in 1992 he joined a fledgling company named COMSAT, which was a player in the satellite television industry.

Lyons worked his way up to the title of CEO, and with it came a new title: sports owner. COMSAT bought the NBA's Denver Nuggets a few years before he joined the company in 1992, so Lyons became its majority owner when he assumed the big chair.

Lyons had big plans to remake the once-sleepy Denver pro sports market into a big-time player. That meant getting a modern arena to maximize revenues in a world in which sports was increasingly seen as a way for businesses to entertain clients in expensive, posh suites. McNichols Sports Arena did have boxes in the concourse that technically could be called suites, but they lacked the emerging new technologies of wireless Internet and fancy video screens. The suites were also located on the main concourse level, which meant the hoi polloi could too easily mix with the 1-percenters.

A new arena also would need a new tenant to generate more revenue, which meant it needed a hockey team. Lyons quietly and effectively brokered friendships throughout the NHL, including Commissioner Gary Bettman. When the Quebec Nordiques came upon revenue problems as a small market, without the hope of a new arena fixing them, Lyons secretly reached out to Nordiques owner Marcel Aubut with an offer he couldn't refuse: $75 million.

The thing is, COMSAT's capital reserve wasn't too deep by normal sports owner standards. While video rentals in hotel rooms was a solid cash-flow business, Lyons knew the window for it to remain a growing industry was small. The Internet was coming, and Lyons knew it would likely cannibalize the business of people paying $10.99 for some movie they could someday get for pennies as part of a Netflix-style operation.

After much wrangling with the city of Denver over the terms and conditions of the Pepsi Center, the building finally opened in 1999. Lyons by this time knew Ascent probably needed to sell the Avs, Nuggets, and Pepsi Center. The video-on-demand industry was already starting to fade, and Lyons also had developed a new love of making movies.

Ascent in the mid 1990s spun off a film company named Beacon Pictures, producer of the 1997 megahit *Air Force One* (which has its own chapter in this book). Lyons became enamored of the Hollywood lifestyle, which contributed to his desire to sell Ascent and try his hand at making films full-time.

Today, Lyons remains a Hollywood player, the managing partner of a new film company named Holding Pictures. The company has produced such films as *Ladder 49*, *The Guardian*, and *Raising Helen*. Lyons also is a licensed pilot, often flying himself to and from business meetings.

Anyone who has ever met Lyons can easily see why he's been such a success in business, despite the lack of any fancy Ivy League degree or silver-spoon upbringing. He just has that certain charm factor that draws people in. He was great to deal with from a media perspective because, although he didn't like to be quoted a lot, he would steer you in the right direction if he thought you had done your homework on a particular story. He knew the media needed some good gossip to sell papers, and he would sometimes give you some. He recognized the benefits of keeping his name and company in the papers too, especially in the days before oversaturation of Internet media and the ability of companies to publish their own news on their own websites.

He was smart that way. He treated the media well, so the media treated him well. Don't ever kid yourself into believing reporters don't like to have their egos stroked by powerful people they cover sometimes, and sometimes they give a bit more favorable coverage to a person or company that treats them nicely.

Everything, in the end, is about politics and personal relationships. Always has been, always will be.

7 The Lemieux-Draper Incident: A Rivalry Is Born

On May 29, 1996, the Avalanche had a chance to close out the Detroit Red Wings. A win in Game 6 of the Western Conference Finals that night at McNichols Sports Arena would do it, and in the end that's what happened. A Detroit team that had set an NHL record for most wins in the regular season (62) and had beaten Colorado 7–0 in a late-season game, had been knocked off by an underdog.

That wasn't the biggest story to emerge from that particular game, however. That came with 5:53 left in the first period. That's when, with the Avs holding a 1–0 lead and a loose puck by the Detroit bench, depth center Kris Draper went to gain control of it. Facing the bench, his head down a bit, Draper was hit from behind by Avs veteran Claude Lemieux. It was a hard hit against a player in a vulnerable position. Lemieux should have been smarter and tried to hold up some, but for some reason he didn't.

Although notorious for being a pest and a trash-talker, with a reputation for embellishing, the fact is Lemieux had never been considered a truly dirty player in his 10 years in the league to that point. He was a guy opposing fans loved to boo and other players didn't like, but he had the respect of his peers as a clutch player and a winner.

But this was just a bad hit, and the physical damage to Draper was severe. His nose, jaw, cheekbone, and right eye socket all were broken, with five teeth bent inward. His jaw would require being wired shut, and he would have to eat food through a straw for five weeks.

Lemieux was given a major penalty for boarding and an automatic game misconduct. He complained vociferously and made a bit of a show exiting the ice, trying to slam the exit door in the east end zone. When the final horn sounded and the Avs were 4–1 winners, Lemieux came back on the ice dressed in a white WESTERN CONFERENCE CHAMPION T-shirt to celebrate with teammates and to line up to shake hands with Wings players. Draper, under medical care and still in the Wings dressing room, wasn't one of them.

Detroit veteran Dino Ciccarelli, after seeing Draper's face, uttered one of the more famous quotes in what would go on to become one of the most heated and competitive rivalries in pro sports history.

"I can't believe I shook his frigging hand," Ciccarelli said.

This incident remains the most replayed, most discussed part of the great Avs-Wings rivalry. I was in the Avs locker room that night and asked Lemieux if he was sorry for the hit on Draper, telling him that the injuries were pretty bad. Lemieux said he never wanted to hurt him or anyone else in his career, that it was an attempt at finishing a check that went bad.

If that is all Lemieux had been quoted as saying about the incident, the hatred he went on to endure from the Red Wings and their fans probably would have been cut in half at least. But another reporter followed up with Lemieux, and to that reporter he said: "I don't want to waste my time talking about Detroit. They were beaten for the second year in a row. I try to hit everybody as hard as I can, just like everybody tries to hit me as hard as they can. Everything is always vicious about us and not them. At worst, I thought it should have been a two-minute penalty. I think that was going to be his first call, but then [referee Bill McCreary] saw blood and decided to change his mind."

As one can imagine, those comments did not go over well in Detroit. Lemieux was suspended for the first two games of the Stanley Cup Finals, by NHL discipline chief Brian Burke. The Avs still beat Florida in a sweep, and Lemieux got his third Stanley Cup ring with as many teams, then got a nice big contract extension that summer.

He was asked at times by reporters over the following weeks if he had any newfound regret for the hit on Draper, and Lemieux stoked the fires more with comments that essentially made Draper out to be a whiner. Cue the outrage from Detroit even more after that.

As of late 2015, Lemieux and Draper had yet to officially reconcile. As will be documented later in this book, Lemieux later paid a physical price from a revenge fight with Detroit's Darren McCarty, and Draper went on to a long, successful career, winning three Stanley Cups with the Wings. Lemieux went on to several more years of good hockey, including another Cup with New Jersey in 2000. Both players were fortunate to have enough success after the hit for it not to become the focal point of the rest of their careers. Yet it will forever be known as the thing that sent the rivalry from heated already to thermonuclear.

Without condoning the hit on Draper at all, I will say that the general public never got to know the real Claude Lemieux well enough. He was actually a very nice man who did a lot for underprivileged kids, most of which went unpublicized. He always had a soft spot for kids who never had a fair shot at life, partially because he grew up with a younger brother, Serge, who was stricken by cerebral palsy at birth.

But Lemieux grew up poor in Montreal, Quebec, the son of a truck driver who had to bum used equipment from people just to play hockey. He was from a world in which you had to fight, literally and figuratively, to escape to a better life. He was from the school of hockey that said you had to do whatever it took to succeed, that there was no sympathy for the enemy. While he would gripe at refs and look like a diva at times, Lemieux never actually whined about anything. The guy took plenty of dirty hits in his career, but if you go back and look at the film and read the papers, he never cried about it. Unfair as it may be, that was the perception Lemieux had of Draper, and some of the things he said in the aftermath reflected those feelings (Draper's mother was even quoted at one point, badmouthing Lemieux).

Lemieux helped the Avs win a Stanley Cup in 1996, and he might have cost them another the following year. The Red Wings used him as the rallying cry for revenge, and when they got it, it changed the complexion of the two teams. But people forget that Lemieux was on the Avs team that went on to dethrone the two-time defending Cup champion Wings in a 1999 playoff series. He also got a taste of revenge on Joe Louis Arena ice.

Almost 20 years after the hit on Draper, Lemieux told me: "Of course, I never would want anyone to get hurt like that. But it's something that happened, and you can't change it. It's a rough sport, things happen sometimes. He went on to have a long career, and so I'm glad for him that he was able to do that."

8 The Crawford-Bowman Screaming Match

First off, if you are squeamish about profanity, skip this chapter. Second, if you are a hockey fan, and if you're reading this I'm guessing you are, you're probably used to it.

Anyone who has ever watched the HBO series *Road to the Winter Classic* knows how much hockey people, particularly coaches, swear. Keep in mind: that's with cameras rolling!

Absolutely everybody uses the *F*-bomb in hockey. Quick story: When Zigmund Palffy did a stint with the Denver Grizzlies of the IHL during the lockout of 1994–95, I sat down with him to do a story. He was probably the best prospect in the New York Islanders system, so this was a good chance to talk to a likely future NHL star.

Palffy, a 22-year-old Slovakian, could speak little English. The interview was painful. He just didn't know the language. We should have had a translator. But he did know one English word: the *F*-bomb. Pretty much every other word was the *F*-bomb. I'd ask something like, "So what do you do for fun?" and he'd say "I go to the fuckin' store" or "Watch fuckin' TV." I think he thought it was just a normal word, to be honest. And in hockey, it is.

So that brings us to the famous shouting match between Avs coach Marc Crawford and Detroit coach Scotty Bowman during

Game 4 of the 1997 Western Conference Finals. It happened toward the end of a blowout Detroit victory, which would put the Wings up 3–1 in the series.

The Avs were getting humiliated on the Joe Louis Arena ice for the second time in about two months, and Crawford had had about enough. There were a bunch of noncalls by referee Paul Devorski too, which had him steaming.

Crawford called Devorski over to the bench and let him have it. If nothing else, Crawford would get in a little primal scream therapy and that would probably be it. But Bowman was always conscious of working the referees, whether he was doing it or his opponent. He walked over to the end of the bench to listen in on Crawford's rant, and started to say something to a linesman. Crawford didn't like that Bowman was edging into his private rant, so he started going after Bowman too.

Nearly 10 years after this all happened, I got my hands on a videotape of the incident—an unedited videotape, with sound. I documented what was said in my book *Blood Feud: Detroit Red Wings v. Colorado Avalanche: The Inside Story of Pro Sports' Nastiest and Best Rivalry of its Era.*

Crawford started off the confrontation with Bowman by referencing the plate in his head. Legend had it that, after a gruesome head injury as a junior hockey player, Bowman had a plate surgically implanted in his head. The thing is, it never happened. There never was a plate in Bowman's head. Crawford had referenced it the year before in the playoffs, and there he was again, trying to ridicule him over it on the bench.

That's when Bowman said the line that was one of the few true ones documented by the media afterward. "I knew your father before you did," Bowman told Crawford.

What was never reported by the press was what Crawford said next: "Yeah, yeah, and he thinks you're a fuckin' asshole too."

Crawford repeated the line, but Bowman didn't react in anger at all. He just casually told the linesman on hand, "He just wants a rallying point." Then he said as much to Crawford. "You just want a rallying point. You want a rallying point, that's all. It's over."

Not to Crawford it wasn't. He was just getting warmed up. Crawford started yelling "Are you gonna apologize? You gonna apologize?" in reference to Detroit's constant hammering at Lemieux over the previous year for not apologizing for the hit on Kris Draper.

Detroit assistant Barry Smith intervened, trying to pull Bowman away from the situation. That prompted Crawford to lean over the glass partition between the benches and scream, "Are you gonna apologize for that? Are you gonna apologize for that, you old fuckin' cunt?"

I told you, you should skip this part if you're squeamish about language.

But it went on. Crawford called Bowman a few more choice words, and then he started yelling at the entire Detroit bench, yelling over and over: "Are you gonna apologize for that?"

Finally, someone on the Wings bench was goaded into saying something back. "Fuck off. Sit down," said Detroit defenseman Aaron Ward, who had had a skirmish with Crawford in the hallway outside the Avs dressing room following the March 26 game.

That set Crawford off even more. He motioned with his index finger toward Ward and yelled, "Come on, Ward, come on. Any fuckin' time, boy, any fuckin' time. Any fuckin' time, ya fuckin'—you're all a bunch of pussies. Especially you, you little fuckin'…"

Bowman started to walk back down toward the middle of the bench, and Crawford seemed to want to jump on the Detroit bench and go after him.

"I'll fuckin' kill you. I will. I'll get you, you cocksucker," Crawford yelled, his face beet red. Crawford had to be restrained by assistant coach Mike Foligno at that point. After yelling a couple more times how he would "get" Bowman, Crawford turned his attention toward Assistant Coach Smith: "Whose fuckin' ass ya kissin' now, Barry? Whose ass ya kissin' now? Whose ass ya kissin'?"

That was about the end of it but, wow, what a show. Crawford was fined $10,000 by the league and gave a halfhearted apology the next day, saying his emotions "got a little out of line."

Nearly 20 years later, this was what Crawford had to say about the incident:

"That's just how intense it was with that rivalry. Scotty knows how much I respect him as a coach, and always did. Yeah, they had gotten under our skin by that time in the series. And I probably did want to stir something up, to get a rallying point for our club, as he said. People might not remember, but we came back and really smoked them the next game [a 6–0 win]. I think it did help fire us up some. But we just couldn't win that Game 6 back in Detroit. They were just playing better hockey at that time than we were."

It might be an overstatement to say both sides can "laugh about it" now. Make no mistake: both teams truly hated each other, and that feeling will never totally go away. But of course time has a way of mellowing everything out. Bowman never took the incident personally; he knew he had the series won right then and there, in fact, that his team had definitely gotten into the heads of the defending Cup champs. Maybe if the Red Wings had blown the series, he wouldn't look back on it with the same kind of nostalgic air he does now.

But while there was mutual hate, there and remains mutual respect. "It was the best rivalry I was ever a part of," said Bowman, which is saying something. "Pretty much everyone who was involved in it for any length of time had something bad to say about everyone else at one point."

Fuck yes, was that ever true.

9 The Ray Bourque Trade

It was a warm night in Calgary in March 2000, and Rick Sadowski and I both thought our work was over for the night. Although we were competitors as respective beat writers for the *Rocky Mountain News* and *Denver Post*, Rick and I also were friends. He was an impossible guy to dislike, which was a relief to me when I first met him, because I was worried about hating a guy I knew I'd probably have to spend a lot of time around in the coming years.

On that night, Rick and I saw each other at the downtown Marriott hotel late in the day and decided to grab dinner together. There wouldn't be any potential Avalanche news until the next day, we both thought, so we headed across the street to a popular place called Joey Tomatoes.

Very often when we spent any time together on the road, Rick and I would kid each other all the time about some potential scoop the other had just gotten. "Did you hear the news yet?" one of us would say, and while we would always go "Very funny," there was always that one second of terror that maybe the other guy had something big. Before the Internet was all-pervasive and keeping secrets for long became impossible, we were never quite sure something hadn't bubbled up quietly.

So Rick and I enjoyed a nice long, leisurely dinner on our companies' dimes, confident there would be no "breaking news" to worry about. As we walked back to the hotel and into the lobby, we both noticed something weird: Peter McNab, the longtime excellent Avalanche TV color analyst, was being interviewed by a TV crew. *Hmm, maybe they're just getting some Avs analysis for some Flames broadcast,* I thought. It was Canada, after all. Hockey never sleeps there.

As we walked closer, we heard the name Ray Bourque. Still, what would this have to do with the Avs? There had been nothing—nothing—in any media outlet about Bourque possibly coming to Colorado. Sure, he was on the trading block, we all knew, but everyone thought it was a done deal that he was being shipped out of Boston to Philadelphia after 20-plus years as a Bruin. McNab actually played with Bourque in Boston, so he was probably just giving his input into any possible deal. That's when we both saw Avs PR man Jean Martineau standing near McNab's interview.

When Martineau greeted us with a "Where have you been?" look (neither of us had a cell phone at the time), he handed each of us a white piece of paper on team letterhead. Neither of us could believe our eyes.

"Colorado Acquires Defenseman Ray Bourque from Boston" read the top of the media release. At first I thought it might be an early, elaborate April Fool's joke by the Avs. In all my years covering the team, if I didn't get the first trade scoop myself, I always prided myself on always having *some* inkling a possible deal *could* happen. Not this one.

GM Pierre Lacroix pulled his best masterpiece of subterfuge on this one. Not once did I hear anything about Bourque being a possibility to come to the Avs. Nor did anyone else; it shocked everyone.

When Martineau assured us it was no joke that Bourque would be on a plane from Boston to Calgary the following morning, Rick and I dashed for the elevator to get up to our rooms and onto our computers. We had a website then, but breaking news like that was almost never posted right away in those days. Still, thanks to our night of leisure at Joey Tomatoes, there wasn't much time until the first edition deadline.

I remember having about an hour to pull a big story together. Suddenly, the food wasn't digesting so well. Luckily, I was able to get Dave Reid on the phone. Remember, kids, no cell phone for me then, so if I was to get Reid, he would have to be in his room, answering the landline. Reid was in and picked up, and I wound up getting some great quotes about what it was like to play with Bourque for a few years in Boston.

For the time I had, the story turned out to be a perfectly respectable one. Although getting the scoop ahead of time was always the goal, at least I had my bases covered for the next day's paper. (How quaint that all sounds as I type this now, in 2015.)

Bourque and Dave Andreychuk, included in the trade, were indeed at the hotel by early the next afternoon for an impromptu press conference. It was definitely surreal for all involved that he was an Av, after two decades as a veritable institution in Boston. I mean, I was a teenager living in New Hampshire, and a Bruins fan, when Bourque first came into the league in 1979. Suddenly he was right here, a new member of the team I covered.

Thank God Rick and I decided not to go anywhere after dinner for a nightcap.

10 Mission 16W: Bourque Lifts the Cup, with an Assist to Sakic

Bourque still would call it the greatest assist in hockey history 15 years after it happened, and he was the beneficiary.

Bourque played his first 21 seasons as a premier NHL defenseman but never won hockey's biggest prize—the Stanley Cup. The first 20-plus seasons saw him in Boston, where the Bruins won a lot of games but never a Cup.

After a near-miss at getting one with the Avs in 2000, Bourque signed a contract for the 2000–01 season and told friends no matter what happened it would be his last.

The Avs of 2000–01 were one of the best teams in NHL history, winning 52 games and breezing to a President's Trophy. But they needed to win 16 more games for that Cup, and so the slogan "Mission 16W" was born.

Players wore caps and T-shirts with the inscription, and it became the official rallying cry for a team that badly wanted to win that first Cup for Bourque—a classy, team-first man who might have been the most respected player in the league. The first four *W*s, against the Vancouver Canucks, were easy. The second four, against the Los Angeles Kings, came a lot tougher, with the Avs needing to go to seven games to win their Western Conference Semifinals series.

The third set of four, against the St. Louis Blues, look easy on paper, as the Avs won in five games. But Bourque has actually called that series one of the toughest he ever played in, and years later he recalled the moment in which he said the team faced perhaps its biggest gut check of all.

"It was before overtime of Game 4 in St. Louis," Bourque said. "We were only up 2–1 in the series and we came into the dressing room tied 3–3, and we'd had a 3–0 lead in the game. We were on our heels, their crowd was booming, and we'd just lost the previous game in OT. We lose that game, and now it's all tied up and they have a ton of momentum, and that was a real good team."

Not only had the Avs blown the 3–0 lead, they needed a couple miracle saves by Patrick Roy late in the third period, against Scott Young and Keith Tkachuk, to even get to OT. It was then that Bourque stood up to make a short speech to the team. While never afraid to speak his mind as captain of the Bruins, in Colorado Bourque deferred to Avs captain Joe Sakic when it came time for big locker room speeches. This time, however, Bourque felt compelled to say something.

"He basically just stood up and said, 'Do we really want this? Because we're not playing like it, and we've got to put a stop to it right now.' I think that made guys refocus a little better and we came out and won it pretty quickly. When it's Ray Bourque standing up to say something, guys' ears perk up pretty quick," recalled Avs teammate Dave Reid, another locker room leader who played with Bourque in Boston.

Indeed, one game after he was the goat (taking too long and getting stopped on a wide-open short-and-easy shot in OT), Stephane Yelle was the Game 4 hero, tipping in a Rob Blake shot past Roman Turek at 4:37 for the win.

Only one opponent stood in the way of Bourque getting that elusive Stanley Cup, and it was a tough one. The New Jersey Devils came in to the 2001 Cup Finals as the defending champs, with not only a great core of veterans who knew how to win (Scott Stevens, Martin Brodeur, Ken Daneyko, Bobby Holik, Brian Rafalski, Randy McKay, Scott Niedermayer, John Madden) but a bunch of other really good players as well (Alexander Mogilny, Jason Arnott, Petr Sykora, Scott Gomez, Patrik Elias). The Devils had a reputation as a trap team that took all the fun out of offensive-minded hockey, but that 2000–01 squad was the top-scoring team in the NHL.

Without Peter Forsberg in their lineup, because of a ruptured spleen suffered a couple weeks prior, the Avs entered the series as underdogs in the eyes of many hockey pundits, despite home-ice advantage. After the Devils won fairly easily in the rubber Game 5 at the Pepsi Center, most everyone (myself included) wrote off the Avs. Hockey writers everywhere were getting ready to write stories comparing Bourque to Ernie Banks, the great Chicago Cub who could never quite get that World Series ring. Mission 16W would end at only 14 *W*s.

The Devils came out looking for the kill in Game 6, just swarming all over the Avs in the first 10 minutes of the opening period. At Continental Airlines Arena, the press box was actually in the lower bowl of the building, right across the middle of the ice (that seems comically absurd in today's world of huge-money lower-bowl seats) and fans were really letting us Denver media have it—my *Denver Post* colleague Woody Paige, in particular.

Earlier in the series, Paige had written a column making fun of New Jersey as a place to live, with *Sopranos* references and the like, and fans kept walking up the aisle screaming insults at Paige and anyone else who looked like they might be from Denver. Extra security actually had to be called over.

But while the rest of the Avs looked ready to just give in to the Devils, Roy refused. He, and he alone, kept the game scoreless entering the late stages of the period. He stopped Madden on a breakaway, and he stopped Elias on a couple three-footers in front and other blue-chip chances. Then Adam Foote got a little lucky. Coming over the blue line for a slap shot, the normally low-scoring defenseman got a goal when the shot knuckled a little on goalie Brodeur and past his blocker, far post.

Instead of being blown out, the Avs came into the dressing room of a much quieter Continental Airlines Arena thinking, *Hey, we can still win this thing.* They did. Ville Nieminen, who blocked a shot and then set up Dan Hinote for a great goal in a Game 3 victory, tipped in Martin Skoula's shot at 2:28 to make it 2–0. With 1:33 left in the second, Chris Drury scored his 11th goal of the playoffs and third unbelievable goal of the series. Drury, who scored four goals overall in the Finals, faked the pants off Devils defenders at key moments of the series, highlight-reel goals that make for great YouTube watching today. He particularly turned Devils defenseman Colin White inside out all series, leading to some dumb frustration penalties by New Jersey's snaggle-toothed player.

When the Avs finished up with a 4–0 win, they knew the series was over. "We weren't going to lose that Game 7 at home, no way," Reid said. "Everybody was just very, very confident."

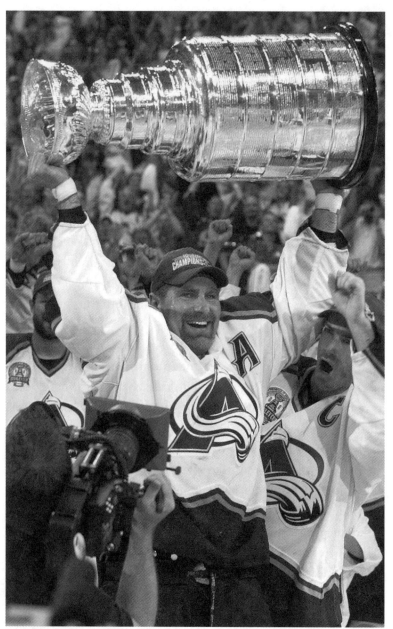

Bourque hoists the Stanley Cup (with Sakic standing by) in celebration of the Avs' 2001 championship win.

"Yeah, teams have seemed to struggle on home ice, but I don't think that's going to be a factor next game," said Sakic, who rarely said anything like that.

Sakic, in fact, was so confident he went up to Bourque after Game 6 and tried to tell him of his plans for what he'd do with the Stanley Cup when NHL commissioner Gary Bettman handed it to him first—as is tradition. Bourque, though, told Sakic to keep quiet, that there was still another game to win. He didn't need any jinx at this stage.

But Game 7 would indeed be a coronation for Bourque, an ending every player dreams about. Alex Tanguay got the first goal, a bottle-knocker turnaround wrister from the right side after circling the net, the exact same shot Brodeur thwarted at the end of Game 2, a 2–1 Devils win. Roy had just made his first tough save of the game the shift before, on Gomez, when Hinote made a great play to help set up Tanguay's goal—a play that didn't get enough attention at the time. Hinote chipped the puck in deep then beat Stevens to it in the left corner. Brodeur came out of his net to play the puck deeper into the corner, but that allowed Tanguay to get to it first. He then beat Rafalski around the net with the puck. Hinote then essentially set a pick on Stevens that prevented him from getting to Tanguay on the other side too. Was it interference? Maybe, but it wasn't enough to call, and Tanguay's goal gave the Avs a lead they never relinquished.

The final minutes took forever, with long stops between whistles and lots of icing violations by the Avs, who were just trying to kill the clock with dump-in-and-change hockey for the final 10 minutes. Rob Blake left the ice with 20 seconds left to let Bourque be on the ice, and as the horn sounded everyone mobbed around him in front of Roy's net. Roy scooped up the final puck and handed it to Bourque. All that was left was for Bettman to hand the Cup to Sakic. This time, Sakic deferred to Bourque.

"I remember Bettman handed it to me, and I tried to take it right to Ray right away, but Bettman goes, 'Picture first,'" Sakic recalled. "So when you look at the tape, you see me give this little forced smile, and all the while I'm thinking, *Let me get out of here so I can give it to Ray.* When I was able to hand it to him, it was like time stopped for a second. It was a great, great moment for all of us. We all worked really hard for it."

One of the most memorable moments from the celebration was seeing tears run down the face of Bourque's youngest son, Ryan.

"Joe was probably the classiest guy I ever played with," Bourque said, 15 years later. "He didn't have to do that, but I'm forever grateful he did. I remember that was the first time I'd actually ever touched the Cup, and I just remember thinking for a second, *So this is what it actually feels like. It's heavier than I thought.*"

Mission 16W had become Mission Accomplished.

11 Peter Forsberg—Mr. Cool

Nobody who has ever played for the Avalanche was as cool as Peter Forsberg. He had quite the charmed life—big, fancy houses, millions of dollars, swarthy Swedish good looks, unbelievable skill as a hockey player. He also had more bad luck health-wise than most any player who ever suited up in Denver. But let's focus on the positive.

Forsberg was the best player I ever saw in his prime, at least among forwards. Anyone who watched him with any regularity will usually say the same thing: he could do it all. Great skater, great passer, unbelievable stick handler, a sixth sense for what would happen next on the ice before it happened, very tough and physical, very tough in the clutch—there was nothing Forsberg couldn't do well on the ice.

The one thing he couldn't do very well after around 2001, however, was stay healthy consistently. Bad ankles were the primary culprits for his career being cut short, but Forsberg had just about every other kind of injury you could imagine. Groin pulls, shoulder problems, broken fingers, pelvis problems, back problems, concussions, charley horses—you name it, Forsberg had it.

He tried hard to find solutions for his ankles, especially the right ankle, including undergoing a procedure in Philadelphia during which the entire bottom third of his ankle bone was sawed off and soldered into a different spot in an attempt to relieve pressure. It didn't work.

Forsberg's career was good enough to warrant inclusion in the Hockey Hall of Fame in 2014, however. His career points-per-game average (1.25) remains among the top 10 all time. He won two Stanley Cups and two Olympic gold medals with Sweden, including the famous shootout goal on Canada's Corey Hirsch in 1994 that was memorialized on a postage stamp. He won a Hart Trophy, an Art Ross Trophy, and led all playoff scorers in 2002 despite missing all of the regular season and despite playing only three rounds.

Still, there is some sorrow in how Forsberg's career developed. He played in the wrong era in some ways. The NHL of the late 1990s and through 2004 was a butcher shop of a league, in which marginally talented defensemen could get away with hacking and whacking at guys of Forsberg's talent. If I had a dollar for every time I saw Forsberg take some egregious infraction that went uncalled, I'd be able to eat out at Morton's every night for the next two weeks. So many times, Forsberg would beat a defender with a fake or his speed around the end, and so many times the defender would just bear hug him and haul him down, with no call.

And yet Forsberg could be his own worst enemy with that stuff. He invited too much trouble with his style of game. Whereas teammate Joe Sakic played a quick give-and-go game and avoided big hits, Forsberg would hold on to the puck forever and stubbornly try to make his way to the net with battering-ram force. But he became like the bull with too many rodeo cowboys on his back after a while. Because opponents knew they could get away with most anything, and because Forsberg had too much of a temper to turn away from a confrontation, they could too easily lure him into a war of attrition rather than a game of skill.

Teammates such as Adam Foote and Claude Lemieux and many others were always telling Forsberg not to take the bait, to walk away, but he just couldn't help it. Every slight had to be addressed.

I went to Sweden in the fall of 2014 to visit Forsberg, shortly before he was to be inducted into the Hall of Fame. I finally discovered where he really came from and how he was so cut from the mold of his hometown, Ornskoldsvik. It is a rugged logging town, but one of breathtaking beauty. A majestic harbor sits right in the middle of two large hillsides. That contrast fit the stories I wrote for the paper from there, a kind of *Beauty and Beast* theme of his career.

Unfortunately I was sick as a dog the whole time there, and slept much of the time in a closet-sized hotel room. But the times I got to spend around Forsberg there were something I'll always cherish.

One day I met him at a swanky restaurant in downtown Stockholm for lunch, and as he was to just about everything, he arrived late. But suddenly there he was, only he was pushing a stroller. He had brought his infant daughter, Lily, along, and while she slept the whole time, Foppa and I had a great, leisurely lunch while he discussed his career. It was so strange to see the guy who seemed he might forever be the eligible bachelor, who wore cool, stylish clothes and always hung out at the best parties and nightspots and yet still kept a private mystique about him, suddenly doting on a baby daughter. He also had an older son, Lennox, who just might carry on his NHL legacy someday, at least if the early scouting reports from the Forsberg living room are to be taken into account.

A couple nights later, I drove the four or five hours to Ornkskoldsvik in my tiny, manual transmission rental car and was supposed to meet him at the home arena of his Swedish League team, Modo, where he starred as a player and now was the part-owner and general manager. I stopped off at a pizza parlor next to the arena named Mamma Mia, where the owner, Giordano Sternad, talked about the days when Forsberg was just a kid coming in for pepperoni pies with his friends.

Suddenly, in walked Forsberg with his father, Kent, and other friends. I wasn't expecting him and he wasn't expecting me. So I actually sat a couple tables away, alone, while they dined at one near the front. It was a little bit awkward for me because, well, I kind of expected him to invite me to their table. But that was the real Forsberg too. He was very private, very hard to really get to know. But just when I was about to walk out feeling like a jilted date or something, Forsberg got up, said he'd be out in a few minutes and that he'd give me a ride to that night's Modo game, against rival Skelleftea.

Suddenly, I was in the passenger seat of Forsberg's super-nice Audi, listening to him tell stories of landmarks around "Ovik," seeing the first hockey rink he skated at and where his boyhood house was, and getting all kinds of other juicy little tidbits about his life for use in my stories. He was as friendly and accommodating as could be. As I walked into the arena with him, whisking past all security and walking up to his private luxury suite, I thought I was his best buddy in the world.

Then he told me: "I can't watch the game with you. I get too into it." So off I went again, to another box, where father, Kent, and mother, Gudrun, also sat. They knew better than to think they could watch a game with him too. He really was that privately competitive about his team and didn't want to be distracted. Modo got hammered 7–3 that night, and Forsberg was quite upset afterward. We had made tentative plans, on the car ride over, to meet up after the game to maybe down a couple beers and talk more, but the loss sent those plans right into the harbor adjacent to the building.

So I walked back to the nearby hotel alone—the hotel that was owned by one Peter Mattias Forsberg. Not only did he own the hotel—a really nice, new one—and part of Modo but he owned an airline (NextJet) and a golf course in town. Talk about the life, right?

And yet the next morning I was eating the totally free all-you-can-eat buffet breakfast, thinking my time with Forsberg was over. Suddenly, there he was, getting a plate and getting in line for some of the delicious variety of meats and other very good items, making zero show of anything. This time he invited me to join him, and we had another great talk, and toward the end, he dialed his brother, Roger, to arrange a lunch meeting with him a few hours later.

While Forsberg went back to the local airport for a flight back to Stockholm on his own airline, I sat with Roger at some hilltop restaurant with a ridiculously gorgeous view of the city and harbor below, listening to great stories of what it was like to grow up with a younger brother who just happened to be one of the greatest hockey players of all time.

The next day, after 14 hours or so of flying that included a layover in Helsinki, I was back in my Thornton, Colorodo, bed saying, "Did that really all just happen?"

That's sort of what it was like covering his career. It was wonderful and it had some great memories. And yet it seemed like it went by way too fast, too quick to really realize how great it all was at the time.

12 Patrick Roy—The Man, Myth, and Legend

Patrick Roy's name has already been used several times in this book, as it should have been, and it will be used more. No player in the team's history had as big an impact as he did following his acquisition in 1995 from the Montreal Canadiens.

Honestly, I never thought enough was made about the sheer unbelievable fashion in which Roy came to Colorado. What were the odds a guy who had won two Stanley Cups already in Montreal, who was only 30 years old, and who had won a Conn Smythe Trophy just two years before would end up as the Avs' starting goalie in their first season in town?

It was such an unlikely row of dominoes that fell in the Avs' favor to land him, but they did, and it forever changed the face of the franchise in his time.

Other chapters in the book detail Roy's trade to Denver and the great accomplishments of his career, so this one will talk more about Roy the man. He was then, and remains, one of the most unique people I've ever met, and I know I'm not alone in saying that.

But let's admit something: winning is what made Roy so interesting. Really, he wasn't all that different from most hockey players. He had his superstitions (steak and peas for dinner before every game, skating in on the net from center ice before each puck drop to make it look "smaller" in his vision, never skating on the red or blue lines), and he said mostly the same things before and after every game (every game was always a "challenge" and every win was "a great win for us").

What made Roy such a fascinating subject was how he spanned different eras as a player and always maintained his excellence. In fact, his career statistics technically show he got better as he got older (his two best seasons for goals-against average were his final two, at 1.94 and 2.18, respectively).

Roy did not invent the butterfly technique (falling to the knees, closing the five-hole shut with the pads), but he perfected it. Only a few goalies played the butterfly before Roy (Glenn Hall, Tony Esposito), but most everyone did after he came along.

Even though I had a few run-ins with Roy the player and coach, I never had anything but the highest respect for him. And let me dispel some common notions about Roy:

First off, he was not a guy who ranted and raved and was out of control. Yes, there were times on and off the ice when he could get very mad, but the Roy I remember 99 percent of the time was always very calm and conscientious of his status. He had stardom thrust on him at a very young age, in the city that invented hockey, so it was natural that he had a good-sized ego from then on. But Roy the person was almost always a real gentleman.

Case in point: people forget this, but even after the Avs lost an emotionally wrenching 6–5 overtime decision to Detroit on March 26, 1997, perhaps the most anger-inducing loss in team history, Roy made a grand gesture to Detroit goalie Mike Vernon right after Darren McCarty's winning goal.

Roy knew the win was Vernon's 300th of his career, and he took the puck out of his own net and tossed it down to him before exiting the ice. How many players would take the time to do that in the heat of the moment? How many players would even know anything about the other guy's personal stats? Roy knew, as he knew about pretty much everything about the opposition.

He had something of a photographic memory. Ask him about some weird game in Calgary three years before on a Tuesday night, and he'd remember who won and who scored the key goals. He remembered kids who asked for autographs one year and came back for another the next, and would sometimes say, "No, got you last year."

He was a golf freak. Hockey and golf—that was pretty much his whole life, and is even today. When the hockey season is over, he usually goes right to a home he has in Florida and plays 18 holes every single day. He's a very good player too, about a 2 handicap. They don't have as many celebrity sports golf tournaments anymore, but Roy could have been the Pierre Larouche of hockey players on the celebrity circuit. Larouche was a pretty good player with Pittsburgh for a while, but he'd get more publicity sometimes as a winner of celebrity player tournaments.

Roy knew a million people, but he was a tough person to get to know. He kept people at an arm's length usually, but it wasn't because he was a jerk or a snob. He was just a very type A personality who was always thinking about his next game, his next challenge.

Roy had a fear of flying that would flare up badly sometimes. On an Avs team flight once, he went into the bathroom and didn't come out for a long time. Claude Lemieux had to coax him out. It was ironic that he hid in the bathroom, because Roy also was bothered at times by claustrophobia. He didn't like elevators much because of that, often taking the stairs.

When Roy was confident about a game, or a series, forget it. It was over. The other team had no chance. You should have seen how relaxed he looked after Game 1 of the 1996 Finals against Florida. He stood in the hallway outside the locker room and just casually laughed and chatted with any reporter who came by. He was a keen judge of the opposition's talent and resolve, and that year he later acknowledged he knew the Panthers had no shot. And he knew the Panthers knew that.

Other times, Roy could run into periods where his confidence disappeared on him. One of those times was after Game 1 of the 2001 Western Conference Semifinals against Los Angeles, which the Kings won. Roy was genuinely nervous about the series and his play. Teammate Ray Bourque played a big role in getting his spirits back up again. Bourque hung out with Roy a lot between Games 1 and 2, just telling him to relax and stop worrying about winning one for him. Roy did start to relax again, and was great pretty much from there on out in winning the Cup.

To me, Roy was the greatest goalie of all time. A lot of people like to bring up Martin Brodeur, because he won more regular-season games, but neither he nor anyone else accomplished what Roy did.

Roy is the only player in NHL history to win a Conn Smythe Trophy in three different decades (1986, 1993, and 2001). He won four Stanley Cups with two teams. Brodeur won three. And, of course, Roy won the only head-to-head matchup against Brodeur in their careers, in the 2001 Finals. Roy was 36, Brodeur was 29.

It's an interesting question to ask: would the Avs have won a Stanley Cup in any of those mid-1990s or early 2000s years without Roy? Could Stephane Fiset or Jocelyn Thibault have been good enough, with all that other talent in front of them? I highly doubt it. Nothing against those two, but Roy not only was a great talent, he was a *presence*. He just transformed the team from a bunch of good young players with a lot of potential to one with a genuine killer in goal, a player with some of the greatest pure will to win of any athlete in sports history.

The team had a swagger they never had before Roy and haven't had since he retired. He helped get some of it back in his first year behind the bench as coach, but Roy the coach could never be as great as Roy the player.

13 Nine Straight Division Titles

It is almost as much a source of pride within the Avalanche as their two Stanley Cup titles. Almost. While nothing can top the thrill of winning it all, the Avalanche franchise still holds the distinction of owning the NHL record for most consecutive division titles. From 1995 to 2003, the franchise finished first in its division. We must use the word *franchise* here, because the first of the nine division flags came as the Quebec Nordiques, in the lockout-shortened 1994–95 season. All nine flags came under GM Pierre Lacroix.

Even longtime Avs fans forget this, but the first three division titles in Denver came with the team in the Pacific Division. The Avs' division rivals included all three California teams, so there were a lot of late-night games broadcast back home in those years. The final five titles came in the newly formed Northwest Division, which no longer has that name.

Probably the toughest title to win was the last one, which is what made it so satisfying. Another thing Avs fans forget: the Avs trailed the Vancouver Canucks by one point, 104–103, entering the final game of the 2002–03 season, and the Los Angeles Kings were the visitors at Vancouver's GM Place. The Kings by that game were banged up health-wise and out of the playoff picture. They had nothing to play for, while everyone in Vancouver was ready to savor knocking off the Avs and clinching a top three seed in the Western Conference Playoffs.

The Avs had the St. Louis Blues at home on the final day and won easily. The Kings-Canucks game was played later in the day, so everyone gathered around TV sets at the Pepsi Center to watch the action and find out whether the Avs would set a record or not.

The Kings came through for Colorado, shutting out the Canucks 2–0. Not only did the Avs sneak past the Canucks in the standings at the end, but so too did Peter Forsberg over Vancouver's Markus Naslund for the NHL scoring title. In quite a coincidence, Naslund's point lead over Forsberg entering the final game was the same as the teams in the standings: 104–103.

While Naslund and the Canucks were shut out by L.A., Forsberg scored a goal and two assists in the Avs' win over the Blues. He won the only Art Ross Trophy of his career, and the Avs set an NHL record, on the last day. While Forsberg never really cared that much about individual honors, he got great satisfaction in beating out his boyhood friend Naslund.

Even though they were from the same hometown of Ornskoldsvik, Sweden, and played on several national teams together and were friendly off the ice, Forsberg and Naslund had a strong rivalry on the ice that occasionally got testy. Forsberg sometimes would lay a hard hit on Naslund, or the two would joust with their sticks and exchange cross looks. One thing I remember well was Forsberg's father, Kent, being at that final game in 2003 and scoffing when I mentioned Naslund's name. To Kent, Naslund was too much of an individual player who didn't work hard enough defensively like his son did. I remember Kent mocking Naslund's plus-minus numbers (plus-6 in 2002–03 while his son was at a whopping plus-52).

The other eight division flags the Avs won rather handily. You can see them all, in chronological order, hanging from the rafters of the Pepsi Center today. The Avs would not win their next division title until 2013–14, another one won on the final day of the regular season.

14 Adam Foote

He is in the pantheon of Avalanche greats, whose No. 52 forever hangs in the rafters of the Pepsi Center.

Adam Foote never played in an NHL All-Star Game in his long career, but his skills as a player were valued enough to be selected for two Canadian Olympic teams—about as high an honor as a hockey player can get. He was a mainstay on the Avs' first two Stanley Cup teams and became the obvious choice as the player to succeed Joe Sakic as team captain after he retired in 2009.

I'll always remember Foote as a fierce, tough hombre on the ice who was very relaxed off it. You'd never peg him as a guy who could really lose his mind at times in a game. Win or lose, he was almost always the same even-keeled guy who had a kind of "Hey, that's hockey" kind of attitude about most things.

Foote was blessed with great physical attributes for a hockey player, including tree-trunk thighs and a big, thick rear end that knocked many opposing players on their skinnier asses. But his high hockey IQ is what separated him from the pack of many similarly built D-men.

He was very adept at spotting opposing weaknesses, either systems-wise or mentally. He knew which top players he might be able to make lose their focus with a well-placed stick jab or a verbal taunt. He knew which players not to do that to, lest it fire them up. He knew everybody's tendencies and always adapted his game to better compete against them.

He was a good player with the Avs by the time they came from Quebec in 1995, but he became a much better one after they got Patrick Roy late that year. Yeah, partially that was from Roy just being a great goalie and making every defenseman's numbers better by extension. But in Roy, Foote found someone who shared his passion for analyzing the game and, in particular, the psychology of opponents. The two quickly became roommates after Roy arrived, and would stay that way until Roy retired in 2003. (The picture I always have of them on the road is coming off the elevator together for the bus ride to the game, with Foote looking ready for battle and Roy looking like he had just rolled out of bed, which he had probably just done. Roy almost always slept right to the last minute before joining the team in the lobby.)

Foote was a well-liked, respected teammate, but he also made sure always to look out for No. 1 when it came to business. That made him smart too.

I'll never forget how startled I was when interviewing him alone in the dressing room one day in the late 1990s, in the final year of one of his contracts, and listening to him say, "[It will] probably be my last year in Denver." He was not seeing eye-to-eye with management about an extension at the time, so he used the platform of my newspaper to express his disappointment. Sure enough, he got a nice new extension not long after that, once the panic of the Avs fan base over his words forced the hand of Pierre Lacroix.

Foote got a reasonable offer to stay with the Avs in 2005, when the new NHL salary cap severely handicapped Lacroix's ability to bargain with free agents such as him and Peter Forsberg. But Foote took a better offer from the Columbus Blue Jackets, where he would play until being traded back to Colorado in 2008.

Foote received some bad press in the Columbus media toward the end of his stay there, with stories about how he allegedly engineered his way out of town by making selfish demands and overall indifference to the team cause. I never got into the particulars of that whole situation, but again, Foote did what was best for Adam Foote in the end. That is not a knock against him at all, just part of an overall observation of his desire to be in successful situations personally and professionally.

Adam Foote's greatest hits as a player with the Avs? There are many, but his goal in Game 6 of the 2001 Cup Finals in New

Adam Foote gets aggressive with Sharks right winger Teemu Selanne during a 2002 game.

Jersey has to be right near the top, as it gave them a 1–0 lead in a game that had been all Devils before that and righted the ship to an eventual championship. He had a great series against the St. Louis Blues in the 2001 conference final, including getting Blues star Keith Tkachuk off his game mentally with his physical play (he did that a lot against him as a Phoenix Coyote too). And his many memorable battles against the Detroit Red Wings, many of which are documented elsewhere in these pages, helped make Foote a team icon.

15 To the Extreme

If it had been up to Charlie Lyons, the Colorado Avalanche would instead have been named the Rocky Mountain Extreme.

Lyons never forgot his "extreme sports" days skiing the moguls and back trails of the state's biggest mountains. He thought the name was perfect for a team in the go-go mid-1990s.

Why did that name never happen, despite the fact logos were designed and other marketing materials were drawn up? Well, I'll take my share of credit for that. Or the blame, if you still think that's a better moniker.

To sum it up in a nutshell: I got the early scoop on the new hockey team's name, and wrote a story in the *Denver Post* exposing it to the world in late summer 1995. Other than getting the actual scoop that the team would be sold and moved to Denver from Quebec, this was going to be the second-biggest exclusive of my early career, and I can't describe my excitement when I picked up the same day's *Rocky Mountain News*, our bitter rival at the time, and saw nothing about it.

Believe me when I tell you it was a real newspaper war back then, where we fought over every little morsel of news like two hungry lions over a scrap of meat. All day long, I reveled in the scoop, accepting literal and figurative pats on the back from colleagues and readers.

And then *The Dave Logan Show* happened. A former NFL wide receiver with the Cleveland Browns and Denver Broncos, Logan hosted a popular sports talk radio show on the state's biggest AM station, 850 KOA.

The day of the story, Logan fielded call after call from fans just ripping the hell out of the hockey team's new name. It was just an, ahem, avalanche of negative public opinion. Everybody hated it.

But what did I care? I had the scoop, and so who cared how bad it was? *It's in the books*, I chuckled to myself. Except it wasn't.

"Hey, Adrian, it's Shawn Hunter," said the voice on the other end of the phone. He was the president of the new team.

"Hey, Shawn, what time is it?" I remember mumbling. It was about 6:00 AM or so.

"Hey, I don't think what you had in the paper is going to be accurate," Hunter said.

And then I knew right away what was going to happen: burned by all that bad publicity the day before, the Extreme would get cold feet and pull the whole concept, then deny it ever was a possibility.

And that's exactly what happened. As I woke up and grabbed that day's *Rocky Mountain News* off my apartment's front stoop, I suddenly felt like I'd been whacked in the head by a baseball bat.

Stripped across the top of the front page of the sports section was a story by *News* columnist Bob Kravitz, the gist of which can be summed up as: "Extreme? What Extreme? There was never going to be any Rocky Mountain Extreme. That other inconsequential paper got it all wrong."

It's a bad feeling when you get scooped by the other paper. It's an even worse feeling when the other paper has a lead story saying yours was all wrong. I felt like I wanted to dig a hole in the front yard, jump inside, cover up, and never come out. I had just gotten the full-time beat of the new team, just a couple months removed from covering prep and some college sports on an ad-hoc, freelance basis. Now, I knew people around the office had to be wondering: *Did we make a mistake on this kid? Maybe that other story was just a fluke.* It went from a great day to a really bad day in a hurry.

I doubled back to my sources, wondering what the hell had happened. "How could you let me hang out to dry like that?" I sternly said (OK, I yelled) to a couple people.

I quickly came to realize they hadn't hung me out to dry. The story was right. At the time, anyway. But the early scoop and the horrible fallout from it with the fans made it so the team could still scrap the idea and just blame it all on me. Would I have liked to have had someone from the team say, *"Yeah, the story was right. We were going to go with that, but we now see the light. Adrian Dater is a hero for his scoop, for stopping the train wreck before it happened!"*

Yeah, I would have liked that, but of course it didn't happen. All I could do was take one snarky *"Nice scoop, pal! Way to get it all wrong, Woodward and Bernstein"* remark after another, along with the news, which for several days kept saying something to the effect of, "As erroneously reported in another Denver daily the other day…"

All I could do was say, "But it was true at the time. They were going to be called the Extreme! Really, they were!" But what I lacked was any visual proof. That was always the problem with the story. Somewhere around that time, I did find a new team advertising logo that showed a hockey player on a sign with the words EXTREME CAUTION on it. I said this was part of the visual proof, but

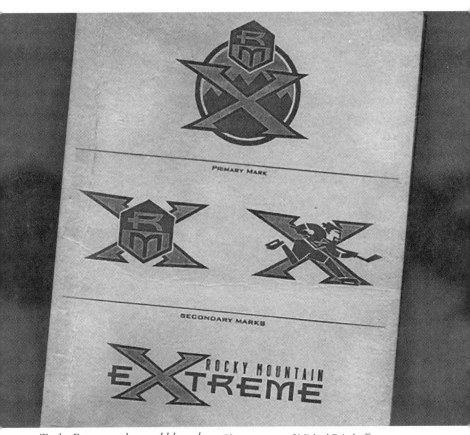

To the Extreme: what could have been. Photo courtesy of Michael Beindorff

I'd never gotten my hands on the actual logo designs that would go on the uniforms.

But the man who designed those logos, a man named Michael Beindorff, released them in an e-book on his Facebook page. Beindorff, along with Dan Price, designed the subsequent Avalanche logo, the team name that was chosen by fans in a "Feedback Forum" where they could choose that or seven others—Black Bears, Rapids, Cougars, Outlaws, Renegades, Storm, and Wranglers.

So there, nearly 20 years later, is your visual proof. Thanks to Beindorff for publicly showing them, and for allowing us to show it here.

And *you're welcome* for doing that original story when I did. It caused me a lot of grief, but we can laugh about it now. Otherwise, you would have been stuck with an *Extreme*-ly bad team name!

16 The Very First Game and First Road Trip

Nobody, but nobody remembers this fact: The first time the Avalanche ever suited up as a team, in any form, was not in Denver or any other big North American city. It was in the town of Cornwall, Ontario, population 46,340 as of the last census, taken in 2011.

It was a game against the Montreal Canadiens, on September 17, 1995. A sold-out crowd of 4,168 convened at the Aces' barn, the former home of the Quebec Nordiques' AHL farm team but now beholden to some strange team from Denver. We stayed at the Holiday Inn in Cornwall, and being a kid just off the boat from New Hampshire, I thought this was a five-star hotel. While other players snickered when we first got our room keys, I was in awe. Your own bed, your own bathroom, your own TV, your own view out the window!

The name of the airline that ran the Avalanche's charter flight outfit was Champion Air. That first night in Cornwall, PR director Jean Martineau took me and other assembled media (just Rick Sadowski from the *Rocky Mountain News* and me and Norm Jones and Mike Haynes from radio) to the best restaurant in town, which just happened to be called Chumps. (When the Avs won the Cup after the season, I would dutifully record in a story that the Avs started out on an airplane called Champion and first dined at a place called Chumps, and the former prevailed. That's why I got the big bucks as a writer. Like Dickie Dunn in *Slap Shot*, I was just there to capture the spirit of the thing.)

The Avalanche took the ice in their brand-new uniforms for the first time ever, and wow did they look weird. Seeing Joe Sakic in these crazy burgundy-and-blue getups, with a giant *A* on his crest with what looked like a melting snow cone on it…it was just a little too much for this quiet minor league city to take in. People forget this was the first time the uniforms had ever been seen on a player. The uniforms had only been fully created about two weeks before the trip.

Despite it being the former AHL home of the Nordiques, most in the crowd cheered for the Canadiens. Not that the Avs gave much for the old Nords fans to cheer about.

Montreal won 6–3, on the strength of 18 saves from a Habs goalie named Patrick Labrecque. Stephane Fiset played fine for the Avs in the first half of the game, but his replacement, Richard Shulmistra, allowed goals to Mark Recchi, Vincent Damphousse, and Oleg Petrov, with Recchi adding an empty-netter.

Colorado's three goals came, in order, from Owen Nolan, Rene Corbet, and Janne Laukkanen.

The next night, I stayed at the Hotel Bonaventure in downtown Montreal, and I swear I thought I was in heaven. First off, the windows from my room looked right out onto a humongous rectangular pool that lined the inside first floor of the hotel. The room was so big too! It had a bathroom separately connected to the bedroom only through a long parlor walkway. What was this, the Taj Mahal? In later years, these were the kinds of rooms I would take for granted, which was the first sure sign of some burnout.

The Avalanche beat the Canadiens in the preseason game that next night, with Patrick Roy starting in net for Montreal. It was your typical preseason NHL game—boring, meaningless—except it proved to be a very important road trip in so many ways for what would become a Stanley Cup–winning team. It was not yet the fully formed team, in roster or in character, it would soon become. Roy, Mike Keane, Claude Lemieux, Sandis Ozolinsh, and Dave Hannan were still in other uniforms by the time the Avs' charter took off for Cornwall on September 16.

The rest of the road trip wound through Hamilton, Ontario; Ottawa; Toronto; and Hartford, Connecticut.

It has become a cliché somewhat, but it's true: teammates often become much closer during and after extended road trips. While most of the Avs roster had played together the year before in Quebec, the move to Denver opened players' eyes to a whole new way of life. They were no longer in the geographically small, one-team town of Quebec City anymore, where the Nordiques were the who, what, where, and when of just about every sports story in the newspaper.

They were in the wide-open, big-sky spaces of the Rocky Mountains in the American West, and everybody was just trying to take it all in and adjust to what was a true culture shock. Pretty much everyone had to uproot their entire lives. While people in pro sports are used to changing jobs and addresses, rarely does it happen for everyone in the same organization all at once.

What many will never forget: Quebec Street. There they were, most players and team personnel, coming to Denver for the very first time, and one of the first street signs they saw coming in from the airport was an exit sign for a street bearing the name of their old workplace.

"To me, that was unbelievable, seeing that," Martineau said. "I thought it was a joke at first. That was the first street sign I saw."

While players and team personnel tried to get used to a whole new environment, so did I as a rookie reporter. Along with being amazed at a simple Holiday Inn, there were other things I just couldn't believe.

Such as: Seeing Owen Nolan, who would be traded to San Jose for Ozolinsh in a couple weeks, ask a clerk to change in some money at a hotel front desk in Hamilton. I think the amount was $500 in US dollars, which would have translated to about $750 in Canadian funds in 1995. I don't think I'd ever seen anyone with $500 of any national currency in hand until then. Remember, I was a kid from New Hampshire who got four dollars from my parents for mowing big front and back lawns from roughly 1977 to 1983 (no raise).

Nolan practically yawned when handed the seven or so Canadian $100 bills and change. This was a player who would go on to make more than $44 million in his hockey career, which ended in 2009–10. By 2003–04, he would be making $6.5 million a season with the San Jose Sharks. Divided over 52 weeks, that's *$125,000 a week.* And, of course, hockey players don't work 52 weeks a year.

It was my baptism to another side of life, one where people carried big wads of cash and didn't sweat it, one where people went to fancy restaurants and didn't look at the prices on the menu, one where people drove big cars and lived in big houses. I would later learn that much of this supposed "good life" was very temporary for most involved, whether they knew it or not.

But while it was good, it was very good. The Avalanche was lucky in many respects. They were a team that just happened to be in pro sports at the dawn of charter travel, where they boarded their own plane and didn't have to fuss with any of the hassles of commercial travel. Before 1990 or so, few teams ever traveled by charter, except in special circumstances. They flew on the same planes as the rest of us, going through the same security lines and sitting in the same middle seats as anyone else.

On the modified team charter run by Champion Air, there were no middle seats. It was two seats side by side, with another two seats facing those, with plenty of space in between. Up front, there were no facing seats, just two side by side, with wide berths to stretch out.

One of the gestures made by the Avalanche to the new press corps in their new city was to invite the beat writers—Rick Sadowski and me—onto the charter for many trips in the first and second years. That first preseason road trip saw us accept the invite and pretty much live the same life as the players—minus the bigger paychecks.

That meant really nice meals on the flights, with most any kind of drink we wanted. That meant walking into really nice hotels (after the Holiday Inn) and having a big room for each of us. That also meant riding the bus to games, hotels, and to the plane, and listening in on all the chatter.

One of my first funny memories is of Mike Ricci and Uwe Krupp ragging on each other in Hartford, the end of the trip. The team didn't play too well in the Hartford Civic Center, and everyone was a little tired on the bus ride to the airport.

Krupp, always reading a book, usually about some heavy-hitting sociological or historical subject, would snicker at Ricci's less-than-intellectual bus banter. All that did was make Ricci's taunts even louder. "Aw, come on, ya big Kraut," Ricci would yell at the 6'6" German.

Krupp would respond with some Italian epithet without looking up from his book. Several months later, Krupp and Ricci would hug each other after winning a Stanley Cup. Probably nobody on that team bus would have believed it months earlier.

They were a transplanted team playing in a new conference in a new city that hadn't seen NHL hockey in 13 years. That first road trip, though, played a significant role in bonding everyone together. It was the beginning of what would be a great journey for Denver's new NHL club.

17 March 26, 1997: Payback for Lemieux

It was one of the worst nights in franchise history, a night Avs fans do not want to relive in any form. But it has to be documented here. While it was a night that absolutely derailed a team likely headed to an easy Stanley Cup, it also had one or two tangible benefits down the road.

It was March 26, 1997, the infamous "Bloody Good" night for the Red Wings at the appropriately named Joe Louis Arena. It was a night when there were probably more punches thrown than shots taken on net.

In a nutshell: Claude Lemieux, whose hit from behind on Kris Draper in Game 6 of the previous year's Western Conference Finals turned the Avs-Wings rivalry from intense to all-out war, got beaten up by Detroit's Darren McCarty late in the first period.

The Avs came into Detroit well ahead of the Wings and every other team in the West as the regular season was winding down. They had just come off an easy win in Hartford over the Whalers (one of the last games played at the Mall), and this essentially was nothing more than a tune-up for the playoffs for the defending champion Avs.

Keep in mind: Detroit still had a reputation still as being a team of skilled softies who couldn't win the big ones. Detroit hadn't won the Stanley Cup since 1955; the Avs hadn't won one since the previous June.

The Avs had beaten the Wings three out of three times already, so who cared who won this last, meaningless game? As it turned out, it would irrevocably change the fortunes of both teams.

That's not to say Avs people thought nothing might happen. Extra security had to be ordered for Lemieux around the team hotel, the Atheneum. There was already plenty of security on hand at the hotel, though, because as chance would have it, First Lady Hillary Clinton was staying there the night of March 25, on the same floor as Avs coach Marc Crawford.

On the morning of the 26th, the *Detroit News* carried a front-page sports column by Bob Wojnowski titled "A Time For Revenge." In the column, which showed Lemieux's face in an old-fashioned "Wanted" poster graphic, Wojnowski called for the Red Wings to stand up and fight back against Lemieux for the Draper hit.

"Wings fans shouldn't shower him with octopi tonight," Wojnowski wrote. "They should honor him with turtles, because when danger lurks, Lemieux retreats." The word *turtle* would haunt Lemieux's reputation forever after.

After Peter Forsberg and Igor Larionov, of all people, had a scuffle near the Detroit bench at the 18:22 mark of the first, McCarty and Lemieux just happened to be on the same ice together. While everyone else was looking at Forsberg and Larionov trading ineffectual punches, McCarty saw his chance to sneak up on Lemieux and clock him.

McCarty, best friends with Draper and pound-for-pound the toughest guy on the Red Wings—and who had promised his friend he'd get Lemieux back—reared back and threw the hardest punch of his life at the shield-wearing Avs veteran. The punch hit Lemieux square in the face and dropped him straight to his knees.

Lemieux tried to cover his head from the coming onslaught of follow-up punches, and in the process he gave photographers on hand the perfect shots on which to plaster the "Turtle" headlines that would follow the next day.

Lemieux would later claim McCarty sucker-punched him, and it depends on one's definition of the term whether that was true or not. Replays do show, however, that Lemieux was looking straight at McCarty when he threw the first punch.

"I cold-cocked him," McCarty told me years later, for my book on the great Avs-Wings rivalry, *Blood Feud*. True, but Lemieux never really saw the punch coming. It happened a millisecond after he faced McCarty.

Lemieux would later blame himself for not being better prepared for what might happen that night. "I should have been more on my guard than that," he said. "I should have known they wanted a moment like that to rally around and build off of. I wasn't as good a fighter as McCarty, but if I had prepared myself better, what happened wouldn't have happened. I fought him the next year, and thought I did fine for myself."

True, Lemieux got his balls back, as they say, the following season in a real, honest-to-goodness fight with McCarty. But for the rest of the 1997 season, the Avs had all their swagger transferred to Detroit in that first McCarty punch.

Despite Patrick Roy's attempts at salvaging Fight Night in Detroit against aging Wings goalie Mike Vernon, the Avs looked like the losers in the macho part of the game. Then, in overtime, the Avs lost the actual game on a…wait for it…McCarty goal. Referee Paul Devorski later admitted to me, for *Blood Feud*, that he should have given McCarty a game misconduct for jumping Lemieux unprovoked.

But none of that mattered come playoff time. The Wings gained a ton of confidence from the night and went on to beat the Avs in six games of the 1997 Western Conference Finals.

"We had to win that game too, not just the fights," McCarty recalled. "Winning the game made it so that we could come into the dressing room and say, 'We're as good as that team, and we can beat them in the playoffs. That's what happened.' If we lost that game, we still wouldn't have been able to say that."

The '97 series started out well for the Avs—a tight Game 1 victory. They had a 2–0 lead in Game 2 as well, before the roof caved in. Detroit's super puck possession finally started to wear down the Avs, and they took Game 2 with Scotty Bowman slapping the boards in jubilation when it was over.

"When I saw that, I started to worry for the first time in earnest," Crawford said. "Scotty rarely did anything like that. They had the momentum, and they capitalized on it from there."

The Avs lost Games 3 and 4, and neither was very close. They had one last champion's punch in a 6–0 Game 5 win at home but ran out of gas in Game 6. The Wings finally had their true revenge for the events of a year earlier.

18 Joe Sakic—Almost a Ranger

On July 28, 1997, the New York Rangers—only three years removed from winning their first Stanley Cup since 1954—lost their captain, their best player, and their heart and soul in veteran center Mark Messier. The Vancouver Canucks swooped in and stole Messier away with a three-year, $20 million free-agent contract.

Nearly 10 days later, on August 7, the Rangers shocked the hockey world by offering Joe Sakic a three-year, $21 million contract as a Group 2 restricted free agent. Under the rules of the NHL at the time, the Avs had the option of either matching the offer down to the final dotted *i* and crossed *t* or accepting a raft of draft picks from the Rangers as compensation.

With a payroll that was only $16 million for their Cup-winning team of 1996, this was a serious hand of poker played at the Avs by the deep-pocketed Rangers. At an average of $7 million a year, this would be far and away the largest salary of any player on the team, which to that point was Patrick Roy at a little more than $4 million per. In fact, it would make Sakic the highest-paid player in the NHL, guaranteed.

There was a big catch to the contract too: $15 million of it would be paid up front in one gigantic check as a signing bonus. The Avalanche's entire Stanley Cup payroll of $16 million would have to be nearly matched in one signed Charlie Lyons check within seven days if they were to keep their 28-year-old captain and recent Conn Smythe winner.

The Rangers structured the deal in a way they thought Lyons and Ascent wouldn't be able to match. The Avs had a great team, but they'd already shown signs of not being able to keep their financial house in order. The fact was, Ascent was not a very deep-pocketed company in relation to most team owners. Their No. 1 stream of revenue was receipts from hotel room movie rentals, and even in 1997 the smart computer people could see the writing on the wall that such a business's salad days would be numbered because of broadband technology.

This happening in August, I was caught completely unaware of the offer. Hockey reporters like me usually don't work much in August. The deal with most newspapers, at least in the older days, went something like this for beat reporters: We'd work at least five days a week during the season, and usually more than that. Anything beyond five days worked technically would put one day of comp time in our bank, and we'd take that comp time, plus our regular one to four weeks of vacation, in the summer months. Essentially, we'd get most of the summer off, with pay, as a winter sport beat writer at a big paper. It was good work if you could get it. At the time, I lived in jealousy of the reporters at the *Rocky*

Mountain News because of their pay system. Not only did *News* reporters get a comp day added to their personal account for anything beyond five days, they also got a day of overtime pay.

Oh, and the *News's* expense account system was a beauty. At the *Post*, we had to have a receipt for anything more than $10 spent on the road or elsewhere using company funds. No receipt, no reimbursement, and I lost a lot of receipts in my day.

The *News* only required a receipt for anything more than $75. That meant that, wink wink, you could have a meal for $74.99 and not provide a receipt—and still get reimbursed for it! All *News* reporters had to do was say, "Yeah, um, dinner for $74" or "Cab to church, $74" and they'd get a reimbursement check for that very amount without having to account for it. No wonder Scripps Howard, their owner, lost big-time money on the paper.)

Compounding Ascent's money problems at the time of the offer sheet was a mass of red tape that was bogging down construction of the planned Pepsi Center, which would wipe away any cash-flow problems with more than 100 luxury suites that had already been presold. The Pepsi Center and the two Denver winter pro sports teams, the Avs and Nuggets, would be sold to former Memphis State college basketball star Bill Laurie and his Walmart heiress wife, Nancy Walton, in a combined package for $400 million.

But Ascent still was haggling with the City of Denver over lease terms and other sticking points, and in the meantime Ascent was on the clock to try and come up with $15 million in cash to hand over to Joe Sakic if they wanted to keep him.

Avs GM Lacroix always liked to drive a hard bargain over contracts, but he very nearly burned a bridge with Sakic when negotiations toward a new deal started early in the summer. Lacroix gave Peter Forsberg a nice three-year $18 million contract before Sakic had gotten a new deal. Lacroix's best offer to Sakic, as July got closer to August, was four years at $20 million. Sakic had just come off mediocre playoffs that spring, so maybe his market value had gone down some in Lacroix's estimation.

Either way, Sakic wasn't amenable to the offer. Though he was never ruled by money as a player, he felt he should still be paid more than Forsberg. Certainly, he shouldn't be earning $1 million less per year. He had several outstanding years already on his résumé, with a record-setting Conn Smythe performance in 1996. Forsberg, as great as he already was, still was just a fourth-year player.

Then came the surprise offer. The Rangers called Sakic's agent, Don Baizley, to inform him a formal offer would be coming his way via fax. Baizley was stunned when he saw the numbers, and quickly phoned Sakic.

Sakic later recalled his response to Baizley was, "Well, I think I'd be pretty dumb to turn that down."

What happened after that has always been cloaked in a bit of mystery, but not the main points, which are: Ascent quickly signed over a 6 percent share in the Pepsi Center to Liberty Media, a local Denver cable and media giant at the time, in exchange for the $15 million in cash to keep Sakic. Peter Barton, the No. 2 man at Liberty, essentially formulated the deal with Lyons. Four years later, Barton died of pancreatic cancer.

The *Denver Post* caught the scoop on all the major particulars of the deal a day in advance. Mike Monroe, the Nuggets beat writer, and I worked in tandem to break the news on the top of page 1A. I still remember Mike walking up to me quietly before the press conference announcing what already was in our paper and saying, "Uh, we nailed it."

By the last of the seven days, with the financing they'd need secured, the Avalanche gave their response to the Rangers in a most unique way. Along with a fax saying they would meet the offer and Sakic wouldn't be going anywhere, the Avs sent over a framed picture of former Democratic presidential nominee Nelson

Rockefeller's famous one-fingered salute to protesters at the 1968 National Democratic Convention in Chicago.

Lyons, a former intern for Rockefeller in Washington, delighted in sending the photo to Rangers GM Neil Smith and president Dave Checketts. At one point during the week, during a conversation on the phone I had with Sakic, he said he would have been excited to play with his boyhood idol, Wayne Gretzky, and that the schools in New York were presumably as good as those in Denver for his young kids.

But when the Avs matched the offer, Sakic, ever the diplomat, smiled and said he'd be happy staying where he always wanted to stay. Of course, those 15 million new reasons didn't hurt his affinity for Denver either.

There was another unlikely source of income that helped keep Sakic with the Avalanche, which we'll get to in our next chapter…

19 Harrison Ford to the Rescue

While Ascent Entertainment Group had a nice cash flow from its hotel pay-per-view business in 1997, they knew they'd need to search for other revenue streams before long to still be able to piss in the tall grass with the big dogs of the sports ownership club.

Ascent CEO Charlie Lyons had a jones to get into the movie business somehow, and around early 1996 he formed an umbrella movie company named Beacon Pictures, and lo and behold, Beacon was able to line up the financing for a new Harrison Ford star vehicle titled *Air Force One*, a tall tale about the president of the United States being taken hostage on the plane by Russian evildoers. The film ran up a budget of about $95 million—with

Ford's salary alone at $20 million—before nearing release on July 25, 1997.

This had the makings of a possible turkey. Much of the dialogue was just plain cliché, and the stunts were ridiculously unrealistic, such as the president holding on to the wing of a jet aircraft while in flight—something that is not humanly possible. As for the Russian villains, led by English actor Gary Oldman in a not-very-convincing Russian tongue, you could have just stamped 1970s Cold War Stereotype on all of them and had them not speak at all. Some of the advance reviews from critics were not kind to the film, and Beacon employees braced for the possible ends of their short careers in the movie business.

But, hey, was anyone really going to bet against Harrison Ford? *Air Force One* became the smash hit of the summer in 1997 and to date has grossed more than $315 million worldwide. When the film opened to then-record weekend box-office numbers, it gave Ascent the financial breathing room it needed. They knew the money would be coming in to cover the contract and then some, and so all true Avalanche fans should always have a copy of *Air Force One* in their DVD library.

Beacon Pictures had two films in the can by the summer of 1997, but originally *Air Force One* was slated for a later fall or Christmas release. The Jessica Lange–Michelle Pfeiffer film *A Thousand Acres* was originally going to go out in the summer. That film turned out to be the real turkey, costing $23 million to make but taking in less than $8 million at the box office.

If *A Thousand Acres* had come out in the summer, the Avs might have had to say good-bye to Sakic. Ascent would have suffered heavy losses on the film and probably would have had to cut the budgets in other areas, and certainly having to come up with a $15 million check would have been more problematic.

Those seven days between the Rangers' offer and the Avs' decision day were permeated by great box office numbers for the Ford flick, and it gave Lyons the confidence to go ahead and match the deal but also with a little help from Liberty, which received 6 percent equity in the Pepsi Center.

When the final decision was made to keep Sakic, the duty of handing over the $15 million cashier's check was given to Lacroix. He drove over to Sakic's house and presented it to him in person, probably a little sheepishly.

20 "No More Fucking Rats!"

When Rob Niedermayer scored to give the Florida Panthers a 2–1 lead on the Avalanche at the 11:19 mark of the first period in Game 3 of the 1996 Stanley Cup Finals, plastic rats rained down on the Miami Arena ice.

Why plastic rats? Supposedly, Florida's Scott Mellanby killed a rat with his stick in the Panthers' dressing before their home opener that year, then scored two goals with the same stick. Panthers goalie John Vanbiesbrouck told reporters that although Mellanby just missed out on a hat trick, he did manage a "rat trick."

Once that got into the papers, a fan threw a plastic rat on the ice the next game after a Florida goal. Then more and more fans started doing it. Pretty soon, the manufacture of plastic rats became a growth industry in south Florida. By season's end, it was routine for hundreds of the rats to flood the ice, which caused a considerable delay after goals.

So when Niedermayer scored, Patrick Roy was pelted with the rats. Some goalies hid from them in their net, but not Roy. He just stood there and took it. But he let it be known in the dressing room after the period that he wouldn't take it anymore.

"No more fucking rats!" Roy yelled to his team.

"You knew he meant it too," teammate Claude Lemieux recalled.

Guess what? There were no more rats. That Niedermayer goal was the last one scored by Florida in the series. That included the next two periods of Game 3, won 3–2 by the Avs, and more than five periods in Game 4's 1–0 clincher in triple OT.

Patrick Roy looks on as the rats rain down.

The rat theme was big with our paper that series. The headline after Game 1 included "Rat-A-Tat-Tat" after a 3–1 win. After Game 2, it was our own "Rat Trick," in honor of Peter Forsberg's three-goal game.

It was big with Miami waiters before Game 3 too. On the night before the game, an Avs party that included Pierre Lacroix sat down for dinner, and when the waiter removed a silver cloche atop a dish, there was a plastic rat garnished on a bun.

Everybody laughed, including Lacroix, but he was not about to be one-upped. Lacroix unscrewed the top of his saltshaker and emptied the bottle all over the rat. "Sir, your rat has been buried by an avalanche!" Lacroix crowed.

21 Marc Crawford

He was one of nine children born to Floyd and Pauline Crawford, in a family so hockey crazy that some of the toughest games he ever played, he said with no hint of exaggeration, were in the backyard with six of his brothers.

Many hockey fans know Crawford as Crow, a nickname he picked up during his coaching days with the Canucks, but his nickname as an NHL player was 747, because of the frequent flights he made between the Vancouver Canucks and their top farm team in Fredericton, New Brunswick. He paid a lot of dues growing up and getting into the NHL as a player, but his path to NHL coaching success was relatively quick and easy.

He got his first NHL head coaching job at 33, with the Quebec Nordiques in 1994. By 35, he had a Stanley Cup and Jack Adams Award on his résumé.

"I tried to appreciate it at the time," Crawford said nearly 20 years later, "but I probably didn't really. I didn't really have much else to compare it to in those early years, except a lot of winning."

Crawford's move from Quebec to Denver made him the first coach in Avs history, and in those early years he was a popular man, saluted by fans everywhere and with all the sponsorship deals he could handle. He plugged everything from cars to satellite TV systems, and had his own shows on radio and TV.

With his perfectly coiffed hair and dimpled smile, Crawford was Mr. Popular in those early Avs years. But just two short years after winning it all, he was gone. A few years later, as coach of the rival Canucks, he was part of a controversial night involving Steve Moore and Todd Bertuzzi that made him a villainous presence in Denver.

Why it didn't last longer between Crawford and the Avs was always something of a surprise, but the fact is coaching in the NHL is a thankless business. After a first-round playoff exit in 1998, GM Pierre Lacroix reassessed every aspect of hockey operations, known as the "dust-settling" period.

Crawford had one year left on his contract and, despite the loss to Edmonton in the first round, felt he was deserving of a long-term extension if he were to stay. The most Lacroix would go was one extra year, though, which didn't sit well with Crawford. So he quit.

Crawford was willing to forego the salary due on that last year and sit it out, then sign with another team in 1999–2000. He did some color commentary for the CBC and was enjoying it when the Canucks fired Mike Keenan and immediately looked to Crawford.

With some good talent on the Canucks and his familiarity with the franchise, Crawford felt it was a good fit and wanted to take the job. But the Avs and Lacroix decided to play hardball, saying they needed compensation from the Canucks to let him out of the last year on his deal.

A contentious standoff ensued, and it wasn't solved without the intervention of NHL commissioner Gary Bettman. The Canucks had to give the Avs a second-round draft pick and $200,000 for Crawford. (That pick, forward Serge Soin, never played in the NHL.)

Despite his youth and a career as a depth wing plugger, Crawford had no fear of standing up to star players, some of whom were older than him. He would bench a top player who wasn't producing, and get right back in his face if he complained about it.

One of my earliest memories of Crawford's intensity happened at the old University of Denver Arena—razed in 1997—where the Avs practiced that first season. Andrei Kovalenko, who would be traded to Montreal in the Patrick Roy deal, wasn't hustling enough in Crawford's estimation, and Crow let him have it. When practice ended, Kovalenko said something to Crawford as he left the ice, and began walking down the steps to the dressing room.

Crawford practically came running after him, cursing the whole time. They took it behind closed doors, but all you could hear was Crawford's high-pitched screaming voice. Documented elsewhere in this book, Crawford had it out with enforcer Chris Simon at practice in the 1996 playoffs, and standing up to Lacroix in the contract standoff took some guts.

Crawford didn't like Lacroix at times in those early years, and my theory is they were both so new to their jobs, and success came so fast, maybe their egos couldn't always fit in the same room. But Crawford later came to respect Lacroix's methods. "He was really good at creating a family atmosphere in those early days, especially right after the move to Denver," Crawford said. "I think he did a good job of communicating to everyone what our objective as an organization was going to be, that we were always going to go all out to win it all. That set a very high bar, but I think everyone began to really embrace that kind of attitude. I was just very intense then. I still am but, you know, with age comes a little more maturity."

Crawford also coached the Los Angeles Kings and Dallas Stars before being fired by Dallas in 2011; he spent the next few years coaching in Switzerland. In a 2015 interview, the suddenly 54-year-old Crawford hoped for another chance at the Cup that came so quickly in his career.

But no matter what, nothing can take away the great memories he'll always have of Denver. "We were all very blessed to have the team we did, to have the people in the organization that we did," he said. "It will always be a special time in my life."

The Plane Ride Back from Dallas, 2000

For the second straight year, an Avalanche season was ending in a plane ride back from Dallas as losers of a Game 7 of the Western Conference Finals. Neither was any fun, but the second one, in 2000, was as grim as it could get.

The Avs were a better team than Dallas in 2000. They outshot the Stars 204–170 in the series, which isn't a huge margin, but there was a definite disparity in the quality of scoring chances throughout. And yes, Ed Belfour outplayed Patrick Roy in the series. Eddie *was* better, as the chants from Stars fans went.

But the Avs beat themselves in that series. They missed countless bunny chances around the net, they hit the post numerous times, they just couldn't finish anything. The final moments of Game 7 encompassed everything.

Ray Bourque took a shot from the point with time running out. Adam Deadmarsh tipped the puck and it appeared ticketed to a corner of the net, which would have tied the game 3–3. But the puck rolled away from the goal line and into the post at the last second, stopping harmlessly as time ran out. The Stars scored two very fluky goals in their 3–2 win.

The frustration was immense in the dressing room. Deadmarsh just sat at his locker for a long time, in full uniform, staring at the floor. Peter Forsberg took the final game sheet, looked at it for a second, crumpled it up, wound up, and threw it hard into the trash can. It all came down to Dallas having a big advantage by having Game 7 on home ice for the second year in a row.

Most of the plane ride back, witnesses say, was stone silent. But toward the end, on arrival into DIA, a group of veterans gathered near the back of the plane. Included were Bourque, Roy, Joe Sakic, and Dave Reid.

"We made a vow, right then and there, that we would not have any Game 7 on the road the next year," Reid recalled. "It was like, 'We will *not* have a *goddamned* Game 7 on the road *at all* next year.' And then we said we'd see each other at camp and that everybody had better be ready to go, because we're not going to go through this again. Next year, we're winning."

That, of course, is exactly what happened. The Avs of 2000–01 were one of the best teams of all time, going 52–16–10–4, winning the Presidents' Trophy and the Stanley Cup. Yet the Avs needed to win two Game 7s in the playoffs—one against Los Angeles and one against New Jersey. Home ice made the difference again.

"We knew we were going to win that Game 7 against the Devils," Reid said. "That was another plane ride [on the way back from New Jersey after Game 6] where we all kind of looked at each other and knew what would happen. There was no way we were going to lose that seventh game at home, not with a Cup on the line and Bourquie's last game and all."

23 The Steve Moore– Todd Bertuzzi Incident

It remains probably the most stomach-churning incident I ever saw while covering hockey, although I didn't actually cover the game in which it happened.

Denver Post colleague Terry Frei was assigned to cover the Avs' game against the Vancouver Canucks on March 8, 2004, at General Motors Place. The Avs had played the night before, losing at home in ugly fashion to Calgary. The NHL trade deadline was the next day, so most of everybody's focus was more on that than what might happen in the game.

The Avs had been scuffling badly entering the game, but absolutely everything went right in the first two periods, and they built themselves a huge 8–2 lead by the third. One of the goal scorers for the Avs was a hardworking depth center named Steve Moore, an Ontario native who played college hockey at Harvard.

A few weeks before, Moore had injured Vancouver's most skilled forward, Markus Naslund, with a big open-ice hit at the Pepsi Center. The Canucks vowed revenge on Moore, with enforcer Brad May saying, "It'll be fun when we get him."

The Avs and Canucks played another game not long after that, at the Pepsi Center, but with NHL officials such as discipline czar Colin Campbell at the game, nothing happened. But much like the Detroit Red Wings did in 1997 with Claude Lemieux, the Canucks waited until getting on home ice to get down and dirty.

Most everyone expected someone on the Canucks to make a run at Moore or drop the gloves, or both, and Moore did indeed fight Vancouver's Matt Cooke in the first period of the game. Thing is, if the Canucks wanted physical retribution on Moore, they didn't get it with the Cooke fight, as Moore more than held his own against the sneaky, dirty player Cooke always was.

So with the score an embarrassing rout and the Canucks still looking for a pound of Moore's flesh, Canucks coach Marc Crawford sent out one of his other bigger and tougher players, Todd Bertuzzi.

As Moore was trying to skate out of the Avs' zone and join the play up ice, Bertuzzi made no pretense at playing hockey anymore. He skated behind Moore, tugging at his jersey, trying to get him to turn around and, presumably, fight.

But Moore wouldn't turn around. Bertuzzi outweighed him by probably 35 pounds, and he thought he'd already stood up for himself earlier in the game by fighting Cooke and absorbing a couple other cheap shots. When Bertuzzi didn't get the face-to-face confrontation he wanted, he took the coward's way out and punched Moore in the head from behind.

The blow was hard enough to knock out Moore before he hit the ice. Bertuzzi wasn't just content to let Moore fall by himself, though. He crashed down on Moore's body from behind, driving his head and face harder into the ice, then kept sucker-punching him some more. Avs teammate Andrei Nikolishin tried to pull Bertuzzi off him, but by then Moore lay unconscious, his blood reddening the ice beneath his face.

It was just a sickening act, the pure definition of yellow-bellied cowardice. Not only had Bertuzzi picked on someone not his own size, he had hit a man with his back turned. The crowd roared its approval of seeing Moore down but got very quiet when Moore wouldn't move and bloodstains kept getting larger.

Medics brought out a stretcher, and Moore's neck was immobilized. Doctors would determine that Moore had suffered a concussion, facial cuts, and three cracked vertebrae. His season was likely over. It would turn out, sadly, that so was his career. Moore never played again.

Andrei Nikolshin comes to the aid of teammate Steve Moore as Todd Bertuzzi keeps coming.

A genuine media circus ensued. That night, having seen the game live on TV, I made a couple calls to NHL sources to get a sense of how bad Bertuzzi might be punished. Bertuzzi, I was told, would be suspended for a long time, possibly all the way through until the next season.

I went on a Vancouver radio station that night as a guest and reported what my sources were telling me. The host was skeptical it would be that harsh, and so were other Vancouver media types when they heard what I said.

So they must have been shocked a couple days later when the NHL announced Bertuzzi would be suspended for the rest of the regular season and the entire NHL playoffs.

The *Post* sent me up to Vancouver to cover the scene there, including Bertuzzi's tearful press conference, in which he apologized to Moore and said he never meant to hurt him like that. While I maintain that Bertuzzi's actions were despicable, I genuinely believe he was sincere in his apology to Moore at the press conference. I was sitting right in the front row, and Bertuzzi's tears weren't fake.

I remember vividly the cover of the Vancouver tabloid the *Province* the day after the suspension was announced. It had Bertuzzi's mug shot surrounded in black, with no words anywhere on the entire page.

Moore never did accept his apology, which went somewhat against the norms of hockey culture and turned many of the game's purists against him. He was just a "Harvard boy," after all, too good for the game's blue-collar ethic. Even the nastiest of fights are supposed to end with both sides shaking hands and putting it behind them.

But aside from a press conference of his own back in Denver a few weeks later, as part of a night in which the Avs honored him as a guest in a luxury suite, he stayed mostly quiet. Meanwhile, the British Columbia attorney general filed formal assault charges against Bertuzzi, which he pleaded down to in exchange for 80 hours of community service.

Moore later filed a civil suit, which started a nasty smear campaign against him from unnamed Canucks sources, who said he was just milking his injuries looking for a big settlement, that their own doctors had concluded he wasn't hurt as badly as he let on.

That, plus the lack of acceptance of his apology, seemed to again harden Bertuzzi against Moore and the entire situation. In pretrial depositions, he later accused Crawford and the Canucks of ordering him to harm Moore. The whole thing attracted worldwide media attention of the kind the NHL most certainly didn't want.

It would be 17 months before Bertuzzi would play his next NHL game. The 2004–05 season was lost because of the lockout, but by training camp of 2005 NHL commissioner Gary Bettman lifted the suspension. When the Canucks played their first game in Denver that season, media from all over flew in to cover it.

In all my years, I've never heard booing of an opposing player as intense as Avs fans gave it to Bertuzzi that first game. Every time he got near the puck, the boos just thundered down. The Avs won easily, and while Bertuzzi would play several more years in the league, he was never the same player.

Asked his reaction to the booing after that first game, Bertuzzi would only continually mutter, "It is what it is."

In the summer of 2014, at the NHL's annual awards gala in Las Vegas, I turned a corner at the Wynn Resort and Casino, and there was Steve Moore. He was there to be with his brother, Dominic, who was receiving the Masterton Trophy.

I didn't break out any notepad, so the conversation will remain private. But we talked for about 20 minutes, about everything associated with the incident and all he'd gone through. He said the headaches from the concussion still bother him, and at no time had he milked the injuries looking for a big check.

A big check is what he ended up getting a few months later, however. After years of the court case dragging on, he and Bertuzzi/ the Canucks came to a confidential financial settlement.

In the time I got to cover Moore as a player, I was always struck by his genuine joy at being an NHL player, of being a guy who overcame the odds to make it in the highest of all leagues. That check no doubt has created a comfortable life for him financially, but I also have no doubt he would give it right back if it meant he could have gone on to have a normal rest of his career, even if it had only been for two or three more years at a fourth-liner's salary.

24 Roy Does Damage in Anaheim

During a December 1999 game in Anaheim, Patrick Roy was lifted from the game for a few minutes by first-year coach Bob Hartley. The Avs were on a power play and needed a goal to take the lead, but Hartley's players were tired from an extended shift. So he decided to change goalies to get his team more of a breather, inserting Craig Billington in for Roy when the power play resumed.

The Avs scored, and it proved the game-winning goal. Billington, because he was in the net for the game winner, got credit for the win despite never making a save. Roy made every save otherwise in the win. Everyone in a burgundy red sweater was happy coming off the ice at the Arrowhead Pond, except for one player: Roy.

Feeling he was slighted, used as a pawn by Hartley, Roy seethed after the game in an otherwise jubilant room. He decided to take a walk to the visiting coach's office, where Hartley savored the win with assistants Bryan Trottier and Jacques Cloutier, and video coach Paul Fixter. With his goalie stick in hand, Roy confronted Hartley in heated French.

Hartley suggested they talk about things in the morning, as there was a bus to catch out of the arena. Roy would have none of that. He then took his stick and smashed up a TV and a VCR. Roy felt Hartley should have just used his one remaining timeout to give his tired power-play unit a breather, instead of taking him out for Billington. Sure, the move worked, but Roy felt it was minor league.

The Avalanche kept the blowup under wraps for nearly two weeks, when I got tipped off to the whole thing. Even though it was by then an old story, my bosses at the paper and I felt it was still newsworthy. I called Roy, and he acknowledged the story was true.

But then he got really upset with me after the story actually hit the paper. It just so happened Roy's former team, Montreal, was in Denver the day the story was published. It was a pure coincidence, nothing more. Believe me, we would have published it much sooner if we'd known. But Roy accused me of waiting until Montreal came to town to run the story, to make him look bad in front of all the traveling Canadiens writers who were sure to put their own spin on the story. Roy then took his accusations to a new level. Because I had a good relationship with Paul Theofanous, the agent for Avs players Sandis Ozolinsh, Valeri Kamensky, and Alexei Gusarov, Roy thought one of the three had to have leaked it to Theofanous, who must have then leaked it to me. None of them were my source, which remains known only to me and the other person.

When Theofanous' clients told him they were being fingered by Roy, Theofanous got upset too. He just happened to be in town that day as well, and he insisted we clear the air then and there after an Avs practice at McNichols Sports Arena.

So for at least an hour, maybe more, Theofanous, Roy, Kamensky, and I sat in chairs all facing each other. I told Roy that none of the people he thought were the leakers had actually done so. He didn't believe it, and we just went around and around and around on it for what seemed like forever.

By the end, though, Roy seemed to have calmed down and we finally departed on what seemed like good terms. I never took anything Roy said about me personally. It's part of the job. Hey, I wouldn't like a story like that about me in the paper either. But there was another aspect to my relationship with Theofanous that I did get very upset about.

A rumor got around that the reason I had gotten a decent number of scoops from Theofanous was because I was paying him for them. Excuse me? First off, I was a *print* journalist. I didn't have wads of cash for a secret slush fund. Second, I had a little more integrity than that.

I got really upset over that one, and I knew I had to nip it in the bud. So I then stormed into Pierre Lacroix's office and essentially said I'd sue him and the rest of the organization for defamation and slander if they wanted to keep such a rumor going. Lacroix played dumb, saying it was only something he'd "heard" but didn't believe. OK, I said, but I was red-hot over it for a while.

Years later, we just laugh about it. Roy and Hartley laugh about the incident anytime they see each other, and the same with Lacroix and me. It's sports; it was never that serious.

1996 Playoff Series Against Chicago

If ever there was a series almost too weird, to the point that if it were written fictitiously it might have been considered too far-fetched for publication, it might be the 1996 Western Conference Semifinals between the Avalanche and Chicago Blackhawks.

The following happened: Some Blackhawks players claimed to have been poisoned by lyonnaise potatoes at a Morton's restaurant in Denver before Game 2 of the series. Chicago's best overall player, Chris Chelios, missed Game 4 because of an "equipment problem" that turned out to be too much numbing agent administered by the team doctor. Chicago star Jeremy Roenick called out Avs star Patrick Roy, and Roy responded with a (well-rehearsed) riposte that remains a classic.

Let's start with the classic Roy line, which most serious Avs fans will know. It came after Game 4, when the Avs pulled out a triple-overtime win over Chicago at the new United Center to even the series at two games apiece. Roenick was blatantly tripped from behind by Sandis Ozolinsh in one of the overtimes, as clear a penalty as ever existed in the history of the sport. It should have been a penalty shot, and at worst a two-minute power play.

But referee Andy Van Hellemond—still part of the single-referee system of those days—let it go. Roenick was robbed on the play that would have given the Blackhawks a 3–1 series lead. As we reporters asked Roenick before the next game about his thoughts on the noncall, he took a shot at Roy, saying if he'd had a clear shot on him Roy's "jock would be still be hanging from the rafters of the United Center" like a previous breakaway goal he scored in the series.

Roenick's verbal blast came at about 12:30 PM that day, at McNichols Sports Arena. The Avs were practicing later in the day, and Roy had gotten a heads-up from Mike Keane about what he said. When it was time to interview Avs players later in that afternoon and Roy came to the podium, he had his answer ready when asked about Roenick. "I can't really hear what Jeremy says, because I got my two Stanley Cup rings plugged in my ears," Roy said in his broken English. He got a huge laugh from the press on hand (play the video on YouTube and you can still hear Terry Frei's cackle right away).

The lyonnaise potatoes incident went something like this: On the night before Game 2, a group of players went to Denver's Morton's steakhouse for dinner. Ed Belfour and Murray Craven did not play in the game because, they said, they got food poisoning after eating at Morton's—and specifically blamed the lyonnaise potatoes they each had.

Was that the truth? Neither Craven nor Belfour ever said much more about it, but the Morton's management people were not happy, claiming there were no other reports of people being sick from eating them that night.

In Game 4, an epic contest won when Joe Sakic redirected Alexei Gusarov's shot from the blue line in triple overtime, Chelios never played because of what the team described as an "equipment problem." It turned out Chelios, nursing a moderate sports hernia at the time, was given a needle shot in the wrong place just before Game 4 by the team doctor, Louis Kolb.

Chelios couldn't feel his right leg in warm-ups. Every time he pushed off, he fell down. He tried everything to relieve the numbness—taking hot tubs and riding a stationary bike—but it never wore off. Until right after Sakic's goal, that is. If the game had gone to a fourth OT, Chelios would have been out there, and maybe the game—and series—would have turned out differently.

The Avs won the series back in Chicago in Game 6, another double-overtime affair. Ozolinsh, with irony, won it with a goal in front of Belfour. The Avs could have lost that series in so many different ways, but they got all the breaks. Not only did Chicago play without star goalie Belfour in the rubber Game 5 because of alleged food poisoning, and Van Hellemond swallowed his whistle in Game 4 in a game Chelios never could play, but Chicago lost top young forward Tony Amonte early in Game 4 to a leg injury after being hip-checked by Adam Foote into the boards.

The Avalanche dressing room changed after Game 3 of the series. Colorado lost in overtime on a Sergei Krivokrasov goal in which he capitalized off a turnover by veteran defenseman Craig Wolanin. In the dressing room afterward, Claude Lemieux stood up and ripped Wolanin—a former teammate in New Jersey. Roy's glares at Wolanin made it evident he wasn't absolving him of blame, and when reporters approached Wolanin's stall to get his reaction just to the loss—not the rip job in the room, as nobody had any idea by that point—Wolanin was in tears.

Wolanin never played for the Avs again. Take a look at the video of the Avs after they beat Florida in Game 4 of the Stanley Cup Finals and you can see Wolanin half-heartedly taking part in the celebration. Despite the awkwardness of the Wolanin situation, the Avs became a "stop being polite and start getting real" kind of team. Nobody cares about people's hurt feelings anymore.

Roy and Lemieux were true killers on the ice. They didn't care about feelings, just results. Other players might have wanted to comfort Wolanin, but after seeing Roy and Lemieux's no-prisoners attitude, they started to harden in their outlook.

The team lost only two games the rest of the playoffs with that newfound attitude.

26 2001 NHL All-Star Game

If you really want my most vivid memory of the 2001 NHL All-Star game, which was held at the Pepsi Center, it's this: me standing in front of the 1980s pop artist Thomas Dolby and being too timid to say hi to him and tell him that "She Blinded Me with Science" was and still is one of my all-time favorite songs.

I just never wanted to be *that guy* around famous people. One time in Vancouver, I was standing in line to rent a car, and who did I notice standing *right behind me?* None other than movie star Ethan Hawke. I never said a word to him, despite the fact that we were the only two people in line, and don't you always say *something* to the person when it's just you two in a line, one foot apart?

Other encounters with famous people over my 19 years of almost constant travel covering the Avalanche: sitting one seat ahead of the lead singer of the Bay City Rollers on a small plane to Calgary and listening to and watching him get absolutely tanked after six or seven scotch and sodas; standing one spot ahead of Martin Sheen at LAX once; my tablemates and I saying hi to Dave Matthews at the Sherlock Holmes bar in Edmonton, and pleading with him to take over for the terrible one-man band that was playing onstage; seeing Bill Clinton inside the White House during a private NHL tour at the 1998 Stanley Cup Finals; seeing Cuba Gooding Jr. a couple times; and seeing Sylvester Stallone at a Flyers game.

The 2001 All-Star Game in Denver on February 4 was a real happening for the city, largely because of all the Avalanche players who took part. Representing Colorado were Joe Sakic, Peter Forsberg, Patrick Roy, Ray Bourque, and Milan Hejduk. The game featured North American players vs. the rest of the world, and North America won 14–12.

The game remains memorable to many Avs fans because of the opening faceoff, between Sakic of North America and Forsberg of the World. Sakic, Forsberg, and Hejduk went on to score goals in the game, which was also memorable because of the recent return to health and action of Pittsburgh Penguins superstar Mario Lemieux. Bill Guerin was named MVP for his hat trick performance.

NHL All-Star Games are excruciating for real hockey fans to watch. There is virtually no hitting, almost never a penalty, and the players couldn't care less about the game. The game has never done very well in the ratings either, and some think it will go away eventually and be replaced by more outdoor games.

But this was a good game. So many Avs in front of the home fans made for a truly lively event. The official NHL All-Star party was interesting too. It was held on the dirt floor of the Denver Coliseum, where the National Western Stock Show had occupied it about two weeks before. The whole place still smelled like cow shit, but that only gave it more of a real Colorado feel.

27 Bob Hartley— Always in Motion

His father died when he was a teenager. He had to give up some of his personal hockey ambitions to go to work at a young age, to help support his family. Most of that work was at the local windshield factory in Hawkesbury, Ontario—about halfway between Ottawa and Montreal.

It was through sheer toughness, perseverance, and a legendary work ethic that Bob Hartley made it out of that windshield factory and into the big time of hockey.

Hartley coached the Avalanche from 1998 to 2002 before being fired midway through his fifth season. In the four full years he coached the Avs, they made it to the Western Conference Finals all four times and won a Stanley Cup in 2001.

In all my time covering the NHL, I never saw anyone with the sheer energy of Hartley. Sitting still and/or not talking seemed impossible for him. He was always on the go, always on to the next thing, always thinking about his next game, his next practice, his next play.

He never played in the NHL, never even in the minors. His formal education, partly because of his life circumstance, was limited. But that never stopped Hartley either. He was and remains a master communicator. He probably would be the greatest sales-man of all time if he worked for some company pitching their product. He could converse with anybody, rich or poor. He had a booming voice.

He was and is totally obsessed with the game of hockey. He never stopped talking about it…never. Because of that, he could sometimes drive his players crazy. Nobody who makes it to the NHL as a player is lazy—it takes a brutally strong drive. But Hartley's zeal for the game was 24/7. He never got tired of being at the rink and working. In the off-season, his idea of relaxation was

Bob Hartley argues his case during a 2002 game.

to teach hockey at a camp he founded in York, Pennsylvania, in 1997 while he coached with the nearby Hershey Bears of the AHL.

Hartley won a championship with the Bears, and when Marc Crawford departed in 1998, he won the promotion to the Avs. Things didn't start so well, however.

The Avs lost their first four games under Hartley. They came into Los Angeles 0–4–0 and trailed the Kings by two goals with less than two minutes left in the third period. A mini-miracle later, the Avs salvaged a 5–5 tie. Hartley gradually got his team better, but things looked hopeless by the second round of the playoffs.

The two-time defending Cup champion Detroit Red Wings won the first two games in Denver, and Hartley looked foolish in sending out his fourth line at the end of Game 2 trying to stir up trouble. Hartley seemed totally overmatched against the legendary Wings coach, Scotty Bowman.

That presumption proved very wrong. Hartley got a break for Game 3 with the return of Valeri Kamensky from a monthlong wrist injury, which allowed him to spread out his top three lines better. Then Hartley devised a new defensive scheme. Essentially it was a neutral-zone trap, something he'd been loath to try all season because of all his star forwards who might chafe at such a system.

Instead of squelching his own offense, though, the trap brought about more goals. The Wings were confused by the new system and started to make a few turnovers, which the Avs turned into a lot of odd-man rush goals against veteran goalie Bill Ranford, and later Manny Legace. The Avs stormed back to win the series in six games, and any headlines about the Wings' coming dynasty never saw their way into print.

Hartley's team beat Bowman's Wings again the following season, in a five-game series. After successive seventh-game Western Conference Finals losses to Dallas, Hartley and his players vowed if there was to be any seventh game of a playoff series in 2000–01, it would be at the Pepsi Center. The Avs would need two such games—in the second round against Los Angeles and the Cup finals against New Jersey—to earn a ring.

The 2001–02 Avs needed seventh games to win the first two rounds of the playoffs, and had another one against Detroit in the conference finals. By then, the Avs had little left in the tank and lost big.

It was still something of a shock, though, when Hartley was fired the following season. Four years and four conference finals, with one Cup, wasn't good enough to allow him to see through a fifth season? But nobody ever said life was fair for NHL coaches. And the fact is, Hartley's relentless drive and demeanor probably had burned out some of his top players on him by then.

Hartley went on to some success as coach of the Atlanta Thrashers before getting axed there too. He remade himself as a TV analyst for a few years before taking an opportunity to coach in Swizterland. After a championship there, the Calgary Flames gave him another shot. In 2015 the Flames were a playoff team again.

In the movie *Wall Street*, Gordon Gekko praises Bud Fox for his persistence, saying his face should be in the dictionary next to the word. Bud Fox's, and Bob Hartley's.

28 Columbine

April 20, 1999, was a practice day for the Avalanche. It was slated for 11:00 AM at Family Sports Center in Centennial, about a 30-minute drive from my apartment on West Mansfield Parkway in Lakewood. Recently divorced, I lived in a Spartan two-bedroom place save for one luxury item—a giant 60-inch television laid right at the foot of my bed, one of those older TVs that came in a black, faux-wood, four-sided square with about 20 inches of depth. When the divorce happened, it was the one present I gave to myself.

Because this was a playoff practice and all, I got up a little earlier than usual and drank my normal two or three cups of strong coffee while reading the morning papers. Right at about 10:00, I locked the front door and hopped in my black Honda Civic. My usual route to get to practice was to drive south on Wadsworth Boulevard, then make a left on Bowles Avenue followed by a right turn on Broadway, about 10 miles or so, then a left on Arapahoe Road for the last six or seven miles to the facility.

The drive was uneventful. Driving East on Bowles, I passed one of Colorado's largest high schools, Columbine, on the right. I'd been in the school a couple times in my prep sports writing days, covering basketball mostly. Many times I visited the public library right next to the school. Known as a strong school academically and athletically, Columbine was one of the more desirable public schools in the metro area.

It was settling into a spirited but otherwise routine practice by the time a news flash filtered around the rink, something about a school shooting. The details were vague at first, and everybody mostly went back to paying attention to the practice in anticipation of a first-round playoff series at home against the San Jose Sharks.

Right around noon, though, more details began to emerge. The shooting was at Columbine. 911 calls were coming in to dispatch, some from kids in the school on cell phones, saying at least two gunmen had opened fire and that explosives had been detonated. Before long, it was all over every TV station, including CNN.

Two Columbine students named Dylan Klebold and Eric Harris carried out an attack they had been planning for months. Armed with machine guns, shotguns, and other weaponry, they began shooting at 11:19 AM. Not even an hour later, 12 students, 1 teacher, and the perpetrators themselves were dead, and 24 others were wounded. At that point, it became the most deadly shooting at a public school in US history. Sadly, that number has been eclipsed since.

As players began to come off the ice, they learned the horrible news along with the rest of us. By that time, I knew I wouldn't be writing any conventional stories about the Avs preparing for Game 1, and so did everyone else in the media. The TV crews on hand to film practice left on orders to get to the school and help provide coverage.

Some of the reporters from San Jose also were told by their editors to get over to Columbine. By 1:00 or so, nobody was talking about any hockey game anymore. As the beat guy covering the Avs for the *Denver Post*, though, my job was to stay with the team and write any developments that might come, from a hockey perspective.

From that standpoint, the most pressing question quickly became: Would Game 1 still take place as scheduled at McNichols Sports Arena? Avs GM Lacroix, who lived near Columbine in the town of Littleton, soon was in contact with the NHL league office in New York. So too was Sharks GM Dean Lombardi. New Avs owner Bill Laurie soon became involved, and a decision was made: Game 1 would be postponed to a later date.

What happened next, though, was something of a shocker—but perfectly understandable: The Avs agreed to move the start of the series to San Jose. Instead of the usual 2–2–1–1–1 format, with Games 1, 2, 5, and 7 slated for Denver, it was agreed the series would have the first two in San Jose, Games 3, 4, and 5 in Denver, Game 6 in San Jose, and a Game 7 in Denver. The Avs still technically maintained their earned home-ice advantage, but one loss at the Shark Tank to start the series would give it away.

I was with the team every day, and I can honestly say nobody on the Avs cared about any home-ice advantage anymore by the next day. The scope of the tragedy of April 20 became an international story that transcended sport. It would have been wrong, everybody agreed, to hold a sporting event so soon in a grieving city.

Players from the Avs and Sharks visited the school the next day to pay respects. The Avs would wear a patch on their uniforms the rest of the playoffs in memory of the victims. Everybody was shaken up as they continued to learn more, but especially so were the players with children of their own.

Driving home later that day (via a different route), I just couldn't believe it. I'd just driven by the school shortly before the attack. Who knows, maybe I'd driven right past the shooters on the road somewhere. It was chilling, but all I could do was think of how terrible it must have been inside that school.

The Avs won the first two in San Jose but then lost the next two at home. They caught a break when Sharks coach Darryl Sutter, for some odd reason, elected to start backup goalie Steve Shields in the rubber Game 5 at Big Mac, instead of veteran Mike Vernon, who had been strong the previous two games.

The Avs easily put pucks past Shields for a lopsided win, then closed out the series in overtime on a Milan Hejduk goal. As meaningless as sports can often seem, they can sometimes lift the spirits of a community in times of crisis. The Avs, grateful stewards of hockey in a city still only four years old to them, were happy to be able to put some smiles back on peoples' faces.

The Columbine tragedy remains a very dark place in the minds of everyone who lived in Colorado then. May the memories of the victims, and the heroes who saved others, never be forgotten.

29 McNichols Sports Arena—RIP

I really miss McNichols Sports Arena, otherwise once known fondly by Colorado people as Big Mac. If only I could walk through it one more time, to experience the sights, smells, and feelings associated with what for Denver was its top sports arena from 1975 to 1999.

The first time I was ever in the arena was to see a Denver Nuggets game with a friend while on a Colorado visit from New Hampshire in 1990. Five years later, I would call it my practical working address, covering a new NHL team in town.

McNichols Sports Arena opened in 1975, named after a former Denver mayor, Bill McNichols. It cost $16 million to build, quite a princely sum at the time, and was considered state-of-the-art in all manners of technology. The first band to play the venue, ZZ Top, was also the last to play there, in 1999. But by the late 1990s, the building looked antiquated, and owners of the Avs and Nuggets couldn't wait to get out of there for the lucrative luxury suite–filled Pepsi Center.

Hockey fans fondly remember McNichols because there really wasn't a bad seat in the house. From the second deck, you were closer to the ice than at the bigger Pepsi Center. Of course, the Colorado Rockies played there from 1976 to 1982, before moving to New Jersey. The Rockies had a fan named Crazy George, who pounded on a drum and shouted insults to the opposition the whole game, most of which could be clearly heard by everyone because there were usually few fans in the building.

Along with the Rockies and Avalanche, McNichols was home to hockey teams such as the Denver Grizzlies (IHL), Denver Spurs (WHA), and Colorado Flames (CHL). The Avs never won a Stanley Cup on the ice of Big Mac, but they did clinch a Western

Conference championship there, against Detroit, and a large crowd watched the Avs win the Cup against Florida on the Big Mac Jumbotron.

Visiting teams didn't much like the accommodations at McNichols. The visitors' hockey locker room was spartan, just a few benches, hooks on the wall, and a small shower room in the back. When visiting players stepped out of the locker room, they stepped into a hallway the media could pass through to their room. In fact, the media room was only about 30 feet down the hall from the visitors' room, so everything players said before going out on the ice could be heard by anyone in the media room. Lots of "C'mon boys, c'mon boys!" but occasionally you'd get more than that, like a coach ripping into his team or a player getting in another's face.

When the Chicago Blackhawks played the Avs in the 1996 Western Conference Semifinals, Blackhawks GM Bob Pulford became annoyed at the media traipsing through the area and demanded the Avs or NHL do something about it. A black curtain was installed thereafter that gave some privacy to the players, and the Avs installed an engraved piece of gold metal on the curtain that read Pully's Curtain.

The hockey "press box" at Big Mac wasn't really one at all. About 10 rows of an upper deck section were blocked off with tables stripped above the seats. The media essentially sat with the rest of the crowd during games, but I always liked that. To me, being in a sterile, soundproof press box is a bad way to experience covering a game. It *could* be a little annoying fighting through crowds in the concourse after games to get down to the pressroom, where we wrote our stories.

Today, most modern press boxes have elevators that take you down to event level, so you never have to mix with the riffraff of the fans. After the final games were played at Big Mac in 1999, the city didn't waste much time demolishing it to open room for a parking lot that would serve the new football stadium, first called Invesco Field at Mile High.

I wish I'd gone in for one last, quiet look. So many of my greatest memories as a beginning sportswriter happened in that place, not to mention the countless memories for generations of Denver sports fans.

30 The Rob Blake Trade

Rob Blake wanted more money than the Los Angeles Kings were willing to pay, so exit visas were imminent in February 2001. Blake would be an unrestricted free agent after the season, so he made the perfect rental-trade player. The Avalanche was known to be interested in the big, blond defenseman.

Still, it was something of a shock when it happened, especially considering whom the Avs gave up to get him. Adam Deadmarsh, always hugely popular with the fans, was traded to the Kings along with Aaron Miller, a first-round pick, prospect Jared Aulin, and future considerations.

Deadmarsh traded away? He was still a top-flight young power forward, a member of the Avs' vaunted "core," a gamer and one of the most liked players in the dressing room. Peter Forsberg, his best friend on the team, wasn't happy when he first heard of the trade. Not just because he was losing a friend and teammate but because Deadmarsh's wife, Christa, was in the late stages of a difficult pregnancy.

But those are the occasional hardships that pro athletes have to be ready to absorb. And the fact was, getting a player like Blake just wasn't going to come cheap. Not only was he physically dominant in his own end and a terrifying open-ice hitter, but Blake had one of the hardest slap shots in the league.

The trade had its second-guessers, though. Why would Pierre Lacroix risk breaking up the chemistry of a team that was already well on its way to winning a President's Trophy? Wasn't the defense good enough already, with Ray Bourque and Adam Foote leading the way?

Let history record the trade as a winner for Lacroix. The Blake-Bourque-Foote top three was just a monster, and he made the power play that much better. Bourque fired bombs from the left point, and Blake from the right. When they didn't feel like shooting, Forsberg, Joe Sakic, Milan Hejduk, Alex Tanguay, and Chris Drury could do a few things with the puck down low.

He is largely forgotten in Avs history now, but Steve Reinprecht, the throw-in by the Kings on the Blake trade, did a lot of important things for that championship team. He wound up being a valuable player, especially in the playoffs when Forsberg was lost after the second round.

Christa Deadmarsh wound up having two twin girls, who were born premature but grew up perfectly healthy. Adam Deadmarsh immediately did Avs fans a favor by scoring the winning overtime goal that knocked the Detroit Red Wings out of the playoffs in the first round. The second-round matchup for the Kings: the Colorado Avalanche.

31 Deadmarsh vs. Blake, Avs vs. Kings, 2001 Playoffs

It wasn't like the return of Wayne Gretzky to Edmonton in the 1989 NHL playoffs, a year after the trade heard 'round the world that brought him to Los Angeles. But it was still a very strange thing to see in the spring of 2001.

The Avalanche had an easy time of it in the first round of the playoffs against the Vancouver Canucks, sweeping them. The Kings upset the Detroit Red Wings in the first round, capped by an overtime series-clinching goal by Adam Deadmarsh. That put the Kings into the Western Conference Semifinals against the Avs, just about three months after the teams had a blockbuster trade together.

The Kings weren't supposed to be much of a playoff threat, especially after trading Blake to the Avs. But they got hot down the stretch and slipped into the postseason, and there they were, at the Pepsi Center for Game 1.

The series went seven games and the Avs took Game 7 by a seemingly laughable 5–1 final. It was anything but a laugher, and when you talk to Avs players today about that whole playoffs, some think their toughest challenge came not from the Devils in the Cup Finals but from the Kings in the second round.

For starters, it was a hugely distracting series for Blake to play. He had spent close to a decade with Los Angeles and was one of the last players with ties to the "Hockeywood" days when Gretzky played there.

Blake still had a house in Manhattan Beach and young children, and was still trying to get used to his new surroundings—not to mention the pressure of being the supposed final piece of a championship team. Now he had to face his former teammates in a playoff series and had to answer a million media questions about it all.

The Kings stole one of the first two games in Denver, so L.A. had home-ice advantage at the Staples Center by Game 3. When Blake first touched the puck, boos rained down on him. It wasn't just for the first few times either. The booing was long and loud every time he touched it. Blake tried to shrug it all off, but the fact is, it bothered him some.

How embarrassing would it be to lose to the team you thought you'd outgrown, to be the alleged missing piece of the puzzle only to be knocked out by the team that didn't think you were worth the money? The anxiety of such a scenario wore on Blake.

By Game 5, though, Blake's worries seemed over. The Avs struck back with wins in Games 3 and 4 in L.A., including a goal on Felix Potvin by Blake from outside the Kings' blue line that stunned the crowd.

But if there was one thing that bedeviled Bob Hartley's Avalanche teams, it was the tendency to let up with a lead in a playoff series, especially in potential closeout home games. Kings coach Andy Murray challenged his team after a tough Game 4 loss, wondering to the media "whether we'll have a full plane or not" to Denver.

The Kings pulled out a 1–0 victory in Game 5 on a Luc Robitaille goal, and to the aggravation of everyone, there would be another trip to Los Angeles for a Game 6. The final there: 1–0 Kings, on a Glenn Murray overtime goal. Suddenly, the Avs couldn't score anymore.

"That one in Game 6 was pretty frustrating," Avs veteran Dave Reid recalled. "A team with our talent getting shut out twice in a row? That was a bit of a shock to us. But we knew we still had Game 7 at home, and those were the games we worked hard to have in the regular season."

Despite Bourque, Blake, and Foote on defense, nobody on the Avs had any answers for the Kings' top line of Deadmarsh, Zigmund Palffy, and Jason Allison. They were simply dominant with puck possession down low, constantly bearing down on Patrick Roy with pressure on every shift.

In the late stages of Game 6, though, Allison hurt a thigh. By Game 7 he could barely walk. Although he played, Allison just didn't have any push-off with the bum leg. The Avs caught a big break with his injury.

The score after two periods in Game 7 was 1–1. It was nail-biting time in a big way. Would this Mission 16W team choke a 3–1 lead and the series to the Kings? Anything seemed possible as the puck dropped for the third, but finally the Avs broke through again against Potvin.

Drury—who else?—scored the clutch, tie-breaking goal. Ville Nieminen, a likable Finn off the ice who was a great agitator to opponents on it, followed that up with a long slap shot from the left boards.

When the game was over, you could see a visible difference in Blake's demeanor. His sense of relief was palpable. He warmly shook the hands of and hugged most ex-teammates but was very happy not to have to see a Kings logo again for a while.

There was a lot of celebrating that night for Avs players, with most doing so at the Denver ChopHouse & Brewery. For Peter Forsberg, however, the night did not end well (more on that in the next chapter).

32 The Night Peter Forsberg Lost His Spleen

Peter Forsberg was tired, had a bit of a stomachache, and wanted to just go home. But teammates talked him into going to the Denver ChopHouse & Brewery to celebrate the Avalanche's 5–1 victory over the Los Angeles Kings, a win that put them into the 2001 Western Conference Finals for the fifth time in six seasons.

That reluctant decision probably saved his life. Why? Because in the spring of 2001, Forsberg was living quite a ways from town, in a big house near the mountains. The nearest hospital was probably at least a half hour drive away.

Most of the team went to the ChopHouse, to a private room near the back, for a late dinner and assorted beverages. Sitting at a table together were new Avs owner Stan Kroenke and GM Pierre Lacroix, and as Forsberg walked by they noticed him looking a bit off. Forsberg said his stomach was hurting a little. But hey, it had been a tough series, and bumps and bruises and aches of all kinds were to be expected by that stage of the playoffs.

Forsberg then went upstairs to a more private part of the restaurant, reserved mostly for staffers and friends of the place's manager, Bill Schallmoser. While glasses clinked in celebration and a good time was being had by all downstairs, the pain in Forsberg's stomach started to get much worse. Soon, the great Avalanche center was doubled over in pain and he was losing color in his face.

Schallmoser asked what was wrong, but Forsberg could barely grunt an answer. Schallmoser wanted to call for an ambulance, but Forsberg didn't want that kind of scene. So Schallmoser and others drove him straight to the emergency room at Denver's Rose Medical Center.

At about 3:00 AM, doctors discovered Forsberg's spleen had ruptured. A fist-sized organ in the upper abdomen, the spleen mostly filters foreign objects in the blood. Yet the spleen itself is not necessary for survival. You can live a perfectly normal life without one, with the right medication. But when the spleen ruptures, it can be life-threatening. There is loss of blood, and people can go into septic shock quickly, and death is a real possibility if not treated in time.

If Forsberg had been home up in the mountains, he might not have made it in time to get the right treatment. As it turned out, he received a successful surgery that night, with the prognosis of a full recovery.

The bad part: he would be sidelined for a few months while everything healed. The Avs' most talented player would miss the final two rounds of the playoffs. For someone who lived to play in the biggest of games, this was quite a blow.

"I just couldn't believe it at the time," Forsberg recalled more than a decade later. "I still don't know how the injury happened. It was probably the most pain I ever had in my life. It felt like my whole stomach was on fire or something. I thought I was going to die for a little bit. It could have happened, I guess. I was lucky."

Forsberg was soon out of the hospital and went to the rest of the playoff games. Before Game 7 against the Devils, the game for the Stanley Cup, Forsberg actually tried to talk the team into letting him play.

"I wanted to do it," Forsberg said. "I wanted to try, anyway. I did a little skating even. But the doctors wouldn't let me even think about it. I thought, *Maybe I can just go out there for a few minutes, maybe play on the power play.* But I'm sure that would have been a bad idea."

Forsberg did take the ice in skates to celebrate with the rest of the team after they had won the Cup. He lifted the Cup over his head and everything. At least he had that.

"That was still really brutal, not being able to play. I think it's a little hole in my career, that I didn't get to play in that second Stanley Cup. But at least we won it. I would feel a lot worse if we'd lost," he said.

Memories of Florida, 1996 Finals

Since a lot of this book was written in the first person because, well, I was there for just about everything in it, I thought some old memories of the 1996 Stanley Cup Finals that never made it into print might be fun.

Twenty years later, as I write this, everything that happened hardly seems possible. How was it that we were in south Florida in June 1996, when the spring before there was no NHL team in Denver? How was it possible a *Stanley Cup* was on the line, between a team that didn't exist a year before and a Florida Panthers opponent that was only three years old itself?

How was it possible that I forgot to pack any shorts before leaving for Miami for Games 3 and 4 of the series? For me, one of my favorite personal memories of the few days we had in Florida is *Denver Post* columnist Mark Kiszla (whose nickname was Kiz) sadly shaking his head at me right after I told him I didn't have anything but jeans and suit pants when he suggested we walk around the beach the afternoon of Game 3.

Kiszla immediately walked me into the gift shop of the Sheraton Miami Beach, where a selection of board shorts hung on metal racks. Kiszla told me to pick out a pair and he would pay for them. I still have those shorts today, and still wear them to the pool sometimes.

Kiszla and I walked the beach, me in my wildly designed, purple-and-gray 1990s-style shorts, and marveled at the fact that we were walking on the beach on the day of a Stanley Cup ice hockey game in Florida, in June, against a team from Denver. I just kept thinking to myself, *How is this happening? How is this happening?*

A couple days before, after Game 1 of the series—which Colorado won 3–1—Kiszla wrote a column attacking the Panthers' style of play, which was predicated on the neutral-zone trap that New Jersey won with the year before. Panthers coach Doug MacLean actually brought a copy of the *Denver Post* with him to a press briefing and denounced Kiszla and came close to actually demanding an apology.

None would be forthcoming from Kiszla, whose response was a mocking "Ah, what's the matter, you can't take it?" follow-up column. The column became the ire of Panthers fans, and as we walked along the beach I joked I was nervous I might be caught in the crossfire of some angry Florida fan who wanted to take him out.

"They'd shoot you first, for picking that color of shorts," Kiz retorted.

There are so many other little things I remember from that series, such as:

- The time the *Denver Post* misspelled Wayne Gretzky's name in a story done by a news-side reporter who parachuted in as part of our Finals coverage. *Sports Illustrated* noted that Wayne "Gretsky" got his name into our paper's hockey coverage, and man was I pissed. Newspapers love to send non–sports reporters to big local sporting events to add a few more angles, and there is almost always some embarrassing mistake like that. The lesson is: leave the sportswriting to the sportswriters.
- Seeing Pierre Lacroix having to essentially play unwilling BFF with Denver mayor Wellington Webb for the night of Game 4. Lacroix was trying to focus on a triple-overtime Cup-clinching game, wanting to spend the time with his closest hockey aides.

But he and the rest of the Avs staff were continually distracted by questions from Webb and his staff, such as "When will this be over?" or "When do we get to go on the ice?"

It annoyed everyone to no end, but he was the mayor, after all, and in the end, he was on the ice with the team and even held the Cup aloft—breaking just about every postgame Cup-clinching hockey tradition there was.

- The computer I used to write the Cup-clinching story was a Tandy Radio Shack TRS-80, commonly known in the business as a Trash 80. It had the memory to hold—and this is no joke—about four or five stories before they'd have to start being deleted to make room for more.

  With the game going into three overtimes, and having to instantly send a "running" story right after it was over, whenever that would be, I already had about the maximum amount of copy before I'd even sent it. I had to have an "If the Avs win" story all ready to go, and an "If the Avs lose" story too. So I had three or four open files going at once, and trying to update them all on that ancient piece of technology had me reduced to a frazzled mess as the game wore on and on.

  Oh, and it took about two full minutes to send a story of any decent length. Some people at that time still used acoustic couplers to send stories on those things. You would actually put both ends of a landline telephone handset into these big rubber suction cups, and somehow you could send your copy from the computer through the handset to your home paper hundreds of miles away. The only catch: It would have to be pretty quiet in the room when you sent with couplers, because too much noise could foul up the transmission. It was not uncommon back then to hear frantic reporters yell, "Shut up! I'm sending using couplers."

- Golfer Craig Stadler, a Denver resident and big hockey fan, traveled to Florida for the two games. He befriended Patrick

Roy, a golf fanatic, and gave him a great big bear hug after Game 4, in which Roy made 63 saves in a 1–0 shutout. "You fucking brick wall, you!" Stadler said to Roy.

- There were literally no people around the Miami Arena about an hour after the game. I mean, none. It was located in not such a nice neighborhood, and people scattered home quickly after games, even Cup Finals games.

  I actually went back to the hotel in a rental car with a couple writers and editors from the *Hockey News*, where I wrote as a freelancer. It's the strangest thing ever walking to the car in dead silence not long after all the noise and pageantry of a Stanley Cup being awarded.

  The flight back to Denver was at 6:00 AM, so I didn't get a wink of sleep that night—the first of many times that would happen over the next 20 years.

- The time I asked *Toronto Sun* and *Hockey Night in Canada* analyst Al Strachan whether he thought it would be a good series still, after Game 1.

  "Are you kidding? This is gonna be a fucking sweep," Strachan said.

  He was right.

- Not long after the Avs won the Cup, the *Post* made a partnership with department stores to sell T-shirts with the front page of the sports section from the winning day. That meant my story, with all its words clearly visible, was on a frigging T-shirt. I still have one, and it's still the weirdest, neatest thing ever.

34 Say Thanks to a Grizzly

The Avalanche was not the only amazing team to win a pro hockey championship its first year in Denver. In their one and only season in town, the Denver Grizzlies went 57–18–6 and swept the International Hockey League Finals against the Kansas City Blades to win the Turner Cup.

That one season, 1994–95, was a great table-setter for the NHL's return to Denver since the Rockies left for New Jersey in 1982. The Grizzlies, a team I covered, were a phenomenon. They completely dominated most games. They scored 339 goals and allowed 235. They went 16–2 in the playoffs.

Ask real, longtime Denver hockey fans, and they'll nod in agreement: the Avs owe a big debt to the Grizzlies. But the Grizzlies never got much acknowledgement from the incoming team, and the Avs' own transcendence made the Grizzlies quickly forgotten.

The Grizzlies were an expansion team too, owned by David Elmore, who also owned the Colorado Springs Sky Sox of Triple A baseball. Elmore hired away Butch Goring from the Las Vegas Thunder to be his first coach and GM, and hired a shrewd sports marketing specialist, Bernie Mullin, to run the business aspects.

The team was helped out by the NHL lockout of 1994–95, because players who normally might have been playing for the Grizzlies' NHL affiliate, the New York Islanders, were forced to play for Denver. One of them, Zigmund Palffy, dazzled crowds at McNichols Sports Arena with his amazing stick-handling abilities and rock-star hair. Another, goalie Tommy Salo, would win the IHL's most valuable player trophy and finished up a fairly successful NHL career with the Avalanche.

The team's top forward, Kip Miller, went on to play 449 NHL games, and there were a handful of ex-NHL players who blended perfectly with the youngsters, guys such as defensemen Doug Crossman, Normand Rochefort, and Gord Dineen, and forward Andy Brickley.

The Grizzlies also had a pair of great heavyweight fighters straight out of *Slap Shot*, Mike MacWilliam and Jason Simon. MacWilliam played only 30 games but piled up 218 penalty minutes, while Simon accumulated 300 in 61 games. They rarely lost a fight, and the Grizzlies put out a poster of the two together that remains a sought-after collectible among hardcore fans.

The poster was of the bare-chested MacWilliam and Simon posing together with the words BEAR FORCE '95 on the top.

Simon, a First Nations Canadian, played for an incredible 31 teams in his career, mostly all in the minors. He tried out for the Avalanche in the late 1990s but was cut. MacWilliam went on to play a bit role as a Russian player in the 2004 film *Miracle*, about the 1980 US Olympic team.

For me, the best part of covering the Grizz was hearing stories from Goring about his NHL days, and those from Crossman too. Goring was very patient with this first-year reporter who had never covered pro hockey, and I cringe at some of the questions I must have asked. He was famous for using the same helmet his father had given him at age 12 all the way through his NHL career, and for his frugality. Legend had it that he traveled with just a toothbrush for one two-week road trip, with another legend being that robbers took everything but his clothes after breaking into the hotel room he was sharing with a Los Angeles Kings teammate.

Crossman, who played 914 NHL games and almost won a Stanley Cup with Philadelphia, always had a good story about his NHL days—though he positively couldn't stand one of his former coaches, Mike Keenan. Mention Keenan, and Crossman's otherwise genial nature would instantly turn sour.

Another character on the team was Jeff "Mad Dog" Madill, a blue-collar type of guy who possessed a great one-timer from the slot. Madill usually carried a few extra pounds and Goring occasionally got on him about it. One time, Madill came back to his locker to find a bunch of Burger King bags that Goring had stuffed in it, as a subtle reminder to lose a few.

When rumors of the Avalanche moving to Denver surfaced, the Grizzlies knew it would be curtains for them in town. So Elmore and Mullin quietly laid the groundwork for a move to Salt Lake City, where they continue today as the Utah Grizzlies.

You still occasionally see a Denver Grizzlies sweater around town or at an Avs game. While the Avs get all the credit for making hockey cool again in Denver, the fact is the Grizzlies laid the groundwork for an easier entry point.

Peter Forsberg's Six-Point Game in Florida

On March 3, 1999, the Avalanche pulled into Sunrise, Florida, for a game against the Panthers, and things didn't go so well at the start. By late in the second period, in fact, the Panthers had built a 5–0 lead and had chased Patrick Roy from the game. Pavel Bure recorded a hat trick before leaving the game in the second period following a hit from Adam Foote. It didn't seem the Panthers and goalie Sean Burke even needed Bure to get their first win ever against the Avs in Florida.

Reporters like me were already well into their game stories even after Peter Forsberg cut the lead to 5–1 with 1:49 left in the second period. Teams just don't come back often from 5–0 deficits, so a "Panthers win" game story appeared safe to write by then.

Wrong. Two more goals and three assists by Forsberg later, and the Avs walked out of National Car Rental Center with a 7–5 victory. It was the greatest burst of individual hockey anyone who was there that night, including me, probably ever saw or will see.

Forsberg was just *incredible*. And here's the thing: he was absolutely *robbed* by Burke out of three or four more points in those final 22 minutes. Forsberg set a career high with the six points but matched it three years later with a six-point game in Nashville. That win over the Predators was a rout all the way through for the Avs, but the game in Florida was all the more amazing considering how dead the team looked through the first 38 minutes.

But then Forsberg just took over everything. He just kept making one amazing pass after another to teammates, especially Adam Deadmarsh and Claude Lemieux. The Panthers were putting at least two checkers on Forsberg everywhere he went, but he just kept making them look like dogs chasing their tails.

Watching it all unfold sitting right next to me in the press box was newly acquired Avs forward Theo Fleury, who had injured himself in his previous game—his first with the Avs at home against Edmonton. A couple Panthers fans spotted Fleury from just below us and started taunting him as the Avs fell further and further behind. When the final horn sounded, Fleury taunted the fans right back. With his ever-present dip of tobacco in his cheek, Fleury razzed the fans with a gap-toothed grin. You had to be there.

After the game, first-year coach Bob Hartley called Peter Forsberg "Mr. Forsberg" and just shook his head at reporters. "Which coach would you like to speak to, the first and second period coach or the guy who coached the third?" Hartley asked.

Down the hallway, Panthers coach Terry Murray called it the "biggest meltdown I've ever seen, an absolute embarrassment" but gave Forsberg his due, saying, "He just took over out there."

When I met Forsberg in Sweden in 2014 for some stories on him prior to his going into the Hockey Hall of Fame, he said that game in Florida was the closest he ever felt to "being in a zone" as a player.

"It all kept happening so fast. It started to feel like nothing could go wrong. It was pretty nice, I must say," Forsberg said. "I remember thinking *This game is over* after it got to 5–0. Sean Burke was a good goalie, and that was a pretty good team. But then they lost Bure and when we got one late in the second, you started to think, *OK, maybe we can still try for something here.* But six goals in the third period on the road doesn't happen too often."

The game before, Forsberg and Joe Sakic were put on the same line with Fleury in a desperation move by Hartley in a game in which the Avs trailed the Oilers 4–0 after two periods. The trio were amazing together and nearly led the Avs to a win before the Oilers held on for a 4–3 victory.

Fleury missed another three weeks with a knee injury, and to this day laments the lost time because he missed getting a chance to play with Forsberg. "Unbelievable player," Fleury recalled to me about 15 years later. "That was one of the most amazing nights I ever saw. I wish I'd been out there to share in that party."

36 September 11, 2001— In Sweden

I was in our tiny room at the Globen Hotel, writing a story for the next day's *Denver Post* on new Avalanche first-round pick Vaclav Nedorost, when my wife, Heidi, came into the room.

"Turn on the TV," she said.

You always know something bad has happened when someone says that.

We only got about five channels on the TV. One of them was CNN International. Both towers of the World Trade Center in New York were on fire. However long after, both fell to the ground and nearly 3,000 people were dead. I watched it all on the 12-inch TV in the hotel room.

The absurdity of that day for me was that I still had to finish the Nedorost story, and it indeed ran in the September 12, 2001, edition of the *Post*.

What's it like to be overseas when your country is attacked by terrorists? Terrible. I think I can speak for any proud American and say we all wanted to be on home soil that day, to grieve and come together with our own. But it wasn't as tough for me as it was for the several New York–based NHL employees who were also in Sweden that day.

We were all there because Stockholm was where the Avalanche held training camp in 2001, barely four months after they beat New Jersey for the Stanley Cup. It was one of those things where people took family along if they could, as we were supposed to be in Sweden for about a week, then in Finland for a few days. Along with training camp, the Avs were to play some exhibition games, sponsored by the NHL and American Airlines, against Swedish and Finnish pro teams.

Of course, the terrible events of Tuesday, September 11, changed everything. Everybody started congregating in the lobby of the Globen when word of the attacks spread. There were a couple bigger TVs there, but more important, there was an Internet kiosk.

Don't forget, this was 2001. Not everybody had a laptop computer handy, and nobody had the Internet available on their cell phones. So the lone Internet kiosk in the lobby soon had people waiting in line to use it. Thing is, it was deathly slow. It took like five minutes to download a page. I remember most people clicking on the *Drudge Report* and getting scary headlines.

Avs players were just like anyone else, staring at the TVs in disbelief. Patrick Roy spoke for most when he said it was like "watching a movie—you didn't think it could be real."

Also on the trip was *Rocky Mountain News* Avs beat writer Rick Sadowski and his wife, Pam. Despite being competitors, Rick and I always got along well, and on this night we all wound up going to dinner together in downtown Stockholm at some really old, stone-floored, Old Europe type of place. We were all supposed to be going to the American embassy in Stockholm that night for an NHL-sponsored dinner featuring the Avs, but that quickly was canceled. Getting on the light rail downtown, because we looked like tourists from America, several people came up to us to wish us condolences. That sizes up the spirit of the Swedish people pretty well.

A couple bottles of wine later, to try and deal with some of the shock, we all went back to the hotel and probably watched TV for the rest of the night. I know Heidi and I did. The NHL employees from New York were understandably fraught after the initial news, as some had trouble getting in touch with loved ones for the first few hours.

By the next day, all anybody wanted to do was get out of Sweden and back to US soil. Of course, that wasn't possible, with air travel restrictions in place everywhere. When all the details of the attacks became known, Heidi and I realized we'd been in one of the airports from which one of the doomed planes departed just a couple days before. Our layover city on the way to Sweden from Denver was Newark, New Jersey, from which United Airlines flight 93—the one on which the passengers overran the cockpit before the plane crashed in Pennsylvania—departed. The airline Heidi and I flew to get to Sweden: United. We flew right over New York City on the way there, and I still remember looking at the Twin Towers from the window.

On Friday, three days after the awful day, we were all still trapped at the Globen Hotel—a fine place otherwise. Then, as if everyone wasn't in enough shock, Peter Forsberg announced he was taking a leave of absence from the team because of foot injuries. Obviously, that became a huge story for an Avalanche beat writer, so the next couple days became a bad blur of trying to find out what the deal with him was, all the while worrying the whole world was going to blow up or something.

With travel restrictions still in place, the NHL made the decision to hold one of the slated exhibition games between the Avs and Brynas of the Swedish Elite League. None of the players wanted to play, but there was simply nothing else to do, really. So on September 15, the Avs beat Brynas in front of a sold-out crowd at Globen Arena—right next to the hotel—on the strength of an Alex Tanguay hat trick. It was just too surreal trying to keep stats on a game that soon after the awful events of four days prior.

The Avs thus became the answer to the trivia question: what was the only North American professional sports team to play a game of any kind in the week after September 11? Watching the game that night was Avs owner Stan Kroenke, who was working behind the scenes trying to arrange a flight out of Sweden for the team the next day. I spent some time with him in his suite in the arena, just talking like two normal guys trying to make sense of the world.

He was successful in working out the details, and so on September 16 the team flew back to Denver, with a stop in Newfoundland for refueling. But Kroenke didn't just take the team back. He allowed everyone connected with the trip to fly back for free, and believe me, there were many grateful NHL employees who'd otherwise been stymied in getting any flights out of there to get back to New York.

Rick Sadowski and I, and our wives, were and remain grateful at Kroenke's gesture. It was supposed to be a fun trip, and I even had plans to go up to Ornskoldsvik to do stories on Forsberg's hometown. Then it would have been off to see Helsinki. It turned out to be an awful week, but as we all knew on the chartered flight back full of catered food and drink, we were lucky.

37 Chris Drury

October 1, 2002, remains a dark day in the memory banks of Avalanche fans. That was the day the Avs mysteriously, shockingly, traded top forward and fan favorite Chris Drury to the Calgary Flames, along with Stephane Yelle, for Derek Morris, Dean McAmmond, and Jeff Shantz. It was a disaster of a trade for the Avs, probably the worst in the tenure of Pierre Lacroix.

All Drury ever did was score big goals to win big games. In his four seasons with the Avs, he scored 11 playoff game winners and many others in the regular season. He worked hard, had a great, team-first attitude, and was not even in the prime of his career when the Avs dealt him away with the misguided notion that Morris would develop into a Norris Trophy–caliber defenseman.

The loss of Drury was profound. The Avs steadily got worse in the coming years, until they were a bottom feeder by 2009. Drury, meanwhile, never won another Stanley Cup, but he did become a captain with Buffalo and the New York Rangers, scoring 37 goals with Buffalo in 2006–07. Morris was traded two years later.

Drury was a very quiet, very intense guy. He always felt he had to prove himself in the NHL, even after he'd already done so. He was drafted 72nd overall by the Quebec Nordiques in 1994, after having won a national championship as a freshman at Boston University and then the Hobey Baker Award after his senior season.

He gained fame as a 12-year-old in 1989 when he pitched a five-hitter and drove in two runs to lead his Trumbull, Connecticut, team to the Little League World Series title over Chinese Tapei. Hockey was his true love, though, and he excelled despite a shorter, stockier frame.

When he came to the Avs' training camp in 1998, he literally had to fight for respect from NHL teammates. One night at the Avs' annual Burgundy-White scrimmage in Colorado Springs, Drury was challenged to drop the gloves by tough defenseman Pascal Trepanier. Drury more than held his own in the fight, and his respect level started going up from there.

He made the club out of camp but was given mostly third- or fourth-line ice time by first-year coach Bob Hartley, who often rode Drury hard in practice. Drury received more than his share of "What's the matter, college boy?" putdowns from Hartley at first, and he nearly was sent back to Hershey of the AHL a couple times.

But by season's end, nobody could dispute that Drury belonged in the NHL. His 20 goals and 24 assists earned him the Calder Trophy as rookie of the year. Drury wasn't big, but he was solid on his skates, with a low center of gravity. He had that big "hockey butt" that gave him strong power in his core. He had an accurate shot and he would shock you at times with some dipsy-do stick handling through traffic.

In the 2000 playoffs against Detroit, he scored an overtime goal to win a double-overtime Game 4 at Joe Louis Arena, then scored in overtime to beat Dallas in Game 6 of the Western Conference Finals before the Avs lost in seven. In the Cup-winning season of 2000–01, Drury posted 16 playoff points, including a couple huge goals against the Devils in the Finals. He practically went through the whole team before beating Martin Brodeur on a shot in a Game 3 win at the Meadowlands Arena.

He was excellent again in 2001–02, but by then Lacroix wanted to restore a "Big Three" on defense, believing one more top D-man to play with Rob Blake and Adam Foote—like Ray Bourque—was the right formula to win another Cup. So he decided to part with Drury and valuable utility man Yelle to get Morris, who proved to be no Ray Bourque.

Drury was shocked by the deal, and he hated it in Calgary. He constantly monitored the media rumors, hoping he would be dealt away from what was then a terrible team. Lacroix believed there was more than enough offensive firepower left to make up for Drury's absence, but what he forgot about were all the intangibles Drury also brought to a team.

Chris Drury celebrates another clutch goal, this one in the 2002 playoffs.

Nobody worked harder to get to loose pucks in clutch moments. Nobody cared about winning any more than Drury did. He was a quiet leader. As time went on, he became more of a vocal leader in Buffalo and New York, and his teams saw lots of success.

Injuries caught up with him midway through a big contract with the Rangers, and his career ended somewhat prematurely. Even today, though, Avs fans often bring up the Drury trade as the fulcrum for the Avs' slide downward from the glory years, despite the presence of Joe Sakic and Peter Forsberg for many years after.

Drury was Sakic's roommate on the road, and Sakic came to admire his gamer attitude. "When you want a big goal, you look to Drury," Sakic often said.

To the chagrin of Avs fans still, they couldn't look to Drury for any more big goals after 2002.

38 LoDo

If you spend any kind of serious time in Denver, you're probably going to wind up in lower downtown, or LoDo to the locals.

This is where you'll find Coors Field, at 19th and Blake Streets. You'll find dozens of eating and drinking establishments. You'll find lots and lots of young people wandering around looking for the next hot spot. LoDo is both trendy and very traditional, with some great history.

Native Americans, including the original Arapaho tribe, settled the areas around lower downtown in the early 1800s. For a time, it was a thriving area, especially when the gold rush started. For much of the 20th century, however, lower downtown became a vast swath of destitution. By the late 1980s, things started to pick back up again.

John Hickenlooper, who became Denver's mayor and later the governor of Colorado, has rightfully received much credit for revitalizing the lower downtown area. In 1988 he opened the Wynkoop Brewery, which sold its own microbrew. The Wynkoop was one of the first to start the microbrew boom that continues today, and soon many other similar businesses sprouted. The Colorado economy, which used to be predicated on the swings of the price of oil, became more diverse in the early 1990s, with information technology leading the way.

In 1995, when Coors Field opened, LoDo really started to boom. The home of the Colorado Rockies, and the place where the Avalanche played an outdoor game against the Detroit Red Wings in February 2015, quickly became the centerpiece of LoDo. Even though the Rockies were terrible for much of their first 20 years in town, Coors is such a pretty place to watch a game, it will probably always be a big draw.

LoDo officially received the stamp of cool—or the mark of shame, depending on your point of view—by being the location of MTV's *Real World 18* in 2006.

Incidentally, the first place the Avalanche's logo was ever seen publicly was in LoDo, on August 16, 1995, at the Westin Hotel along the 16th Street Mall—a long avenue of shops and restaurants and living spaces known for its free bus rides provided by the city.

In a big conference room, the Avs' first team president, Shawn Hunter, unveiled the logo to a collection of gasps. It remains a very unique logo, which was designed by COMSAT Video Enterprises employees Dan Price and Michael Beindorff.

Many Avs players have lived in LoDo over the years, including Peter Forsberg, who bought a swank penthouse in the Triangle section of the neighborhood. Chris Drury once had a sweet pad in the building connected to the Denver ChopHouse, and recent players such as Ryan O'Reilly have called it home.

Here's the Adrian Dater tip for a good night out in LoDo: Have a drink at the Cruise Room at the Oxford Hotel, one of the coolest bars you'll ever see. Have dinner at the Vesta Dipping Grill on Blake Street—it's fondue at its finest. Don't forget your wallet for that place, but it's worth it. If it's summer, catch a few innings at Coors Field. If winter, the Pepsi Center is a short walk from most any LoDo location. Postgame, have a nightcap at the ChopHouse. And say hi to an Avs player, most likely.

39 Patrick Roy, the Second Coming

A four-year, $7 million offer didn't make it happen the first time. When Patrick Roy turned down that offer in 2009 to be the Avs' next coach, it seemed like the door would be closed forever on a future return. Pierre Lacroix, still the team's president though no longer the GM, went out of his way to entice the legendary former Avs goalie and personal client from his agent days.

Was the bridge burned forever between Roy and Lacroix? That's doubtful, but the fact is that Roy's return as coach and VP of hockey operations coincided with Lacroix's exit from the franchise.

In their recruitment of Roy a second time, new Avs GM Joe Sakic and team president Josh Kroenke went to his home turf of Florida. A golf nut, Roy has made Florida his off-season residence for many years. It was at the Bear's Club in Jupiter, Florida, in the summer of 2013, where Sakic and Kroenke made their pitch to Roy to succeed Joe Sacco. This time, the Avs got their man.

In so many ways, Roy's return as a coach was analogous to his initial arrival in Denver as a player in 1995. The Avs were considered a young, talented team on the rise but needed someone to lead them to be real winners. It worked in '95 and, for the first season at least, it worked again in 2013.

Roy won the Jack Adams Award as NHL coach of the year, guiding the Avs to 52 victories and a Central Division title. It was a remarkable turnaround for a team that had finished 29th overall the year before under Sacco.

Roy brought a ton of energy and optimism with him from Quebec, where he'd spent the previous 10 years working as coach

Coach Patrick Roy addresses the team in 2014.

and executive of the QMJHL's Remparts. He scrapped Sacco's more conservative offensive system for one that emphasized more breakouts up the middle. Players such as center Matt Duchene chafed at Sacco's preferred dump-and-chase systems, calling life under Roy "night and day" compared to Sacco.

It didn't hurt that Roy was handed the No. 1 pick in the 2013 draft, Nathan MacKinnon, who made the squad as an 18-year-old and won the Calder Trophy as rookie of the year.

In Roy's very first game, he made national news by pushing the glass partition separating the benches of his team and the Anaheim Ducks, after a shouting match with Ducks coach Bruce Boudreau. Tempers rose on the Avs bench late in the game, when MacKinnon was given a borderline hit by Ducks defender Ben Lovejoy.

After some squawking by players on the benches, Roy gestured toward Boudreau, and things escalated from there. Roy gave the glass a good, hard shove and it nearly toppled onto Boudreau's bald head. Little did Roy know that the glass wasn't secured too sturdily, so the push created a more dramatic visual than he probably ever expected.

Roy was given a $10,000 fine by the league, and stories proliferated that his "temper problem" would possibly be a hindrance to the Avs. But as far as that kind of thing went, that was it the rest of the year, and mostly it was all sunshine and rainbows for Roy's rookie coaching season.

What was really noticeable that first year was Roy's animation on the bench. He had a sublimely loud, piercing whistle that could be heard all the way up to the press box. He used it all the time in making line changes or trying to get a player's attention. You could hear his high-pitched voice a lot too, barking out orders. Sacco's demeanor on the bench was much more subdued and, fair or not, it seemed to have a disquieting effect on his players after a while.

It should be noted, however, that Sacco was a Jack Adams finalist his first year with the team. Roy won it outright his first year but, like Sacco too, failed to make the playoffs in the follow-up year.

It should also be noted that Roy did guide the team to a 91-point season his second year, but the brutal, Darwinian nature of the Western Conference kept his team out of the playoffs.

40 Kariya and Selanne Fiasco

If there was one thing I was sure of in the summer of 2003, it was that I'd be writing about my third Stanley Cup championship team as a beat writer the following spring.

In fact, I gave up on what would have been a significant career change for a chance to cover the 2003–04 Avs—I was that convinced if I didn't, I would be turning down a chance at covering maybe the greatest NHL team of all time.

In the summer of 2003 *Denver Post* sports editor Kevin Dale took me out to lunch and told me he wanted to move me from the Avalanche beat to that of the Denver Nuggets. Feeling flattered at the nice things Dale was saying about me, and being an NBA junkie as a kid, I said yes. It was to be all set: I would be the new Nuggets beat writer for the 2003–04 season. I couldn't wait to get those courtside seats to watch games, something I'd experienced a few times as a fill-in on the Nugs beat previously and which was, believe me, a strong reason why I would take the job. (In later years, courtside seats for newspaper media would be all but extinct, given away to broadcast rights holders and fans at top dollar.)

A couple weeks later, the Avs signed Paul Kariya and Teemu Selanne as unrestricted free agents. Selanne got $5.8 million on a one-year deal and Kariya signed for the ridiculous discount of $1.2

million—with incentives. It was all part of a plan cooked up by Kariya to reunite with former Mighty Ducks of Anaheim linemate Selanne and go to a team that was ready to win a championship. It was LeBron James–Chris Paul–Dwyane Wade–style team engineering before it started to become more commonplace.

I soon realized I would be giving up some financial benefits from covering the Avs and the NHL. Any newspaper writer will tell you: It's the freelance money you can make on the side that really makes the difference in your life, for richer or poorer. You're just not going to make enough of a comfy living writing for the paper alone. I had some good freelance gigs covering hockey, and would lose them by covering the Nuggets. But that really wasn't the big reason why I begged Dale to get the Avs beat back.

It was truly because I wanted to cover the 2003–04 Avs, a team that already had Joe Sakic, Peter Forsberg, Milan Hejduk, Rob Blake, Adam Foote, Alex Tanguay, and Steve Konowalchuk, and that would now have bonafide, A-list superstars Kariya and Selanne joining the roster.

I couldn't believe it when I looked at the potential top two lines: Kariya-Sakic-Hejduk, Tanguay-Forsberg-Selanne. It would be ridiculous. And for a short time, it was.

I convinced Dale to give me the Avs beat back, and after opening night of the 2003–04 season against Chicago, I was happy with the decision. Under new starting goalie David Aebischer, the Avs shut out Chicago 5–0 in a game that could have been 25–0. The Sakic-Forsberg-Kariya-Selanne-Hejduk-Tanguay top six really did look unstoppable. With Blake and Foote as a top-two pair on defense, who cared who the goalie was? This team would only need a few saves a night to win a Cup.

People forget about that season, but by February 12, the Avs were in first place in the NHL after a decisive win in Detroit. Despite some early injuries to the top guys, including Kariya and Selanne, the Avs looked unbeatable again by their return.

Then it all went bad. Selanne suffered a right knee injury at some point, and it never got better. He tried to play through it but clearly was affected. The coaching staff was led by Tony Granato and Rick Tocchet, and both were guys who had played through tremendous pain in their careers, so any kind of injury excuse didn't work too well for them. If you were out there, you were to be judged on your performance. But the fact was, Selanne should have had surgery on the knee. (He eventually had that surgery during the lost season of 2004–05, and went on to many great seasons in Anaheim, including a Stanley Cup in 2007.)

Meanwhile, Kariya hurt his wrist early in the season but was playing well toward the end when, in the last game of the year at home against Nashville, he suffered a badly sprained ankle. The injury came at the end of a meaningless game, and it was just what everyone around the Avs of that season came to fear. Why was Kariya out there in the third period of a nothing game, with the playoffs about to start?

Why would Granato play so many regulars as he did in that game? Fair or not, it was a decision that would haunt Granato the rest of the way. The Avs managed to win a first-round series against Dallas without Kariya, but lost in six games in the second round against San Jose. Selanne was a healthy scratch for one game of the Sharks series, which totally humiliated the proud Finn. He vowed never to speak with Granato again after leaving the Avs.

Kariya returned for Game 6 at home, but by then the Avs just had too many chemistry problems, and the Sharks were, to their credit, a very good team.

Kariya was a very smart, very polite, and very strange guy. He was impossible to get to know, everyone soon realized. He was very guarded in everything he said. It wasn't just with the press. He could seem snobby, but the reality was he was just really shy. He was embarrassed by autograph seekers and reporters crowding around his locker. He answered questions in a dry monotone, never saying anything more than the minimum required. He was most comfortable around really close friends and family, and that was it. He was a bit of a nerd too, seeming only to get animated when talking about *Star Wars* movies. And he was a terrible dresser too; players rode him unmercifully about his wardrobe, especially his shoes.

Selanne was just the opposite. He was gregarious and funny. He had time for any reporter, whether from the *New York Times* or the Halifax *Daily Herald*. He loved to just sit and chew the fat with anyone at his locker. He knew reporters loved a good quote, and he supplied many. The sad story of his time in Denver was he became more and more morose the deeper he sank into Granato's doghouse. Reporters had fewer reasons to hang around his locker as time went on. He seemed like a sad, washed-up type of player, the kind you see all the time at the end of their careers. He ripped Granato a few times off the record to reporters like me, feeling he was being unfairly punished for playing with pain. In Granato's defense, though, Selanne just wasn't a very good player with the Avs, especially in the second half. He seemed to lose all confidence with the puck, fumbling it away numerous times. With the bad knee, he just couldn't be himself.

Soon after that Game 6 loss, I came to somewhat regret my decision to beg off the Nuggets beat. Not only would the Nuggets be a very good team soon after, but there would be no hockey at all to cover in 2004–05 thanks to a lockout. I was soon covering bowling and high school basketball to fill the time.

You live, you learn.

41 Eric Lacroix's Awkward Exit

He was a very nice person who played hard every second for the Avalanche. That much can never be disputed about Eric Lacroix, who played for the Avs from 1996 to 1998 and later served in various management capacities.

But the following are the events that led to his being traded by his own father, Pierre, in the early stages of the 1998–99 season:

I was in Hershey, Pennsylvania, as part of a preseason road trip, eating breakfast at the Hershey Lodge, when two Avs players—who shall forever remain nameless—sat down with me. A few minutes into our conversation, one of them brought up Eric Lacroix. Then both of them divulged a secret: Eric Lacroix, for the benefit of all involved, should be traded.

It was nothing personal. He was a nice enough guy, both said. The problem was, as one might assume, he was the son of the GM, and nobody could really feel comfortable around him or, it was implied, trust him. Fair or not, they both felt he received favorable treatment from his father, at the expense of other more deserving players. His latest contract, for instance, was done right away, while the elder Lacroix had battles with others over money. "We can't be a team with him here," I remember one of the players told me.

Wow. So what could I do with this? Since neither would go on the record about it, I didn't want to write anything. (And the older I've gotten, I've come to believe that shall always be something of a strike against them. I mean, if you really feel it, you should say it with your name behind it. Unfortunately, there are even more people who hide behind the cloak of anonymity in today's society, partially because of the Internet.)

I essentially held on to the story for a few weeks, because I refused to do an anonymous-source story on something so big. I knew damn well it would turn into a fireball, and I had to be sure I had the backs of a player or two if I started to be questioned on the veracity of it. One day at McNichols Sports Arena, though, things blew up in the Avs dressing room, and then it became too much to ignore.

Denver Post columnist Mark Kiszla had started to hear some of the same things about the issues with Lacroix. And yes, I confided some stuff to him too. But he dug it out on his own at the start. So one day he wrote a column saying there were problems with Eric Lacroix being a member of the Colorado Avalanche, that it was creating chemistry issues in the room. I verified to Kiszla that I'd heard the same things, but that was about it. Once I saw the column, I knew it would be a long day covering the team, and it was. Pierre Lacroix already couldn't stand Kiszla. He once walked around the hallway of McNichols saying "What stinks around here?" when Kiszla began approaching from another direction.

Once Kiszla had revealed the alleged problems with the team with Eric Lacroix around, Pierre flipped out. He ordered first-year coach Bob Hartley to go into the room with the players and, with the paper in hand, insist the column wasn't true.

Maybe because of a language barrier, rookie Milan Hejduk was thought to have been one of the leakers of the disharmony. He wasn't. While I won't reveal whom the two players were, I will say that Hejduk wasn't one of them. What happened next has been verified by more than one player in the room: When Hejduk was blamed and cursed out by Hartley, other players stepped forward to say he wasn't to blame for the leak. Further, they said, the column *was* true.

The whole time of the team meeting, Eric Lacroix stood outside listening in. When he heard what some very reputable players had to say, he saw the writing on the wall. He then went to his father and said, in essence, he should go for the better of the team.

A day later, he was traded back to the Los Angeles Kings for a guy named Roman Vopat. Pierre Lacroix teared up when media surrounded him after the trade was made. It showed his humanity, his love for his son. But to the cynics, it also confirmed Eric had been treated differently. After all, Lacroix never got misty before, such as when he had to let Mike Keane go over money. It was always a business then, nothing personal. Now it seemed personal.

An Avs team that lost in the first round of the playoffs the season before and was kicking around .500 at the time of the trade went on to get within one win of competing for a Stanley Cup. In the end, fair or not, the players who said the team wouldn't jell again until a change was made with a certain player appeared to be right.

42 Sandis Ozolinsh

When Ozolinsh was first acquired from the San Jose Sharks early into the Avs' first season in Denver, even many serious hockey fans said "Who?" By season's end, however, Sandis Ozolinsh was and would remain one of the most popular Avs ever.

Feeling the Avalanche lacked the back end of a "two-pronged attack," i.e. an offensive defenseman, GM Pierre Lacroix swapped proven goal scorer Owen Nolan for Ozolinsh straight up. Lacroix took some heat at the time, as Nolan was considered a top-flight offensive talent, and he would go on to several excellent seasons with the Sharks.

But Ozolinsh made Lacroix look very smart. He proved to be exactly the kind of player the young Avs needed. For years, going back to the Quebec days, the franchise had been plagued by too many one-way, offensively challenged defensemen. When Ozolinsh came aboard, he brought as much or more skill than most every Avs forward, and he was a marvelous skater, honed from a Latvian childhood partially spent as a figure skater.

Ozolinsh posted 50 points in 66 regular-season games for the Avs in 1995–96. One of his first big goals for the team was a marker late in the third period in Montreal against goalie Patrick Roy that gained the Avs a 2–2 tie. When Roy came to the Avs not long after, he came to appreciate Ozo's skill, even though Sandis also caused Roy a few premature gray hairs.

Sometimes Ozolinsh could be caught way out of defensive position from an ill-advised rush, or just make a glaring turnover in his own end. But he almost always more than made up for it at the offensive end.

Probably his biggest goal with the Avalanche came in Game 6 of the 1995 Western Conference Semifinals in Chicago, an overtime goal on Ed Belfour that wrapped up the tough series. It was a typical Ozolinsh goal, where he punched deep into the offensive zone and put back the rebound of a loose puck.

He could have been known as the guy who won the Stanley Cup for the Avs in Game 4 of the Cup Finals against Florida, but he was robbed by Panthers goalie John Vanbiesbrouck on three or four top chances. Uwe Krupp wound up being the hero with his triple-overtime goal.

Ozolinsh was definitely a unique character off the ice. He was unafraid to speak his mind on most things, usually having a funny quip, often at his own expense. He was a free spirit, a lover of fast cars and good times. He could have some funky, colorful outfits at times too, always drawing barbs from teammates. He was often very critical of his own play, usually saying he was "brutal out there" after a loss. But teammates came to just forgive the odd defensive gaffe because he did so many other good things.

He got married and had kids very young, and he acknowledged not being ready for family life as a younger pro. He went through a tough, expensive divorce midway through his career but rebuilt his life and career to the point where he ventured into politics in Latvia after retiring as a player in 2013.

Ozolinsh became a good businessman too, opening Latvia's first 18-hole golf course, Ozo's Golf Club.

He had some differences with Lacroix over money in his Avs years, and was traded to Carolina in the summer of 2000 in a deal that brought a 2001 draft pick who turned out to be Vaclav Nedorost. Ozo went on to play for four other teams, including a second stint with the Sharks in 2007–08.

He finished a seven-time NHL All-Star and finished third in the Norris Trophy voting in 1996–97 for the Avs, scoring 23 goals and 68 points in 80 games. You still see No. 8 jerseys with Ozolinsh's name on the back at Avs games. Ask any longtime Avs fan about him, and you usually get "Man, I loved watching him play. He might give you a heart attack at times, but it was still exciting."

43 Before Kroenke, Ownership Uncertainty

If you want to stump even some of the most hardcore Avalanche fans, ask the question: Who owned the team before Stan Kroenke?

Many people guess his brother-in-law, Bill Laurie, but that's wrong. For about six weeks in the summer of 1999, a man named Donald Sturm owned the team. A Brooklyn-born, former tax attorney–turned–banking mogul, Sturm "won" the Avs, Denver Nuggets, and the new, soon-to-be-finished Pepsi Center in an auction for $461 million.

The team was put up for auction after shareholders of Ascent Entertainment Group, the team's initial ownership group led by CEO Charlie Lyons, sued Ascent. The lawsuit claimed that Lyons had sold too low to Laurie at $400 million. Lyons resigned and the Avs, Nuggets, and Pepsi Center entered into a public auction in which Sturm emerged as the highest bidder. A group led by Broncos legend John Elway and majority team owner Pat Bowlen was one of the bidders, as was a Saudi princess named Thara Baselia al-Saud. There was only one problem with al-Saud: She was an al-Fraud, a con woman from Missouri whose real name was Latonett W. Hollander and whose specialty was bouncing checks.

When the City of Denver attempted to seal lease agreements that would bind Sturm in keeping the teams in Denver well into the next century, complications developed. Sturm said he would keep the teams in Denver but didn't want to sign anything mandating any possible successors in doing so should he die or become incapacitated.

That set off alarm bells in the office of Denver mayor Wellington Webb, and as a result the city threatened to sue, and the teams and arena were put up for sale again. Enter Kroenke, who purchased the package of sports assets for $450 million.

Employees with the Avs were thrilled at Kroenke taking over from Sturm. In the short period working under the Sturm Group, employees privately complained of how the team was being run more like a bank and that there was little communication from the top. Kroenke was not only filthy rich, he was and remains a sports nut.

Finally, the Avs and Nuggets had stability in ownership. The Pepsi Center opened in the fall of 1999, and Kroenke spent a lot of time there. He spent so much time there that he thought, what the heck, why not build a penthouse apartment on the roof?

The 11,500-square-foot penthouse remains today, with an amazing mountain view and what looks like a fancy hot tub on the deck. You can see pictures of it online, but they just don't do it justice. Those who have been inside say it is outrageous, with top-of-the-line everything, including a gym and mini-scale movie theater. It even has a private elevator, so Kroenke never has to go outside should he want to go from home to sporting event and back. No wonder employees at the Pepsi Center refer to it as Stan's Place.

In 2013 *Forbes* magazine reported Kroenke as owning seven homes; 1.5 million acres in Montana, Wyoming, and British Columbia; and several California vineyards. Being a multibillionaire has its perks.

44 Shocker: Forsberg and Foote Depart

Let's just say the summer of 2005 was not the best of times to be an Avalanche fan. The reward for enduring a full season without hockey was to see two of the team's most beloved players, Peter Forsberg and Adam Foote, leave as unrestricted free agents.

How could the Avalanche allow two stars to leave for nothing? A lot of fans still ask that. As much as the team can be blamed for allowing that to happen—and there is some blame to give—the fact is there wasn't much they could do to prevent it.

When the NHL and the players finally came to a new collective bargaining agreement after the lost season of 2004–05, the initial salary cap was $39 million per team. The Avs of 2003–04 had a payroll in the mid $50 million range. Forsberg and Foote both were due new contracts for the 2005–06 season, and GM Pierre Lacroix just had too many players signed already. He just didn't have enough room under the new, draconian cap to make competitive offers to either player.

The Avs did offer Forsberg a four-year, $13.5 million contract. It was the best they could do. But as loyal as Forsberg was to the team, that was just too far under the fair market value for a player of his caliber. He wound up signing a two-year, $11.5 million deal with Philadelphia.

The Avs really couldn't offer any more than $1.5 million a year to Foote, and that just wasn't going to cut it either. So he left for the Columbus Blue Jackets, accepting a three-year, $13.8 million deal. Just like that, two franchise icons were gone. In their place came two players whose best days were well behind them, Pierre Turgeon and Patrice Brisebois.

Lacroix signed both players to two-year, $3 million deals. Although each player had some nice moments with the Avs, they were poor replacements for Forsberg and Foote. It pained Avs fans to see Forsberg do his thing in the orange-and-black colors of the Flyers that first season, as he was tremendous in leading Philly to the best record in the league for much of the season.

Forsberg enjoyed his time in Philly. Just as in Denver, he had a nice bachelor pad downtown and enjoyed the more cosmopolitan life of a big eastern city. Flyers fans loved him too, but they soon discovered the heartbreak that came with being dependent on his health. Forsberg became beset by foot and ankle problems and started missing large chunks of time.

Foote's tenure in Columbus proved less successful. The Blue Jackets continued to be a losing team under their new captain, and Foote wound up wanting out of Columbus. In 2008 he was traded back to the Avs, and Forsberg joined him. Forsberg signed late in the 2007–08 season, and it was like the good old days again—for a while.

After each player helped the Avs win a first-round playoff series against Minnesota, Forsberg got hurt before the second round with Detroit and missed all but one game.

Both players got their numbers retired to the rafters of the Pepsi Center. Their legacies in Denver are secure. But Avs fans just wish they never had to go through that awful summer of 2005. The 2005–06 season actually wasn't a bad one at all. The team made the playoffs and won a first-round series against Dallas. Turgeon and Brisebois were pretty good at times too. But the fact is, Avs fans were bummed out much of the time from seeing franchise icons in other sweaters.

45 A 7–0 Loss, a Drunken Night, and a Turnaround

The Avalanche came into Detroit on March 22, 1996, winners of three in a row, upping their record to 41–21–10. The game against the Western Conference–leading Red Wings was going to be a tough one, everyone knew, but even the most pessimistic of Avs fans wouldn't have predicted a loss as bad as the 7–0 final score that night.

The Avs were given a thorough reminder that they weren't yet in the class of the Red Wings, who set an NHL record with 62 wins that season. The Avs were down to stay overnight in Detroit, which meant players and coaches could enjoy some time on the town if they liked. Nowadays, it is very rare for a team to do anything but take right off for the airport after road games, as teams want to get on their private planes and get to their next destination.

The Avs of 1995–96 chartered to all their games as well, but with their next game not slated for three nights later in Winnipeg, the decision was made to relax in Motown after this one and get a good practice in at Joe Louis Arena the next day. That's technically what happened. But the circumstances went a little differently than Coach Marc Crawford anticipated.

After the loss, the team boarded the bus for the short ride back to the Atheneum Suite Hotel, easily the nicest hotel in downtown Detroit. (Although the city had a terrible reputation then for its lack of ambiance, this hotel was truly luxurious, with every room being a huge suite with fancy sunken bathtubs and fully stocked minibars. Adjacent to the hotel was a fantastic restaurant, Fishbone's, that had the best seafood gumbo ever.)

The bus became ensnared in traffic, which didn't sit well with a group of already angry men. The coaching staff and several players decided to get off the bus and walk the rest of the way to the hotel.

Crawford and his assistants, Joel Quenneville and Jacques Cloutier, decided to hit the bar at Fishbone's. And from Crawford's recollection, they hit it hard. "We got plastered, all of us," Crawford said. "I don't think any of us were feeling too good the next morning. Even when we got on the ice for practice, I think a lot of us were a little shaky on our skates."

More than a few players tied one on too. Yet the hangovers did not correspond with the quality of their play from there. The loss and subsequent soul-searching over a few drinks brought the team closer together, Crawford believes. "We were all pretty humbled, but it made us resolve to be better, instead of us getting all defeated by it," he said. "We knew they weren't that much better than us. And when you look back on it, maybe it made them a little more complacent against us to start the playoffs when we met them a few weeks later."

The team did respond well in Winnipeg, beating the Jets 5–2. For me, that was a memorable game as well. In that first season, the team let *Rocky Mountain News* beat writer Rick Sadowski and I onto the team plane at times, especially at the end of road trips, and that night in Winnipeg was one of those nights. The plane had all the comforts, including big leather reclining seats for all and a fully stocked, glassed-in bar near the front.

After the win, the plane couldn't leave on time because of mechanical issues. So everybody piled onto a bus and headed to another terrific restaurant called Hy's. Known for its sumptuous cheesy garlic bread, Hy's was a chain of steakhouses in Canada popular with hockey teams. (Years later, after a bad loss in Calgary, Avs assistant coach Rick Tocchet memorably yelled, "Get that cheesy bread out of your ass" at a practice the next day.)

Everybody settled in at Hy's for what turned out to be about a three-hour team dinner, with Rick and me as special guests. And the best part for us reporter slobs: the entire check was picked up by owner Charlie Lyons and COMSAT Video Enterprises. That dinner was another good bonding experience for the team.

I remember a few bottles of wine being consumed by everyone, and as the dinner progressed, some very good trash-talking ensued, but in a good way. Adam Deadmarsh kept ripping on Peter Forsberg over his shirt or something like that, and Claude Lemieux kept blowing cigar smoke in guys' faces (yes, he and some others on the team smoked the occasional cigar).

The huge loss from a few nights before, along with some *in vino veritas* ("In wine, truth"), seemed to bring out a kind of confessional honesty that brought everyone a little closer together, Crawford said. "Hey, if I'd known it would do that, we would have all gotten shitfaced a little sooner," he said with a laugh.

46 Newspaper Wars: *Post* vs. *News*

When the *Rocky Mountain News* folded in February 2009, an initial surge of excitement overcame me and, I'm sure if they're honest, every other employee of the *Denver Post* at the time.

"We won!" That was the feeling we had as competitors in one of the last great newspaper wars in America. For us surviving conquerors at the *Post*, the streets would be paved with gold forever and ever. No more worrying about whether the deeper-pocketed corporate owner of the *News*, Scripps Howard, would put the *Post* out of business and people like me would soon be penniless and homeless. No more worrying about some potential deadly new innovation at the *News* to render us obsolete, or some superstar reporter hired to scoop us every day, or anything else job-wise.

The *Post* had become the only daily newspaper in town, and happy days were here again. For me, that feeling lasted for about, oh, two days or so. Winning the newspaper war turned out to be a Potemkin Village kind of victory. Not only did it prove a big loss to the readers and overall citizenry of Colorado, it turned out to be a professional loss for people like me.

Why? On the latter, it was because the competition from the *News* was so fierce, I soon realized, it made me a much better reporter. A reporter's worst fear is getting beaten on a story by a rival competitor, and I lived with that fear every night for about 18 years while I was at the *Post* and the *News* still existed.

That fear of getting beat—and the potential consequences it might have not only for my own career but the survival of the paper (*What if everybody switches subscriptions to read the other paper over my own ineptness?*) made me much better at the job. I wanted all the scoops very badly, and worked as hard as I could to get them.

As discussed in an earlier chapter, my big break in the business came when I got the initial scoop that the owners of the Denver Nuggets had made an offer on the Quebec Nordiques. Exclusives like that are what reporters live for—and also what keeps them up at night, worrying the competition might have one against them in the morning.

When the *News* went away, so too did that fear of losing. And that was the real loss. While I always prided myself on working hard, and still did, the fact is the loss of the *News* did make me a little lazier. Some note about an Avs player that I might have thought imperative to get into the paper in case the *News* might have it too? My thought became: *Meh, we can wait a day on that, maybe. Who else is going to have it but us?*

I actually tried to work as hard as ever, feeling as though I owed even more to the reader then. But without that *fear* of the competition, something just naturally changed in me and probably everyone else at the *Post*. It's just about impossible to avoid the complacency that comes with being a monopoly.

The fact is it was scary being in a newspaper war, but it was also very exciting. For the first 10 years or so of my time at the *Post*, we were actually the scrappy underdog. When I first started in the winter of 1991, taking high school scores over the phone, the *News* had a sizable lead in daily circulation and, boy, did they lord it over us.

Full-page *News* "house" ads would regularly mock the *Post*'s smaller circulation numbers, and I can remember several *News* writers and reporters in those early days trying to nicely warn me I should have my résumé close by to update at any moment, because the *Post*'s days as a paper were numbered.

Scripps Howard, *News* people would always say, was too big to fail. They were a billion-dollar company while the *Post*'s owner, William Dean Singleton's MediaNews Group, was only around to milk what little profit was left before Singleton close the *Post* just like he had a couple other papers he'd previously owned, most notably the *Houston Post*.

But then the *News* started making some mistakes. That "too big to fail" attitude made them complacent in subtle but critical ways. While they ignored us, feeling us beneath them, they let the *Post* up off the mat. A brilliant marketing campaign geared toward people who moved from "broadsheet" parts of the country, people like me who grew up reading the *Boston Globe* over the tabloid *Boston Herald*, won over transplants when first deciding on a Denver paper. Scripps' corporate honchos were all based in Cincinnati, while Singleton moved his headquarters to Denver. That made a difference.

The *Post* had TV ads that ran on local channels about every 15 minutes, it seemed, touting an "It's Bigger, It's Better, It's Free" campaign that had an easy-to-remember phone number—303-832-3232—to call and subscribe. The *News* made a big deal of signing a sponsorship agreement with the baseball Colorado Rockies when they first came to town, calling themselves the "official" newspaper of the team. The *Post* came up with a clever catchall reply. It was to be the "Official Newspaper of the Fan."

Contrary to his reputation, Singleton did not scrimp on the quality of the paper. We had a big, clean, nice-looking paper that was always delivered on time. We started to innovate as a sports department, adding sections such as "Baseball Monday" and "Football Monday" that were complements to the regular sports section. Those sections were full of deep-dive, richly reported features that the sports-crazy people of Denver really liked.

On the Avs beat, I was a relative kid, a hungry newcomer who desperately wanted to succeed. That was the case on other *Post* sports beats too, and we also made the occasionally smart theft from across the street, such as when the *Post* hired Broncos beat writer Adam Schefter away and he subsequently dominated the most well-read beat in the city for a few years before going on to bigger fame at ESPN.

Gradually, the difference in circulation numbers started to close. What once was a difference of more than 100,000 at the start of the 1990s was about half that by 1995 or so. By the end of the decade, the *Post* overtook the *News* in circulation. We lorded it over them something fierce in those house ads too. It was payback time. We mocked them as the "little paper." It felt good to be on our side of the street then.

In 2001 the *Post* and the *News* merged business operations while maintaining independent newsrooms. It was called a joint operating agreement, and for eight years Denver readers had only one paper on weekends. The *News* was a tabloid Monday through Friday but a broadsheet on Saturday, while the *Post* was a broadsheet Monday through Friday and on the all-important Sunday.

It was uncomfortable for all involved. The *News* had their office on the fifth floor of the building, while we were on the sixth. Sometimes you'd be in the same elevator as *News* employees, and it was just awkward.

By 2009 Scripps threw in the towel. Both papers were still practically giving the product away with insanely low subscription prices (you could at one time get either paper for as little as a penny a day. No, really, your subscription bill for the entire year would be $3.65). There was still enough print advertising for both owners to make a profit, but by the time Craigslist and the rest of the Internet came along and started wiping out entire structures of business, especially classified ads, newspapers became a bad business to be in. That, unfortunately, remains the case today.

There appears no realistic hope for a long-term future for print newspapers. Brand names like the *Denver Post* might survive forever, but it'll have to be online only. A *Denver Post* staff of what was once about 350 reporters and editors in the 1990s had dwindled to about 140 by the dawn of 2016.

The readers, the citizenry, are the ultimate losers in all that. Make fun of "lazy, behind-the-times" newspapers all you want—and they deserve some of that, for sure—but people will definitely be the poorer for it when they're gone. The more power goes unchecked by the Fifth Estate, especially at the local level, the more abuses it will impose on unwitting citizens. Local newspapers used to expose all that stuff eventually. Now, what do you get? A lot of Kim Kardashian photos and listicles like "Top 10 Ways to Get Your Cats Noticed on YouTube," that's what.

A lot of people told me over the last few years something to the effect of, "Yeah, it's too bad what's happening to your business, but I get my news from other sources. There's plenty online." Much of that content, though, is stuff purely ripped off from us newspapers and repackaged by aggregators. When the original, organic content goes away, all that will be left for the aggregators, and their readers, is the dreck we see so much of already.

My reply to them was and remains: "Yeah, I used to get my food from farmers. But today I just get it from the supermarket."

Think about it.

47 The Black Helmets

Anyone with a tape of the very first Avalanche game ever—October 6, 1995, against Detroit—has a good memento. A brand-new team decked out in brand-new white uniforms, skating on milky-white ice in a new city. Ever notice something a little different about how the Avs looked in that game, though? If you immediately said, "Yeah, they wore black helmets," you're a true die-hard.

Why the Avs wore black helmets for their first three home games (against Detroit, Pittsburgh, and Boston) remains somewhat of a mystery. But from what I have gathered from my dogged shoe-leather reporting, the black helmets were basically just an innocent mistake, a by-product of the team's harried beginnings.

The helmets should have been white, and the NHL made sure they were changed by an October 18 home game against Washington. One thing that might have caused some confusion from that night is the Avs had a game the next night on the road in Los Angeles, where they would again wear black helmets, this time properly. But that doesn't explain why they kept wearing them against Pittsburgh and Boston. Like I said, it's a mystery that nobody really seems to have good answers about.

48 Milan Hejduk

Milan Hejduk was not exactly well-built, with bony shoulders and birdlike ankles. On the ice, though, he was a force and a leading man of the Avalanche for a long time.

Born on Valentine's Day 1976 in the former Czechoslovakia, Hejduk was the son of a hockey coach whose mother played some tennis professionally. Athletics, therefore, came naturally to him, though coming up through the ranks there was concern about his ability to play the more physical, North American style of pro game.

Those worries were dispelled after his rookie season of 1998–99, when he played all 82 games and led all NHL rookies in points with 48 (14 goals). Hejduk was never a physical player, but he went into the tough areas around the net to score—something he did 375 times in a career that was spent entirely with the Avs.

As of 2015 Hejduk remained one of only two Avs players to score 50 goals in a season, with Joe Sakic the other. Hejduk was the only NHL player to hit the half-century mark, in fact, in 2002–03; his 50 goals won the Maurice "Rocket" Richard Trophy. That came two years after he really broke through, in 2000–01. Playing on a line with Joe Sakic and Alex Tanguay, Hejduk scored 41 goals and 79 points in the Avs' second Stanley Cup–winning season.

The word to best describe Hejduk's career is *consistent*. From 2000 to 2012—12 straight seasons—Hejduk scored 20 goals or more per season. Only Sakic can say as much in Avs history. Hejduk was the right wing on lines with either Sakic or Forsberg for much of his career and had great chemistry with both, but particularly with Forsberg.

For the first several years of his career, Hejduk scored probably at least two dozen goals the same way, on a play like this: Forsberg would have the puck on his forehand circling around the net, looking like he was about to come out the other side to make a play in front. All the while, though, Hejduk would be stealthily trailing the play. While the goalie cheated to the side he thought Forsberg would put the puck on, Forsberg would suddenly turn and whip a pass from behind to Hejduk back to the open, weak side. Before the goalie realized it, Hejduk had already one-timed a shot into the open side. It worked all the time, especially in the 2002–03 season when Hejduk played mostly with Forsberg.

Hejduk succeeded Adam Foote as captain in 2011 but held the post just one season. Toward the end, Hejduk unfortunately started to have problems with Coach Joe Sacco. Hejduk sometimes found himself skating on the fourth line after some slumps, and occasionally even a healthy scratch.

Hejduk's final season of 2012–13 was a sad one, plagued by losses and injuries and tension with Sacco. He scored only four goals, retiring after it became apparent other teams weren't interested in offering him a new contract. It was a tough way for a classy man and great player to finish up. Rare is the player who gets to go out Ray Bourque–style.

Nobody ever had a bad word to say about Hejduk, on or off the ice. He liked to hang out with regular people, not celebrities, usually going to dinners with the equipment guys. By the end of his career, he was an eloquent, thoughtful speaker in English, which he spoke almost none of as a rookie.

Before his first NHL game, *Rocky Mountain News* reporter Rick Sadowski and I approached Hejduk to ask how he felt. His verbatim response was, "I prepare my stick." Hey, he still spoke better English at that moment than either of us spoke Czech.

49 Duchene Gets His Wish— To Be an Av

There is a picture of Matt Duchene as a little kid that shows him in an Avalanche jersey, surrounded by copious amounts of other Avs memorabilia. Despite being from a town—Haliburton, Ontario—that should have made him a Maple Leafs fan, Duchene's heart firmly belonged to the burgundy-and-blue team from Denver.

That picture made all the papers when Duchene was drafted by Colorado third overall in 2009. It made for an even better story when reporters dug in to just how much Duchene idolized guys such as Patrick Roy, Peter Forsberg, and Joe Sakic.

Duchene's timing in his quest to become an Av was exquisite. In any other of the team's first 14 years in Denver, a player of Duchene's caliber never would have been available. The Avs almost always drafted at or near the back of the pack of the first round, the price you pay for being a good team.

But after the disastrous 2008–09 season, the one coached by Tony Granato in his second stint behind the bench, the Avs wound up with the third pick. The draft, held in Montreal that year, saw the New York Islanders and Tampa Bay Lightning picking ahead of the Avs.

John Tavares was said to be a lock with the first pick, and while many scouts had Duchene as the consensus second pick, the Lightning needed defense desperately—not an offensive guy.

Matt Duchene scores a breakaway goal against the Canucks in 2014.

That made Swedish defender Victor Hedman very attractive to Lightning staff.

That's how it ended up. Tavares went first, Hedman went second, and Duchene went third to Colorado. On the night of the draft, though, an online report surfaced from the Long Island, New York, newspaper *Newsday* that said the Islanders would take Duchene. It created a minor sensation at the Bell Centre, as news of the report quickly spread among the players, parents, and agents, and every other hockey person inside the arena.

Duchene to the Islanders? Really? While there were some scouts who thought Duchene was the best player, the vast majority still believed Tavares was the prohibitive choice. I was in the arena that night, and I'd heard the rumors that the Islanders would take Duchene too. Some people with the Avs seemed convinced of it too, and while they loved Duchene as a talent, they would have taken Tavares over him if given the chance.

When Islanders GM Garth Snow stepped to the stage to announce the first selection, there was genuine suspense suddenly. *Newsday* was a very reputable paper, so their word counted. When Snow said the Islanders would be "proud to select, from the Oshawa Generals," the reality of Tavares being their choice all along quickly hit. *Newsday* had gotten it wrong, and the online report soon vanished.

There was still some drama as the Lightning came to the stage. Maybe they would go with the safer choice in Duchene and just try to outscore everybody? But no, things went as expected there too. Hedman became a Lightning, and so the Avs came to the stage with the third pick.

There was little suspense left. Avs GM Greg Sherman wasted little time in announcing Duchene's name, and television cameras caught Duchene doing a fist pump in celebration before hugging his parents and sister.

When Duchene put his Avs sweater on, he truly looked like the kid locked in the candy store. While his first six seasons had plenty of ups and downs, his passion for the team never waned. No, he didn't like his first coach, Joe Sacco, much at all. But the one thing Duchene never stopped loving was that giant *A* in the middle of his chest.

50 The Ryan O'Reilly Saga

The NHL lockout of 2012–13 was a drag for everyone who loves hockey. Seven years after the NHL had become the first pro sports league in history to cancel a full season because of labor issues, there we were again in 2012, with another season hanging in the balance.

By January 1 there was still no hockey, and the headlines weren't optimistic. The owners and players were fighting over the slice of hockey-revenue pie again, and if they could cancel a season once, why not again?

By January 6, though, it was over. That happened to be my birthday, and I got a nice present by breaking the news that the NHL lockout was over on Twitter. Quick story: I covered the Nuggets that night. Hey, they had to have me do something, right?

When I got home from the game at about 11:30, I noticed the NHL movers and shakers were still meeting in New York. Earlier that day, I actually thought I had a pretty good scoop already, posting a story that there was some real "traction" between the parties again. I was hearing they were getting closer to a deal, but nobody had any idea when it would end.

Instead of going to bed after the Nuggets game, I vowed to stay up the rest of the night and try to get the story. Even though dozens of hockey reporters were in New York, just outside the room where talks were ongoing, I felt I had enough good sources to work the story on my cell phone.

So I started texting people. I knew a few players on the NHLPA bargaining committee, and I knew some people on the NHL side. At approximately 2:45 AM, I got a text from a player telling me a deal was done. My first instinct was to post the news on Twitter right away. But what if he had gotten bad information? If I got the story wrong because of that, I would be the scourge of everyone in the hockey world, not to mention my bosses.

I needed another source. So I texted someone I knew at the NHL. My exact, verbatim text was: "[Person's name], I have heard from the other side that a deal has been agreed to in principle. If so, would you give me the honor of a yes?"

After 15 long minutes, when I was almost ready to give up, the text came back: "Yes."

This was a golden source, so I was ready to go with it. As fast as my fingers would go, I typed the news on Twitter. The lockout was over, per the *Denver Post*. I must have gotten about 3,000 retweets and as many or more new followers. It was a nice birthday present.

Right after that, though, it was back to the reporting grindstone, with another unpleasant story: Ryan O'Reilly, the team's leading scorer the year before, was still at loggerheads with Avs management over a new contract. O'Reilly had been playing in Russia to pass the time during the lockout, still without a new deal with Colorado. Most people assumed feelings might soften between the sides once the feel-good lockout-is-over story broke, but it wasn't the case.

The sides remained far apart on a new deal. The Avs gave O'Reilly two options: take a five-year, $17 million contract or a two-year, $7 million deal. Either way, Avs management was resolved not to give O'Reilly any more money on average per year than the $3.5 million Matt Duchene was already making.

Most people were on the Avs' side. O'Reilly had been making $900,000 a year on his previous deal. Wouldn't the Avs' lowest offer of $3.5 million be a nice raise? But no, O'Reilly and his agent, Pat Morris, held firm to an asking price of at least $6 million.

Not only was O'Reilly the team's leading scorer, Morris argued, but he led the NHL in steals and was considered a top faceoff guy. He did more of the little things at the defensive end than a guy like Duchene, he argued, and should be compensated in fair market terms.

There is *no* way O'Reilly would have played for the Avs in 2012–13 if not for one man: Jay Feaster. A former GM of the Avalanche's former AHL farm team, the Hershey Bears—and now GM of the Calgary Flames—Feaster shocked the hockey world on February 27, 2013, with a two-year, $12 million offer sheet for O'Reilly. The deal was structured to have a base salary of $6.5 million in 2013–14, which meant that would have to be the Avs' qualifying offer to retain him the following year.

The Avs were caught blindsided by the offer, but they were forced to accept Feaster's fiendish terms in the end. The Avs could have accepted draft picks and let O'Reilly go, but management decided to swallow hard and match the offer. The O'Reilly saga essentially overshadowed everything about the 48-game lockout season, and despite denials to the contrary, it created a rift in the Avalanche dressing room.

Not surprisingly, Duchene's relationship with O'Reilly was never the same. Duchene had taken a hometown discount on his previous deal, but here was O'Reilly holding up the team after one leading-scoring season on a bad team. Outwardly, the two tolerated each other, but behind the scenes there were bad words about each other from the allies in each camp. O'Reilly's group thought Duchene naïve for taking a short-money deal, while the Duchene group thought O'Reilly selfish.

After the 2014–15 season, in which O'Reilly was mostly mediocre, his relationship with the Avs came to an end. He was traded to the Buffalo Sabres in a blockbuster deal. O'Reilly immediately signed a seven-year, $52.5 million contract, the richest in Buffalo history.

A lot of people in Denver grew to dislike O'Reilly over the money stuff, but let's face it: wouldn't we all want an agent like Pat Morris?

51 Wendel Clark, We Hardly Knew Ye

Pierre Lacroix took Rick Sadowski from the Rocky *Mountain News* and me for a little math lesson sometime in the fall of 1995.

Neither Rick nor I could figure out exactly what the then-current salary was of holdout Avalanche forward Wendel Clark. As training camp neared in the inaugural season for this newly transplanted team from Quebec, Wendel Clark became a name Rick and I would get to know well. I don't remember all the particulars, but I remember Lacroix standing at a chalkboard in his office at McNichols Sports Arena going over the particulars of his offer to Clark and how the Canadian exchange rate worked and other aspects of the negotiations with Clark. It was probably the one and only time Lacroix granted such access to us reporters.

A former beloved member of the Toronto Maple Leafs Western Conference Finals team of 1993, Clark somehow found himself playing for the Nordiques just two seasons later, after a blockbuster deal made by new Quebec GM Pierre Lacroix that involved sending Mats Sundin to the Maple Leafs.

Clark's first year with the Nordiques was the second-to-last year on his contract, which paid $1.05 million. Thing is, that contract was in Canadian dollars, which in 1995 translated to roughly $700,000 or so, give or take the day's market fluctuations of the Canadian loonie to the George Washington American greenback. In the mid-1990s the Canadian dollar was much weaker, so Clark's contract was worth a lot less than it looked like. Sure, he was a Canadian citizen and spent his off-season money in his country, but no player wanted to be paid in Canadian funds back then, and they still don't. In fact, in today's NHL all salaries paid to players are in US dollars—even though there have been times in recent years where the value of the loonie surpassed that of the American dollar.

Clark would have been an unrestricted free agent in 1995 had he been a player in today's age, given his age at the time and length of service in the league. But back then a player couldn't be unrestricted until the ripe old age of 32, and in the fall of 1995 he was still just 28. With one year left on Clark's deal, Lacroix fully expected him to report to camp and honor that last year.

But Clark and his agent, Don Meehan, had other ideas. They wanted to rip up the deal and get what they felt he was rightfully worth in a renegotiation. Before NHL players could become unrestricted free agents after their first seven years of pro service, renegotiations/holdouts were a common tactic of players fresh off big years with time left on their deals.

Clark was a proven scorer in the league, one of its most respected and feared players. He signed the deal that was supposed to give the required $1.05 million in Canadian funds for 1995–96, but so what? Everyone knew he was worth more than that, but without any other viable league to play for and free agency a ways off, Clark's only hope for more money was to hold out.

It quickly became a real standoff between the parties, with venomous feelings on both sides. Lacroix took us reporters aside at any chance to go over the fine print of Clark's contract, as Clark's real salary was erroneously reported at times. Salaries still were not freely available to reporters and/or the general public back then. True, Lacroix said, Clark's salary was in Canadian funds and therefore would cost the newly transferred Canadian-to-American team less in absolute terms. But as Lacroix revealed to Rick and me in his chalkboard math session, there were "easily attainable" bonuses that would likely push Clark's real salary to close to $2 million in Canadian funds.

Clark came to Denver one time as a member of the Avalanche, with one caveat: the team did not have a name yet. Clark was part of a general meet-and-greet with Denver fans shortly after the team was sold to COMSAT Video Enterprises on May 25, 1995, walking through McNichols Sports Arena in a white T-shirt that said COLORADO NHL on the front. Colorado governor Roy Romer introduced the team captain to the crowd, saying to give a warm hand to "Joe Kasic."

At that point, things were still civil between Clark and the soon-to-be-named Avs, but not for much longer. As camp neared and it became clear that Lacroix would not budge off his negotiating stance, which was basically "play the year out or else," Meehan started to bash Lacroix for hypocrisy for playing by one set of rules when he was an agent for 21 years and another as soon as he became a GM with Quebec in 1994.

(The next year, Meehan gave one of the most famous quotes of his era in the NHL. After the Avs won the Cup in 1996, Meehan—perhaps out of some jealousy at an agent turning into a Cup champ GM in just two years—told me over the telephone, "The Zamboni driver could have won a Cup with as much talent as [Lacroix] inherited.")

Lacroix was furious over the slight, and relations were essentially nonexistent for a couple years. It was several years, in fact, before another Meehan client played for the Avs (Jose Theodore).

Anyway, Clark was traded to the New York Islanders for Claude Lemieux on October 3, three days before the start of the opening Avs game against Detroit. It's not a typo—the official trading of Clark has him going to the Islanders for Lemieux, except Lemieux never played for the Islanders. The New Jersey Devils acquired Steve Thomas from the Islanders in exchange for Lemieux, but Lemieux was then quickly pawned off by the Islanders to Colorado for Clark.

Clark wasted away in obscurity for a terrible team on Long Island that wore new uniforms that today show up on many lists for "all-time worst in pro sports history." They are known to Islanders fans everywhere as the Gorton's Fish Sticks uniforms.

Clark soon got his renegotiated new deal from Islanders GM Don Maloney—three years, $6.15 million, in US dollars. But back problems soon became a disruptive presence in Clark's career, and he was never the same player again. Lemieux won a Stanley Cup his first year with the Avs, and it marked Lacroix's first great trade in Denver. Of course, the Zamboni driver could have done it.

52 Mike Ricci

He had lots of hair and few teeth. He looked like an Italian soccer player but was on skates practically right from the crib as a Canadian kid.

Ricci's father, Mario, was a former professional soccer player in Italy and very much wanted his youngest son to follow in his footsteps. But at age two, Ricci already was able to skate around a rink without ever falling down.

As an NHL player with Philadelphia, Quebec, Colorado, San Jose, and Phoenix, Ricci did a lot of falling down, however. In fact, one of the most enduring memories Avalanche fans have of Ricci is him scoring a goal in Game 1 of the 1996 Stanley Cup Finals while falling to the ice. As always, Ricci was parked in front of the net and had just taken a big cross-check before sliding a puck past Panthers goalie John Vanbiesbrouck.

With his crooked nose and mussed-up hair that seemingly blinded his eyes all the time, Ricci looked like Pigpen on skates. That only endeared him more to Avalanche fans. Of all the players I covered as an Avs beat writer, I'd put Ricci easily into my top 10 of most popular with fans, especially women. They just loved his bad-boy look and big, gap-toothed smile. Even today, I still see more than a few No. 9 Avs jerseys with RICCI on the back.

Ricci was quite a character, let me tell you. Though most quotes from the Scarborough, Ontario, native were pretty boring. When the cameras and notepads came out, Ricci usually gave fairly generic answers, and he was a master of hockey's many clichés, such as "We just got to keep things simple" or "We gotta get pucks to the net."

Away from the media, though, Ricci was always cracking jokes—some of them not suited for family publications. He was just constantly cracking on teammates and other club personnel. Whenever there was anything resembling a rough landing, Ricci could be heard from the back of the team plane yelling, "Easy, Bouncing Bob."

Ricci was something of a man-about-town in his days with the Avs, and why not? He was single, though he would marry a girlfriend from his hometown, Beth, on the Fourth of July 1998. More than anything, Ricci just liked to hang out with his buddies, and he made friends easily. One person he befriended was NFL legend John Elway of the Broncos. The two played a lot of golf together and weren't shy about having a few pops at the 19th hole afterward. Longtime *Denver Post* columnist Woody Paige, no stranger to the city's watering holes then, once was with Elway and Ricci at a bar. As Paige recounted, Ricci was approached by a woman who said, "I want to have your baby." Ricci, Paige wrote, took out his false teeth, plopped them in the woman's beer glass, and said, "What do you think of me now?"

It seemed the world was Ricci's Rocky Mountain oyster after he helped lead the Avs to a Stanley Cup in 1996, with a strong 17-points-in–22 games playoff performance. The fourth overall pick in the 1990 NHL Draft (one spot ahead of Jaromir Jagr) by the Flyers, Ricci came over to Quebec in the massive Eric Lindros–Peter Forsberg trade and had three productive years with the Nordiques before the 1995 move to Denver.

Forsberg's arrival, though, wound up greatly cutting into Ricci's ice time. A 30-goal scorer in 1993–94 with Quebec, Ricci was dropped to a third-line center by 1995–96 with Colorado, and his scoring production dropped to just six goals in 62 games that first regular season in Denver. He scored 13 goals in 1996–97, and by 1998 injuries started to nag at him. Despite a relatively slender frame, Ricci played like a power forward, always playing with his back to the net right in front, trying to screen goalies and tip pucks. He took a huge amount of physical abuse playing in that style, and developed a back injury by 1997.

The injury meant Ricci couldn't train as much in the off-season as he normally would, and when he showed up for training camp before the 1997–98 season, a photographer for the *Rocky Mountain News* snapped his bare-chested picture on a team training table with a big smile on his face. Ricci looked in less-than-top shape in the photo, and when he saw it, Pierre Lacroix blew his top.

Lacroix was not only upset at the paper for wasting its front page on a picture of an injured player, but also at Ricci for posing for the picture in the first place. Fair or not (unfair probably, because Ricci was very dedicated to the game) the photo made it look like Ricci was having a grand old time being injured and a bit out of shape. It wasn't long before Ricci was an ex-Avalanche player. On November 20, 1997, Ricci and the Avs' second-round pick from 1998 (who turned out to be a player named Jaroslav Kristek) were traded to San Jose for Shean Donovan and San Jose's first-round pick from 1998—who turned out to be Alex Tanguay.

Ricci's name had been mentioned in some trade rumors before it actually happened, but his stock was low enough that Bob McKenzie, one of the league's most connected reporters, wrote that there were "few takers" for his services. McKenzie was based in Toronto most of his career, and the Avs were in town one night for a game with the Maple Leafs, with Ricci still on the roster. McKenzie was in the locker room after an Avs win, one in which Ricci played well, and he got McKenzie's attention.

"Hey, Bob, lick my balls," Ricci said. "No takers, eh?"

"That one was personal, eh Reech?" McKenzie replied.

It's the kind of thing that happens sometimes between player and reporter. No big deal. Both went on to better days.

53 Valeri Kamensky

Right when the Quebec Nordiques were officially sold to COMSAT Video Enterprises in 1995 and I had a new job and life as the soon-to-be-renamed-team's beat writer, I had a phone conversation with one of the two big beat writers for the Nordiques.

His name was Kevin Johnston, and he wrote for *Le Soleil* in Quebec, otherwise known to everyone there as the *Sun.*

One of my first jobs as the new beat writer for the soon-to-be-renamed hockey team was: find out everything I could about every player, only give it to the readers in about 200 words or less.

Johnston, a terrific journalist, both as a writer and reporter, graciously gave me all the time in the world to go over every player. He was a newspaper pro's pro. Even though he had just lost his team and his beat, he knew I had a story due and he accommodated me until every last one of my I-don't-know-a-wristshot-from-a-wristwatch questions was complete.

Johnston was informative not only in the pro forma sense, he livened up his summations with precious little anecdotes toward the end. He was a combination of the *New York Times* and *Us* magazine at the same time. He knew the readers wanted all the facts first, but also a little juicy personal stuff on the side.

So when it came time to ask him about this guy named Valeri Kamensky, a player who I honestly had never heard of when the team was sold (the ignorance about hockey at that time in my life is covered earlier, right?), I just expected a pro forma answer and then to move on to the next number on the roster.

But Johnston's voice inflected a few notches higher when Kamensky's name came up. This is not an exact quote probably, but Johnston said something like "Wow, is this guy good."

In fact, one of Johnston's quotes about Kamensky was, "He was considered the Russian Wayne Gretzky" once. Wait, what? That was before a broken leg sidelined him, Johnston qualified. By the time the Nordiques had morphed into the Avalanche by late summer of 1995, Kamensky had only then fully recovered from a serious leg injury that many worried would take away from the supreme display of skill he had showed for several years as a kid coming up in the old Soviet hockey system.

When the Avs broke training camp in the fall of 1995, I distinctly remember Coach Marc Crawford telling me, "Wait till Kamensky plays a full year with Forsberg. He'll have the best numbers of his career."

As it turned out, Crawford was right. In the Avs' Stanley Cup–winning season of 1995–96, Kamensky posted career highs in goals

(38) and assists (47) of his 11-season NHL career, playing left wing on a line with Forsberg and Claude Lemieux. He also scored the first goal in Avalanche history, opening night against Detroit.

At the start of the season, though, the Kamensky-Forsberg-Lemieux line was not set in the stone it would become. Martin Rucinsky played left wing on a line with Forsberg and Lemieux a lot in the first two months, before he was shipped off to Montreal in the Patrick Roy blockbuster.

I still remember Lemieux yelling out, "Right here, Rosie!" to Rucinsky during a game at Winnipeg soon before the trade (you could hear everything in the short, overhanging press box above). Lemieux got a tap-in goal on a pass from Rucinsky in a 5–2 win for the Avs. When he and Owen Nolan were no longer among the Avs' top nine forwards, however, it made Crawford gamble with the trio of Kamensky-Forsberg-Lemieux the rest of the way. It worked out.

Kamensky was just a terrifically skilled player. He might have been the best pure skater of anyone I ever saw in the 20 years I covered the team. A word I used many times to describe him as a skater was *elegant*. His feet crossed over when he moved, much like a figure skater's. He skated in quick, geometrically diverse patterns. He was also, other than Forsberg himself, maybe the best pure stick handler with the puck of any Av who ever played.

Quebec signed Kamensky away from Russia in 1991 in one of those early 1990s shady transactions that will probably never be fully detailed. Quebec owner Marcel Aubut had some experience lifting great players out of communist countries by then: he was a major player in the emigration of the Stastny brothers (Peter, Anton, and Marian) from Czechoslovakia to the NHL in 1980.

Things still hadn't loosened up much in the international exchange of players by 1991, so Kamensky took some risk in leaving Russia. He had already just played six seasons for the top team in the Russian League (CSKA) by the time he was in eastern Canada playing for a very bad 1991–92 Nordiques team. That team was the germination of the better teams to come, however, one with Joe Sakic, Curtis Leschyshyn, and Adam Foote as younger players.

By 1995 Kamensky had established himself as a worthy NHL player, but it wasn't until he could play alongside a guy like Forsberg that his full talent was shown. Kamensky was the perfect winger for a guy like Forsberg.

Kamensky scored some of the prettiest goals in team history, none better than a 180-degree-turn backhander in Florida against the Panthers during the 1996–97 regular season. It was later named the Goal of the Year by the NHL. He was a genuine difference maker in the Cup-winning season of the one before too, including a great pass to Uwe Krupp for the game-winning goal in Game 1 of the Finals against Florida.

Kamensky played three more seasons with the Avs after the Cup year, and averaged close to a point per game overall. His return from a broken wrist midway through a playoff series against Detroit in 1999 made a big difference in the Avs' comeback from a 2–0 series deficit. Scotty Bowman said it was the biggest factor in the series.

But by the end of the 1998–99 season, he and his agent, Paul Theofanous, could not agree on his contractual value with Lacroix. After some initial back and forth over the numbers, Lacroix concluded he wouldn't invest long-term in the 33-year-old. Kamensky wound up an unrestricted free agent, and Rangers GM Neil Smith wasted little time in making him a four-year, $17 million offer, with an option for a fifth. It was one of the final few ill-advised signings that cost Smith his job in New York only a few seasons after winning the team's first Stanley Cup in 54 years.

Kamensky lasted two years in New York, scoring 27 goals and 66 points in 123 games. He wound up finishing up his NHL career in obscurity in Dallas and New Jersey. But he later found success as a general manager in the Russian Kontinental Hockey League.

His No. 13 jersey can still be seen at most any Avs game, though. He was a favorite of the fans much like his description as a player: in a stealthy, after-the-fact way.

54 2014 Playoffs—A Cinderella Story Over Too Soon

The task: manage *not* to go 1–4 in the final five games. Just play .500 hockey from there, go 2–2, and then get a ticket punched to the second round of the 2014 playoffs. After taking a 2–0 series lead on the Minnesota Wild, this looked a done deal for the Avalanche. The Wild didn't even have a reliable goalie, having started Game 1 with veteran journeyman Ilya Bryzgalov and switching to Darcy Kuemper, who had no playoff experience and not much of a résumé otherwise. Rookie Nathan MacKinnon had seven points in the first two games at the Pepsi Center, and reporters were already looking up the all-time playoff scoring record, not just for a rookie but for all time. What could go wrong? Everything, it turned out.

The Avs went 1–4 in those next five games. The final loss couldn't have been more excruciating either. The Avs blew four—count 'em, four—one-goal leads in the 5–4 overtime loss. Erik Johnson gave Colorado a 4–3 lead with 8:44 left in the third period, and this time it looked like they could finally hold it until the end.

I remember well Avs fans starting to stand around the final 4:00 mark. The roar started to build as the clock ticked toward three minutes. And then…silence.

Minnesota's Jared Spurgeon, with the puck on the right side, faked a shot, which sent a sliding MacKinnon, trying to block his shot, out of the way. He then loosed a shot that had eyes to the top left corner behind Semyon Varlamov. For the fourth time of the night, it was a tie game, only this time everyone knew the Wild had the momentum going into OT.

It took five minutes and two seconds for everyone to be proven right. Nino Niederreiter won the series for Minnesota at that mark of OT with a shot past a shell-shocked Varlamov.

The Avs dressing room was as crushed as any I'd ever seen. Ryan O'Reilly was actually in tears, still sitting in his full uniform well after the game. Johnson, a Minnesota native, called it a "sick feeling." Captain Gabe Landeskog, who had a two-on-one break with Paul Stastny right before the losing goal, could barely speak.

The series took a turn for the worse for the Avs in Game 3, at the Xcel Energy Center. In the second period of a competitive game, Minnesota's Matt Cooke stuck out a knee and severely injured valuable Avs defenseman Tyson Barrie. Barrie was the Avs' puck-rushing D-man who could single-handedly get the puck out of the defensive zone just with his skates. Otherwise, the Avs usually had to make a couple successful passes to get anything out. Barrie could just fly it out by himself.

Cooke, a loathsome player with a rap sheet as long as his arm, played his usual "What? Who, me? I didn't mean anything by it, honest" routine. Except this time the NHL wasn't buying it. Cooke was suspended for the next seven playoff games by the league, which meant he'd miss the rest of the series no matter what.

The Wild won Games 3 and 4 in Minnesota, but MacKinnon played the hero in Game 5 with an overtime winner. As the series moved back to Minnesota, the Avs got some good medical news: Matt Duchene, out previously with a bum leg, was good enough to go for Game 6. But the Avs' offense wasn't much in Game 6, so it was on to Denver for one last one.

The Wild were just like an annoying rash that wouldn't go away. For the second time in 11 years, the Avs blew a 3–2 lead and finally the series in seven at home to the Wild. The first time it happened, in 2003, Patrick Roy played his final games as a player. The second time was Roy's return to Denver as a coach.

To start the 2015–16 season, the Avs opened with the Wild at home and had a 4–1 third-period lead. The Pepsi Center was rockin', and then...more silence. The Avs blew the game, losing 5–4. If there is one team the Avs really owe one to as the calendar turns to 2016, it is the Minnesota Wild.

55 Mike Keane

He came over as the ultimate "throw-in" on the trade that sent Patrick Roy to the Avalanche in 1995. He proved to be one of the Avalanche's most indispensable players, whose loss was, ahem, keenly felt when he left for the New York Rangers in 1997 as an unrestricted free agent.

The reason why the Winnipeg native was so valuable to the three Stanley Cup champion teams he played on was, first and foremost, because he was a good hockey player. Once the "enforcer, protector" to Theo Fleury as a junior player with the Moose Jaw Warriors of the rough-and-tumble Western Hockey League, Keane wasn't considered NHL material from there. In fact, no team drafted him.

But the Montreal Canadiens were intrigued enough to offer Keane a free-agent contract in 1985. He played well for the Warriors the next two seasons but couldn't crack the Canadiens roster until 1988. By then, Keane had established himself as a good player for the Habs' American Hockey League affiliate in Sherbrooke, Quebec. Five years later, Keane was a Stanley Cup champion on the same team led by Conn Smythe winner Patrick Roy.

Two years later, he was in Denver, the "other" player from Montreal with Roy in the December 6, 1995, blockbuster that sent Jocelyn Thibault, Martin Rucinsky, and Andrei Kovalenko to the Canadiens. About seven months later, he had his second championship ring as a regular third-line forward with the Avs.

Keane had several memorable moments in his first stint with the Avs (he would return to the team from 2002 to 2003), most especially with his mouth. He was a go-to guy in the dressing room for colorful quotes, and he almost never failed to deliver.

One of his most memorable came after the March 26, 1997, game in Detroit against the Red Wings, which the Avs lost 6–5 in overtime. The Red Wings, Keane said, "proved that they're a bunch of homers. I don't think they have the balls to play like that in our building, and, you know, they proved that."

Keane was one of the last of the school of players who thought speaking their true minds to the press was a normal, natural part of their job. When Keane was criticized for not knowing the French language, despite being a captain of the Canadiens, he shrugged it off, saying, "Everybody here speaks English. I don't see the problem."

That comment, to *La Presse* reporter Mathias Brunet in 1995, touched off a small storm of controversy in the primarily French-speaking province of Quebec. It probably played a part in Keane being included in the trade with Colorado, and Avs fans would forever be grateful.

One of my first memories of Keane as a person is him storming down the aisle of the team airplane, yelling, "Hot coffee! Hot coffee here!"

After the second or third time doing that on team flights, it became obvious he was parodying some old flight attendant scene from his past. Keane would say it coming down the aisle, and also any time a flight attendant spilled something, as rare as it was. One bump of an attendant's arm with a cup in its hand, and you'd hear within two or three seconds from the ever-observant Keane: "Hot coffee! Hot coffee here!"

Keane did tangible things for the Avs when he first came over from Montreal, such as give them a much better penalty-killing winger than anyone they'd had. He would team primarily with center Stephane Yelle to give the Avs a strong PK presence up top. He could also score a little.

He scored one of the biggest goals of the Avs' 1996 Stanley Cup run with his overtime wrist shot to beat Detroit in Game 1 of the Western Conference Finals at Joe Louis Arena. It was one of the most nothing shots ever taken, just a long, slow shot from the top of the left faceoff circle. Somehow, it eluded Osgood's grasp and the Avs had a 1–0 lead they never relinquished in the series.

"That shot was heavy," Keane later said with a laugh.

Many of Keane's biggest contributions to the Avs were intangible, things with hidden meanings. When Roy came to the Avs from Montreal, Keane was really the only person in the organization he knew. While they were close in Montreal, they became much closer in Denver.

Roy was essentially a jumbled mess of nerves his first few weeks in Denver, and it often fell to Keane to calm him down. Sometimes that meant a little chat in the back of the team plane. Sometimes it meant a good-natured crack at his expense in the dressing room. Keane sometimes kidded Roy about his less-than-six-pack abs or his seesaw walk. Sometimes Keane would follow Roy to the closed-door part of the dressing room mimicking Roy's walk, as onlookers stifled laughter.

Roy and Keane drove to every game at McNichols Sports Arena together, and ate dinner together many nights at the new Roy home in Parker, a suburb of Denver.

It seemed likely the two would be joined at the hip career-wise after winning their second Cup together in 1996, but in the fall of 1997 Keane left the Avs for a four-year, $8 million free-agent contract with the New York Rangers. Avs general manager Pierre Lacroix was somewhat hamstrung by the budget imposed upon him by owner Charlie Lyons and his Ascent Entertainment Group, but Lacroix's stubborn pride was an issue at the bargaining table.

Lacroix sometimes grew insulted when players didn't accept his last, final, and "fairest" offer. Keane knew he could command more money on the free-agent market but might have stayed in Colorado for anywhere close to $2 million per year. Alas, Lacroix wouldn't go anywhere near it in 1997 dollars for a third-line player, and felt there was enough talent around to make up for Keane's absence.

It proved a costly on-ice mistake. Keane did not excel with the Rangers in 1997–98, but he sure did after being traded to the Dallas Stars at the deadline in 1998. Keane played 46 playoff games for the Stars in 1999 and 2000, 14 of them against the Avalanche in successive Western Conference Finals.

In Game 7 of the 1999 Finals at Dallas' Reunion Arena, Keane scored two goals in a 4–1 Stars victory—every goal against his close friend, Roy. He went on to win his third Stanley Cup with as many teams in just a six-year period.

Keane was reacquired by Lacroix from the St. Louis Blues in 2002 for what looked like it would be another successful Stanley Cup run with his old friend Roy. But after taking a 3–2 series lead over the Red Wings, the Avs lost in seven games. Keane finished up his NHL career as a Vancouver Canuck in 2003–04, on the ice for the awful game in which Steve Moore had his career ended from a sucker punch by Todd Bertuzzi.

Keane just kept right on going, though. He became something of the American Hockey League's version of the fictional baseball character Crash Davis, dispensing his hard-earned wisdom to all the wide-eyed youngsters trying to make it with the Manitoba

Moose. Keane played for the Moose from 2005 to 2010, the oldest player in the league the last two years.

"You know, I loved playing the game. I was fortunate to make a living playing it as long as I did," Keane said during a visit to the Pepsi Center a few years later. "I'll never forget my time in Denver. I played for the organization twice and got a Stanley Cup. I never wanted to leave, but things happen. I will always have the Avalanche firmly in my heart."

56 Denver ChopHouse & Brewery

It is not the same postgame hangout for Avalanche players that it used to be. But that doesn't mean the memories of when it was *the* place to see and be seen with Avalanche players aren't still plastered on the walls of this dining and drinking establishment, which opened the same year the Avs came to town.

I'll never forget the time Eric Messier, a workmanlike forward who won a Cup with the Avs in 2001, asked a group of players where they should all meet after a game one night, probably a couple years before.

"Chopoussse?" Messier proffered in his thick French-Canadian accent. Everybody laughed, and it became a postgame staple for years. All anyone needed to do was turn his head to the air and go "Chopoussse?" and everyone knew where to go.

Before the early 1990s, before a huge migration of young, urban, educated professionals descended upon Denver, the area where the ChopHouse still stands was considered a bad part of town. It was the province of winos and hobos looking to hop a rail at nearby Union Station. After the yuppies came and searched for places to part with their disposable income, the rundown area was reborn as LoDo. Before they were called microbreweries, they were called brew pubs, and LoDo started to get more and more of them by the mid-1990s. Those, and other places known as Internet cafes.

Before long, it was a bustling area, but it didn't really start to boom until the Colorado Rockies moved from Mile High Stadium on the other side of Interstate 25 and planted themselves at 19th and Wynkoop. With the Avs still across the highway at that time, there wasn't much to do around McNichols Sports Arena. When the old hockey Colorado Rockies played there, a place called the Ironworks Brewery was the go-to spot for the players, but it was closed by the 1990s, and the only bar around Big Mac when the Avs first came to town was a place called Brooklyn's.

The ChopHouse—with its kitchen open late at night and its white tablecloths and big, fancy wine glasses and cold beer brewed in-house—became the place to be seen. Most Avs players went there at least once a week during the season, often for a full dinner after games. Most players will eat lightly before a game but not after.

The ChopHouse has been the scene of many Avalanche team events, including their victory parties following their first two Stanley Cup wins. Walk inside its dark, oak-paneled walls, and visitors will see numerous framed pictures from those parties and many others of Avs from the years. In that sense, the place is something of a museum for hardcore fans, a must-stop for anyone passing through town for a night or two.

57 Theo Fleury's Short Stay

I was at the airport gate when Theo Fleury walked off a plane from Calgary to Denver, and I thought, *This guy is a big-time NHL player?* He was just so much smaller than most everyone else in the league. He was about 5'6" and probably didn't weigh any more than 170 pounds.

But yes, Fleury was a very big-time player, and the night he walked off that plane, Avalanche Nation was in full froth mode. Near the trade deadline in 1999, Fleury was acquired, along with Chris Dingman, for Rene Corbet, Wade Belak, and 1998 first-round pick Robyn Regehr.

He would become an unrestricted free agent after the season, so this was clearly a gamble by Avs GM Pierre Lacroix. Could Fleury be the missing piece that would win another Stanley Cup? That was the hope.

It didn't happen. But to call the trade a disaster for the Avs would be inaccurate. Fleury added a lot of excitement to the team and he scored plenty of points in the short time he stayed. The Avs won two playoff rounds with him, including the dethroning of two-time defending Stanley Cup champion Detroit.

And let's not forget Dingman. He was a real contributor to the 2001 Cup team, a big man who served as a physical deterrent and had a pretty smart hockey mind. He made a very key play on the game-winning goal, scored by Adam Foote, in the first period of Game 6 of the Cup Finals against the Devils. Dingman moved the puck away from the boards and helped create the opportunity for Foote to get a long shot off that slipped over Martin Brodeur's pads.

But back to Fleury. He was just one of the most unique players I ever saw. He was small but extremely tough. He never backed down from anyone, always giving lip back to anyone who dared say anything to him. He was a supreme agitator, an expert trash-talker who would get really nasty and personal if need be.

He was a great skater. He had as good a first step as anyone, and had a wide stance that allowed him to glide faster than many could skate with their legs moving. He had such quick hands, able to stick-handle through the tightest of situations.

He loved country music, especially Garth Brooks. He often wore an honest-to-god cowboy hat out and about. He chewed tobacco nonstop, a big bucket of spittle always next to his locker. He hated to wear suits, doing so only grudgingly on road trips. He had very few original teeth left in his upper gums. He used the F-bomb approximately every five words in conversation.

I loved being around him, in other words. He was always good copy, as they say in the biz. He was unafraid of ripping referees in print, or players from other teams, or of giving his opinion on just about any topic. He told it like it was. Well, not quite. Not as a player anyway.

Fleury hid a very big secret his entire playing career. As a junior with Moose Jaw of the Western Hockey League, Fleury was sexually abused by his coach, Graham James. In 2009, after he'd retired, Fleury detailed everything in a superb memoir, *Playing with Fire*, in collaboration with author Kirstie McLellan Day. While many of the details are stomach-churning, I highly recommend the book to anyone who really wants an insight not only into the man but into the era in which he came up.

There had always been whispers in hockey circles that Fleury had been abused by James. It was something of an open secret. But Fleury never addressed the rumors directly. When he finally divulged everything, it put all the troubles he had at times as a player in perspective.

Fleury had a big reputation as a party guy, not shy of downing a few drinks after a game at a bar or other adult establishment. That sometimes led to headlines, such as a 2003 fracas at a Columbus strip joint while with the Chicago Blackhawks. Fleury later admitted to being a full-blown drug addict and alcoholic for much of his career, especially the later years. Such addictions are well-established by-products of past sexual abuse, and Fleury was horribly victimized by James, who served jail time.

James later went on to abuse at least one other player, Sheldon Kennedy, on the Swift Current Broncos. He was Joe Sakic's coach there. Sakic was asked a few times about James after he was arrested and convicted of abusing Kennedy, but he said he never knew anything about it.

Fleury did a lot of good things with the Avs, but the 1999 team blew a 3–2 series lead in the Western Conference Finals to Dallas. Fleury missed Game 5 of the series, in Dallas, because of what the team said was the flu. Lots and lots of rumors were whispered that some other reason was to blame, but to this day nothing has ever come out to prove anything otherwise. Fleury was not the type of guy to miss a rubber game of a playoff series over a flu bug, but whatever. The Avs won that game anyway.

Fleury turned his life around in retirement. He successfully overcame his addictions and became a tireless advocate on behalf of victims of sexual abuse. He's a very smart guy, very intuitive about people now. He can sniff out a phony in a nanosecond.

He refused to stay a victim, and today he is an inspiration to many, including me. The life of a sportswriter is a good incubator for addiction, and I battled a couple myself. Living out of a suitcase most of the year may sound glamorous to many, but it can be a lonely thing, and it's easy to try to fill the boredom with things that aren't always good for you.

58 "Deader"

When the Avalanche first came to Denver, I thought Adam Deadmarsh was an equipment boy or something. Not having seen much Quebec Nordiques hockey the previous year, I didn't know what he looked like. When I saw him for the first time, I thought this was just some 14-year-old kid, part of the team staff somehow.

Seriously, Deadmarsh looked that young as a second-year player. He had this hairstyle that was really long on one side that he continually nodded out of his eyes. He looked like your little kid brother.

Except *little* didn't describe the way Deadmarsh played the game. One of the team's bigger fan favorites in his nearly six years with the team, Deadmarsh played a rough, tough, fast, and skilled game as a power forward. He was a top-six forward in the playoffs for the Avs in 1996, a Stanley Cup champion at age 21.

Deadmarsh led the team in goals the following season, with 33, quite an accomplishment on a team with Joe Sakic and Peter Forsberg. He regularly surpassed 100 penalty minutes almost every season too, many of them from fights. Deadmarsh often fought players bigger than him, sometimes with tough results, such as the concussion he suffered from an Ed Jovanovski punch in Vancouver on November 1, 2000.

Fans might have wanted him to cool it a bit after that, but that wasn't Deadmarsh. After missing a month with the concussion, he challenged Jovanovski the next time they faced each other, and fought without getting hurt again.

Deadmarsh had great wheels. Despite a kind of herky-jerky, choppy skating style, he could really move. He had a great big slap shot too, and scored the kinds of goals one doesn't often see anymore, big blasts coming down the wall.

Deadmarsh was best friends with Forsberg, rooming with him on the road and having him over to his place a lot with Deadmarsh's girlfriend-turned-wife, Christa. Although the Avs had some heavy-duty enforcers in his time with the Avs, Deadmarsh often acted as Forsberg's protector on the ice. If anyone took a run at Forsberg, Deadmarsh quite often would immediately drop the gloves with that player, or he'd get him on a later shift.

Fans loved his style, especially when he'd pick his helmet up after a fight and toss his hair back before putting it back on. A particularly popular shirt worn by fans of his was done up in funky, psychedelic colors to resemble a Grateful Dead shirt, only these said GRATEFUL DEADMARSH. A very popular local brand of pickles, Deadmarsh Deli Dills, flew off the supermarket shelves, with his smiling face on the jar.

Unfortunately, the Avs traded Deadmarsh to Los Angeles in 2001. While history shows the blockbuster that brought Rob Blake in return helped win the Avs a Stanley Cup that year, it was still very tough for many teammates and fans to see him go.

Deadmarsh had a couple very good seasons with the Kings, but his career ended way too soon because of postconcussion syndrome. The worst of his concussions came during a practice, when he took an accidental knee to the head from teammate Craig Johnson. Deadmarsh just never could quite shake the effects of the concussions enough to play again following the 2002–03 season.

He did return to the Avs as a video coach in 2009, and later served one season as a bench assistant to Joe Sacco in 2011–12. But Deadmarsh was still bothered at times by the concussions and decided to retire to a quieter life in Idaho with Christa and their two daughters.

As of this writing, Deadmarsh is slated to be the coach of the Avs' alumni team game against Detroit for the 2016 Coors Light Stadium Series at Coors Field.

59 Joel Quenneville

His face today is synonymous with the Chicago Blackhawks, the team he led to three Stanley Cups from 2010 to 2015 before entering the 2015–16 season looking for more. But there were two periods in which Joel Quenneville played a big part in the Avalanche organization, first as an assistant coach and later as the top dog. He also was a part of the Denver hockey community before that, as a player with the Colorado Rockies.

The man everyone in the game calls Q got his name on the Stanley Cup with the 1996 Avs, as the lead assistant to Marc Crawford. His bushy mustache was part of his trademark, as was his barking voice, which could be heard throughout the rink.

Quenneville was in charge of the Avs' defense in that first season, and he did a remarkable job. He was particularly instrumental in developing youngster Adam Foote into a top-flight D-man, and he was an excellent strategist. He was very influential on Crawford, and he had a major hand in the development of a great game plan in beating the Detroit Red Wings in the 1996 Western Conference Finals. Quenneville thought the way to play Detroit was to pound them harder on the forecheck. It was a gamble, because if someone missed a check, the mighty Wings breakout game could make the Avs pay in a hurry.

But the Avs' speed was as good as Detroit's, and the new attack plan paid huge dividends. The Avs got in on Detroit's D and forced a lot of turnovers and got them out of their usual mind-set.

For nearly 40 years now, Quenneville has continually cashed NHL paychecks as a player and coach, but he is no one-trick pony. He actually worked for a short time as a stockbroker after retiring as a player in 1992, and speaking of ponies, Quenneville is a preeminent horse-racing expert.

Before all those Cups with the Blackhawks, Q was the man in Denver.

He also is an expert on cigars, an off-ice indulgence of his that got started in earnest after marrying his wife, Elizabeth, whose family were tobacco barons from Connecticut.

Quenneville left the Avs midway through the 1996–97 season to coach the St. Louis Blues and led them to seven straight postseason appearances, including a meeting with Colorado in the 2001 Western Conference Finals. He was fired late in the 2003–04 season by St. Louis but quickly found work as the new head coach of the Avs in the spring of that year.

Quenneville coached the Avs until 2008, when he had something of a mutual parting following a second-round sweep at the hands of Detroit. Early in the 2008–09 season, he replaced Denis Savard as coach in Chicago and hasn't looked back.

One of Quenneville's peculiar habits as a coach was always taking a little piece of paper and writing notes to himself after goals against. People always asked him what he was writing, and they were just little thoughts on how the goal happened and the player numbers of those involved. He was also notorious for a Captain Hook mentality with his goalies. One bad game was okay, but two, and the goalie would usually find himself on the bench.

Quenneville was never blessed with great goaltending in his stint as Avs head coach. Peter Budaj, David Aebischer, Jose Theodore, and Vitaly Kolesnik were the primary goalies Quenneville had to work with, and he switched them up often. It was obvious Quenneville was mad about a goalie's play when he would just mumble "He played okay" after a media person asked about an off night.

I always had a good relationship with Quenneville as the beat writer of his teams in Denver. But it was almost over before it started, thanks to an editor changing the headline of an early season story in 1995.

One of the things I did that year was a weekly team column, and once in a while I'd do "Player most likely to..." kinds of things. In one of them, I wrote "Person Most Likely to Be Seen at Arapahoe Park," and that person was Quenneville. Arapahoe Park was a horse-racing track in town, and being the expert that he was on the ponies, I thought it harmless to write about it.

If it had run under the headline I wrote, there wouldn't have been any problem. But an editor decided to change it to "Person Most Likely to Be Seen at a Betting Parlor." There was a practice at the old DU Arena the day the column came out, and man, did Q shoot me a dirty look afterward. I mean, if looks could kill, I would have died that day. What had been just an innocent look at a hobby of his instead was changed to make him out to be a problem gambler.

I tried to explain to him that it was not what I wrote, that somebody else had changed it. But he just walked off, and I felt horrible. Eventually I was able to explain it to him and all was forgiven, but that wasn't the only time I had to explain the inner workings of how a newspaper story was created. In the days of 100 percent print, reporters never wrote the headlines; editors did.

I sent the story into the office, and it got dissected from there by the people on the desk, and they put a headline on the story. But try explaining that to the player who didn't get that, who only saw the headline and got pissed at me for it. It happened at least once a year.

Probably the angriest a player ever got at me over a headline came in 1996, when veteran Troy Murray accosted me in the locker room in Tampa Bay. I also wrote as a freelancer for the *Hockey News* in those days, and a story in which Murray had some "We've got to be better, we haven't been as good as we normally can be" kinds of innocent quotes had a headline that essentially said "Murray Rips Avs Teammates."

I went through the usual routine of trying to explain that I hadn't written that headline, but he stayed mad for a while over that. Editors certainly bailed me out plenty of times by catching my mistakes, but they could create headaches for me sometimes too.

60 Alex Tanguay

He came to the Avalanche in 1998 as the 12th pick overall in the NHL Draft, one of four in the first round the team had that year.

He went on to a very successful career, the best years of which happened with the Avs. He was a Game 7 hero in the 2001 Stanley Cup Finals, scoring two goals in a 3–1 win, all in support of his former landlord, Patrick Roy.

After spending one more year in junior hockey following his selection by the Avs, Tanguay made the big club as a 19-year-old and lived in the basement of Roy's home. He posted 51 points (17 goals) his rookie season of 1999–2000 and followed that up with 27 goals and 77 points on a dominant line with Joe Sakic and Milan Hejduk in a championship season.

Tanguay was traded to Calgary in 2006, after wanting more money than the team wanted to pay. The primary return for Tanguay was defenseman Jordan Leopold, who immediately got hurt in training camp and never panned out as a player in Denver. Tanguay, meanwhile, had an 81-point season for the 2006–07 Flames, playing mostly on a line with future Avs teammate Jarome Iginla.

He possessed that extra second of patience with the puck that just can't be taught. He was an excellent, creative passer and tougher than he looked. He could drive his coaches crazy, though, by his tendency to overpass.

Many times, you could see Avs fans pounding their fists and yelling "Shooooot!" while Tanguay chose instead to make the extra pass. When he did choose to shoot, Tanguay could be deadly. In fact, entering 2015–16 he was the NHL's active leader in career shooting percentage (minimum 700 shots) at 18.7 percent and twice led the NHL in that category, in 2005–06 (23.2 percent) and 2014–15 (21.2 percent).

Tanguay's second stint with the Avs had its good moments, but injuries started to catch up with him. He missed most of the 2013–14 season with a knee problem and suffered a new knee injury early in 2015–16. At the time of the second injury, Tanguay ranked seventh on the franchise scoring list, with 472 points in 560 games.

Tanguay was always a very quiet guy in the dressing room. You had to lean in a little to fully hear what he had to say most of the time. But interviewing him was always worth the time, as he analyzed a game very well and he wouldn't hold back with his honest opinions on things. When he and GM Francois Giguere had a difference of opinion over his worth, Tanguay flat out said he wasn't going to play for any less than $5 million per year. He wound up getting that with Calgary.

He also played in Tampa Bay and Montreal, but his heart always belonged to the Avs, and he was very happy to come back in 2013 when Joe Sakic acquired him from the Flames, along with Cory Sarich, for Shane O'Brien and David Jones.

"I came here as just a young kid in 1999 and had some great, great times playing on some great teams," Tanguay reflected in 2014. "My kids were born here, I won a Stanley Cup here. I'm very proud to have been a part of this organization as long as I have."

61 2002 Western Finals— The One That Got Away

There are two playoff series that the Avs really wish they could have back: one is the 1999 Western Conference Finals, in which they had a 3–2 lead over the Dallas Stars, with Game 6 at home, but lost in seven games. Game 6 saw the Avs take a 1–0 lead, but it should have been 3–0 after the first period. Aaron Miller and Sandis Ozolinsh, however, missed wide-open nets with shots.

The other series was the 2002 Western Conference Finals against Detroit. Again the Avs had a 3–2 lead, after taking a thrilling overtime decision in Game 5 at Joe Louis Arena. Peter Forsberg skated in alone on Dominik Hasek and slipped a shot through his pads, and Joe Louis Arena turned into a library.

One more win, and the Avs would have their fourth playoff series win over the Red Wings in the last five meetings since 1996, and a berth in the Cup Finals against the Carolina Hurricanes. It was likely to become the Avs' second Cup victory in a row and third in six years. Supremacy over the league—and over Detroit in their huge rivalry—would be established.

None of that happened. Instead, the Avs came home and played a terrible first period in Game 6. The offense could do little against Detroit's tightened-up defense, and the power play was terrible. In fact, the Avs failed to get a shot on Hasek for a 15-minute stretch of the first. With less than a minute left in the first period of a scoreless game, Wings captain Steve Yzerman, who had just had a likely sure goal broken up by a poke-check from Rob Blake, had a rebound of a Nick Lidstrom shot come right to his stick.

Yzerman's five-footer to a partially open net was stopped by Roy, who thought the puck was in his glove enough to raise it up high for everyone to see. Problem was, the puck wasn't in it. While he had his arm raised, the puck lay in the crease. Brendan Shanahan swept it in for a 1–0 lead. Goals in the last minute of a tie game are always killers, and this was no exception.

The Avs put only four shots on Hasek in the first period, but 20 in the final two, and the Czech future Hall of Famer allowed nothing. In the second period, Avs coach Bob Hartley challenged the width of Hasek's stick, the kind of gambit the Montreal Canadiens successfully tried against Los Angeles Kings defenseman Marty McSorley and that had swung a 1993 Stanley Cup Finals game.

The Avs had 1:20 left on an existing power play when Hartley called for Hasek's stick to be measured in an official challenge. A penalty on the Wings, and it would be a five-on-three. Hasek's stick proved legal. The Avs were assessed a two-minute penalty, stopping in its tracks the momentum that had been building. Darren McCarty scored to make it 2–0, and that's how it finished.

The Avs had no chance in Game 7. For one thing, Forsberg suddenly had a broken finger, the result of an unpenalized slash from Kirk Maltby. For another, this was the Avs' fourth straight playoff series that went to a seventh game, and by then they were just too mentally worn-out.

Game 7 at the Joe finished in an embarrassing 7–0 rout, the Motown Meltdown. It remains, statistically and figuratively, the worst playoff loss in team history.

"That first period was awful. If we could have gotten out of that first period even close, I think we could have rallied and done something," Sakic said. "But the game was over after the first 10 minutes."

The Red Wings went on to easily win the Cup over the Hurricanes. It was their third Cup since 1997, one more than the Avs. It closed out the great rivalry of its era between the teams, and Detroit got the last laugh.

62 Joe Sacco—His Tenure and Curious Hiring

As a reporter, I always liked dealing with Joe Sacco. He was always professional, always tried to answer a question honestly—which in Avalanche Land often meant having to shade the truth by a few degrees.

With Sacco, I got a pretty straight answer. And after I got to know him a while, I could pick up on his bodily cues as to what he was really trying to tell me. He might say, "Jan Hejda has been playing well for us," but a slight shift in weight or a quick in-and-out eye connection might give me the truth otherwise.

I had to really be able to pick up on those cues in Sacco's final three years of his four-year tenure as Avs coach. He had to tell a lot of half-truths. Those final three years under Sacco, from 2010 to 2013, the Avs went 87–104–21, missing the playoffs each season. The first year went 43–30–9 and earned Sacco some recognition as a finalist for the Jack Adams Award.

Not bad for a guy who wasn't even the team's first choice as coach in 2009, following the departure of Tony Granato for a second time. Sacco was the coach at the time of the AHL's Lake Erie Monsters and was generally credited for doing a good job despite lots of injuries and call-ups from the NHL parent club—the Avs. After the disastrous one-year return of Granato as head coach in 2008–09 (32–45–5), Pierre Lacroix reached out to his old friend and client, Patrick Roy.

Not long after Granato was let go a second time, I got wind that Roy was in town for some reason. I won't give up the source, but let's just say it was someone in the travel industry, and that leads me to a tip for all you wannabe sportswriters reading this: get to know people well in the travel and hospitality industries. It might be a gate agent at a big airline. It might be a travel agent who deals with a lot of celebrities. It might be a parking attendant at the best restaurant in town. It might be a hotel clerk at the biggest hotel in town. It might be one of those people or all of them. As a reporter, you have to get to know some of these people. Get their trust. You'll be rewarded with a scoop or two or three if you do.

Not only did I get the tip that Roy was in town from someone in the travel industry, I got a tip where he was eating dinner with Lacroix one night. It was at Elways's in the Cherry Creek section of town. So I went and staked them out. After a long dinner and a couple beverages at the bar, with assurances they were in the dining room, it turned out I'd just missed them. They had walked out before I got there.

Still, I was able to piece together enough to write a story that Roy was in town and was meeting with Pierre Lacroix, based on "sources." When the story hit the wires, Lacroix and the Avs tried to play dumb. What meeting? Roy who?

But Lacroix was classy enough to eventually give up the ghost. Yes, he was courting Roy, he admitted. But no, it didn't work out. After I published a story saying as much, the Avs made the unusual move of putting Roy on the phone with me. It was no doubt an effort to finesse the fallout of Lacroix's unsuccessful courtship, but that was fine with me. This would be my exclusive too, another trophy on the scoop mantelpiece.

Roy said he was flattered by the Avs' offer to leave his position as coach and GM/part owner of the QMJHL's Quebec Remparts, but he had decided against it in order to keep coaching his youngest son, Frederick. His older son, Jonathan, had just finished his junior career with the Remparts, which included a final season of some controversy. In March 2008 Jonathan Roy was formally charged with assault after a fight with an opposing goalie named Bobby Nadeau. Patrick Roy was his coach, and was seen on video urging

Jonathan to fight Nadeau during the end of a playoff game that had gotten out of control.

Jonathan Roy pled guilty in exchange for an "absolute discharge" (The Canadian legal system? Don't go there. Nobody has ever been able to figure it out.) It essentially amounted to a $5,000 fine. The incident sparked something of a national discussion on violence in hockey, and tainted the elder Roy's image some.

Still, things died down enough for Roy to continue on as Remparts coach, and besides, the Avs' offer wasn't good enough. Roy wanted $12 million for four years to serve as coach and GM, but the team's best offer was four years and $7 million.

With Roy out of the picture, the Avs quickly decided to just give the job to Sacco. He had the credentials to earn such a chance, and after that first year, it looked like a retroactively smart move. The Avs made the playoffs in 2009 as the eighth-place team in the Western Conference. With rookies such as Matt Duchene and Ryan O'Reilly, and a brilliant second half by goalie Craig Anderson, Sacco could boast of being a playoff coach his first year, after a season under Granato in which the Avs finished 29th.

But the final three years were a mess. Players chafed under Sacco's system. The forwards felt it was too conservative. Youngsters such as Duchene and O'Reilly and Gabe Landeskog wanted to get out and skate with the puck. Instead, they felt constrained playing dump-and-chase hockey.

But the fact is, the personnel just wasn't good enough. After Anderson left, Sacco never had a goalie he could rely upon. Some of that probably was Sacco's fault, though. Anderson felt disrespected by Sacco after returning from a knee injury and quickly losing his starting job to Peter Budaj, following a few bad starts. He was traded at the deadline of the 2010–11 season, to Ottawa for Brian Elliott, and went on to make the Senators a playoff team.

By the end of Sacco's fourth year, the players had permanently tuned him out, as had the fans. Everyone got tired of his demeanor, which could best be described in that final year as "shruggish." A typical postgame press conference scene would be Sacco saying something like, "Well, we hung in there for a while until we caught a bad break, and that stuff just happens sometimes."

By then, nobody was buying into any "Prosperity is just around the corner" verbiage from Sacco or anyone else from Avs management. In the summer of 2013, with the promotion of Joe Sakic to the GM job in place of Greg Sherman, Sakic and Josh Kroenke made the decision to make another run at Roy.

This time, they were successful. Sacco went on to be an assistant with Buffalo and Boston. Just like Sacco, Roy made the playoffs his first year (and actually won the Jack Adams Award). Just like under Sacco, the next year the team missed the playoffs.

63 Shjon Podein Refuses to Change

The enduring image of the Avalanche's 2001 Stanley Cup championship is of Ray Bourque holding the hallowed silver punch bowl over his head for the first time, after the last game of his brilliant 22-year career. The enduring smell was of Shjon Podein still being in full uniform a day later.

If there was one player who thoroughly enjoyed his first Cup, who wanted to bask in the glow of every second of it, it was the likable Podein. A curly-haired, spindly-legged Minnesotan with a thick home-country accent, Podein was a grinding third-line player who could score a little but was more counted upon to be responsible defensively and kill penalties.

Podein sweated as much or more than any other Av. His curly locks were mostly straight from moisture after any game. He always seemed to be falling down somewhere, crashing and banging into the boards or taking a beating in front of the net, his back turned toward the goalie setting screens.

When the Avs won Game 7 by a 3–1 score against the Devils, Podein wore a perma-grin that maybe still hasn't come off. One other thing that didn't come off was his uniform, for at least 24 hours.

Like the rest of the team, Podein went to the Denver ChopHouse & Brewery to celebrate. Unlike the rest, he chose to keep his uniform on, pads and all. He did take his skates off, at least.

"I just didn't want to take it off," Podein recalled. "I wanted that feeling to last as long as it could. My wife? Ah, yeah, she made me take a shower by the next afternoon or so."

Podein walked all over town in his uniform, delighting in the stares. He refused to shave for a while too, his Grizzly Adams beard devouring every millimeter of facial skin.

Those who have spent any time in hockey dressing rooms know one thing: it stinks, especially after games. If you want to gag someone, grab a hockey glove off someone who has just played a full game and stick it in the victim's nose.

It smells like rotten garbage in 150-degree heat or something. It's gross. Skates smell too, and socks. Some players use the same equipment their whole careers. Joe Sakic, for instance, wore the same chest protector every game of his career. Brendan Shanahan of the Red Wings did too.

Podein still has the jersey from that Game 7, of course, and the pads and socks and skates. No, they still haven't been washed.

64 Curse of the Ex-Avs

Want to have at least one great game as an NHL player? Easy: Play for the Avalanche, get traded or released or sign as a free agent somewhere else, then play your first game against the Avs. Guaranteed, it'll be a great one for you.

After a while, it became a real thing. People thought it was some kind of jinx against the Avs or something. No matter how good, average, or even bad a player was, he always seemed to have a big game his first one back against the Avs.

Jeff Finger scored six goals in 66 games for Toronto after leaving the Avs as a free agent. Of course, one was against the Avs at the Pepsi Center in the only meeting of the teams that season. Dan Hinote scored five goals for the St. Louis Blues in 41 games in 2006–07, after several years in Denver. Two of those goals came in his first game against the Avs.

On and on it went. After playing one year with the Avs in 2003–04, Teemu Selanne seemed to score in almost every single game he played against Colorado during the rest of his career. The first game Peter Forsberg ever played against the Avs, on a weekend afternoon in Philly, he scored twice, including the tying goal with less than two minutes left.

In the first game he played for the Phoenix Coyotes after being traded for Peter Mueller, Wojtek Wolski scored a last-minute goal to send the game to overtime. Mike Keane tortured his ex-team the first couple years after leaving, including two goals in Game 7 of the 1999 Western Conference Finals for Dallas.

Chris Drury scored a goal for Calgary in his first game against the Avs. Scott Young scored some big goals for St. Louis after leaving the Avs. Anson Carter, Mark Parrish, Robyn Regehr—Avs prospects who never played with the team—all had big games against them right away. Radim Vrbata, traded to Carolina for Bates Battaglia, scored numerous goals against Colorado over the years, mostly for Phoenix. Uwe Krupp left Colorado for Detroit and won a Stanley Cup in 1997–98, though he was hurt most of his time there.

Of course, sometimes it worked the other way around too. Patrick Roy certainly made Montreal pay for trading him, for instance!

65 Nathan MacKinnon's Hot Start

He was the first pick in the 2013 NHL Draft and won the Calder Trophy after his first season. So it all went as planned for Nathan MacKinnon and the Avalanche.

Except for much of the lead-up to the draft, many assumed the Avs would draft Seth Jones with the top pick—and why not? Jones was a big, two-way defenseman, just the kind of player the Avs needed at the time. MacKinnon was a center, and Colorado already had Matt Duchene and Paul Stastny up the middle.

Jones had the higher ranking among many scouts, but things really changed at the Memorial Cup tournament in 2013. Jones' Portland Winterhawks played MacKinnon's Halifax Mooseheads, and MacKinnon dominated, winning the MVP award as Halifax prevailed.

Even if Jones had had the better of things in the tournament, the Avs probably still would have taken MacKinnon. History has always just been too much on the side of the teams that took the blue-chip forward with the first pick than those who went with a defenseman.

MacKinnon's rookie year actually started off a little slow statistically. He only scored one goal his first 10 games, though he did have four assists in his first three. After Christmas, though, MacKinnon just kept getting better and better. From January 25 to March 6, he set an NHL record for longest point streak (13) as an 18-year-old, breaking Wayne Gretzky's old mark.

Then came the playoffs, and MacKinnon was spectacular in the first two games against the Minnesota Wild. He had three assists in Game 1, a 5–4 OT win on a Stastny goal. He had a goal and three assists in Game 2, a 4–2 Avs win. Seven points in his first two NHL playoff games—only two players in league history had done that.

In Game 5 MacKinnon was the OT hero, scoring the goal that gave the Avs a 3–2 series lead. Unfortunately for him and the team, the fun stopped there. MacKinnon failed to get a point and was a minus-6 in the final two games as the Avs lost the series in seven.

Still, his rookie season was good enough for the voters to make him a landslide selection for the Calder. He finished with 24 goals and 63 points, playing all 82 games. He suffered something of a sophomore slump in year two, posting 14 goals and 38 points in 64 games.

MacKinnon entered his third year pledging to get back to the rookie form, only better. He came into training camp more muscular and, as he loved to point out to others, a quarter-inch taller from the last game of 2014–15. He was still a growing boy of 20, after all.

66 Ruslan Salei, Karlis Skrastins, and the Yaroslavl Tragedy

On September 7, 2011, the horrible news flashed across the media: a plane carrying a Russian professional hockey team named Lokomotiv Yaroslavl crashed shortly after takeoff; the team was on its way to Minsk, Belarus, for the first game of its Kontinental Hockey League season. An investigation later revealed pilot error, along with the shocking revelation that one of the pilots had falsified documents in the process of being hired, when he never should have been.

Two former Avalanche players, Ruslan Salei and Karlis Skrastins, were among the 43 people who died when the plane crashed into the ground just after takeoff. Salei, 36, played from 2008 to 2010 with Colorado, while Skrastins, 37, played from 2003 to 2008.

I have such good memories of being around Skrastins and Salei. Both were tough-as-nails, old-school type players who were gentle, good-natured people off the ice. Salei, known to everyone in the game as Rusty, had a dry, devilish sense of humor. He was a guy a reporter could actually talk to, person-to-person, instead of reporter-to-player.

He was a curious type of guy, interested in more than just hockey banter. He would often ask me about the particulars of being a reporter, interested in the things I did in my profession. I remember one time we were talking about our stations in life, and I was telling him how awesome it must be to make big money playing a game.

He said it was, indeed, nice. But he also knew he was getting toward the end of his career, and I'll never forget what he told me after I joked about the huge disparity in our incomes and his privileged status in life. He said, "Yeah, but you get to keep doing what you do long after I will."

That was the kind of thoughtfulness Salei had. Skrastins was like that too. A good-looking blond guy with a thick Latvian accent, he was always in the locker room right after a game, win or lose. So many guys beat it quickly back to the privacy of the shower room after a loss, leaving reporters to swarm over one or two guys still there. Skrastins was always one of those guys still there to give accountability to the public over what happened.

It might not be fair, but I always filed away who stuck around after a loss and who didn't. To me, it showed plenty of the character of each player. It's always easy to hang around the locker after a win and extol the virtues of your game. It's another thing to be there after a bad game too, and to talk about it instead of running to the showers. Salei was always a guy who stuck around too.

Check the newspaper archives from any losses in the years Salei and Skrastins played with the Avs, and you'll see plenty of quotes from them. That's because they knew it was part of their job to deal with the media, in good times and bad.

The tragedy in Yaroslavl had another connection to the Avalanche. Semyon Varlamov, who was slated to start his first training camp with the team that month following his summer acquisition from Washington, played for Lokomotiv for several years before joining the NHL with the Capitals. Varlamov was good friends with many of the players still on the team, and there was even a chance he might have returned to the team had he not been able to agree to a contract with an NHL team for the 2011–12 season. Varlamov could have been on that plane too.

Varlamov was understandably still affected by the tragedy when he came back to Denver, and though he refused to make excuses, his mediocre play that first season with Colorado probably had something to do with his emotions.

It's still a shock to those who knew Salei and Skrastins. Many players all have a little bit of fear in the back of their minds about all the flying they do. It's by far the safest form of travel a human being can do, and most players have no problem sitting through the dozens of flights they take every year. But some have had real problems with it, and it's something I can relate to as well. I flew more than one million miles from 1995 to 2015, and I passed many of them with my hands gripping the armrests.

67 Craig Anderson's Great Year, Then Premature Exit

In the summer of 2009, the Avalanche signed goalie Craig Anderson as a free agent, to a two-year, $3.6 million deal that looked like the bargain of the century after his first season.

Anderson almost single-handedly led the Avalanche to a playoff spot in 2010, the first year of coach Joe Sacco's tenure and the first year of rookie forwards Matt Duchene and Ryan O'Reilly. Anderson won 38 games for a team that allowed 32.1 shots against per game—one of the highest in the league.

Anderson, who struggled in the minors for years before getting a chance with Florida, proved he was a No. 1–caliber goalie at 29 with the Avs. Despite the San Jose Sharks outshooting the Avs by lopsided margins in almost every game, he won two games in a first-round series, including an amazing 51-save shutout in Game 3.

Everything should have been just peachy going into the next season, but by the trade deadline, Anderson was an Ottawa Senator. Why? Money, of course.

But it was more than that. Anderson felt underappreciated by Sacco and upper management when, after hurting a knee during warm-ups in Vancouver, he hurried back to try to get his team back in playoff contention. But he wasn't 100 percent still, and his play suffered. Then Sacco started alternating Anderson with backup Peter Budaj, and relations started to sour. Anderson, a potential unrestricted free agent after the season, wanted an extension worked out while the season was ongoing.

But the sides were far apart on dollars. Anderson felt he'd earned the right to a nicer deal before he could go UFA. Players got extensions all the time, so why not him, especially after he'd proven what he could do the year before?

Craig Anderson shows why Colorado shouldn't have let him go.

With the Avs way out of playoff contention, though, Avs GM Greg Sherman decided to cut ties with Anderson, dealing him to Ottawa for Brian Elliott. Anderson almost immediately signed a four-year, $12.75 million extension.

Many Avs fans had the attitude of "Good, let him go," believing Anderson's attitude was bad. The Avs would not be a playoff team again for four years, while Anderson helped lead Ottawa to playoff appearances in 2012, 2013, and 2015. History shows that dealing him was a mistake (compounded by the fact that Elliott, whom the Avs chose not to sign in 2011, went on to some outstanding years in St. Louis).

The Anderson situation was one that happened too often in Avs history. The Avs too often tried to pinch pennies with key players and saw them go for practically nothing. No, you don't just give players whatever they want. But you don't just let a really good goalie like Anderson go over peanuts either.

68 Peter Mueller's Promising Career Derailed

In the 15 games Peter Mueller played for the Avalanche in 2010, he posted 20 points. That had everyone in Denver really excited as the postseason neared and it became clear Colorado would be one of the eight participants in the Western Conference dance.

Mueller, the eighth pick overall in the 2006 NHL Draft, by Phoenix, scored 22 goals for the Coyotes in his rookie season but was inconsistent in the next few years. The Avalanche had a player just like that in Wojtek Wolski, and at the trade deadline of 2010 the teams decided to swap them straight up.

Mueller, playing right wing on a line with rookie Matt Duchene, was an immediate hit in an Avs sweater. In an April 4 game at home against San Jose, the fourth-to-last game of the regular season, Mueller had two goals and an assist when he went to play a puck behind the Sharks' net. A big Sharks defenseman came to give him a hit.

That defenseman was old friend Rob Blake. As Mueller went to play the puck, he dipped his head some. Blake, seeing an opportunity to teach a player never to do that with him around, drove Mueller into the boards while leading with the shoulder. Mueller went down and stayed down. He would not play a game again for the Avalanche until October 8, 2011.

Mueller's loss was huge to the Avs in the first round of the playoffs against Blake and the Sharks. He was listed as out with a concussion, and that's how it would stay for more than a year. He missed the entire 2010–11 season, plagued with constant headaches. He would play only 32 games in 2011–12, scoring seven goals. He wore a padded helmet that was larger than the normal player's, but he again suffered from concussion symptoms.

The Avs opted to just let him go after that season. He caught on to play 43 games with the Florida Panthers in 2012–13, but injuries again hit.

Mueller was an interesting person. He was smarter than your average bear of a hockey player, so one could talk to him about things other than hockey. While sidelined with his first major concussion, Mueller found religion and would sometimes quote scripture with a reporter. He really went through a trial with the concussions but never felt sorry for himself.

After his time with the Panthers ended, Mueller found a home in Switzerland for two years, playing for a pro team there. For the 2015–16 season, Mueller signed with a team in Sweden, making $700,000 in US dollars. So while life could have turned out worse for Mueller, it remains something of a minor tragedy in Avs history that his career was derailed by concussions.

Concussions are a difficult thing for any pro athlete to play with, but maybe even more so for hockey players. With all that motion, all that light and noise from the rink, and all that physical contact, reinjury is common.

Avs fans came to really dislike Blake for a while after the hit on Mueller. He was booed almost as vociferously when he touched the puck in Denver during the 2010 first round as he was in Los Angeles while playing for the Avs against the Kings in 2001. But by 2015, he was being cheered again, as part of a 20th-year, all-time team reunion. That's hockey.

69 Uwe Krupp Leaves Denver for Detroit

It was tantamount to treason at the time—a player switching sides in the heat of the famous Colorado-Detroit rivalry. To do it as an unrestricted free agent, by *choice*? That turned Uwe Krupp from beloved Avalanche playoff hero to the city's hockey version of Benedict Arnold with the stroke of a pen.

In the summer of 1998, Krupp, who had been unable to agree to terms with the Avs and was slated to become a UFA, shocked everyone by signing a four-year, $16.4 million contract with the hated Red Wings. Just 24 months before, he was tossing his gloves in the air in celebration of a Cup-clinching, triple-overtime goal in Florida. Then there he was, decked out in the Winged Wheel, smiling with Scotty Bowman, Ken Holland, and Mike Ilitch.

History would prove it a bad signing by the Wings. Krupp played just 30 games for the Wings during the four years, and was suspended for 722 days without pay in a dispute that centered on management accusing him of being injured from racing sled dogs—one of the big German defenseman's hobbies. The sides eventually settled for an undisclosed sum in 2003, but it was ugly before that, with one unnamed Red Wings management person telling the *Detroit Free Press* that Krupp was a "con man."

Krupp was anything but a con man, I can vouch for that. He was a very approachable, friendly person in general, someone who in my early years as a reporter taught me a lot about the inner workings of the NHL and what players really thought about things. He became a real go-to guy for me in the locker room, always good for a quote or some bits of gossip.

Krupp was not your typical hockey player in many respects, starting with the fact he was 6'6" and German. He also enjoyed talking about more than just hockey, including music, history, and current events. When most teammates were reading the sports page, Krupp often was reading a novel or listening to jazz or progressive rock.

When the Red Wings signed Krupp, his sled-dog hobby was well known, as was a history of some pretty serious injuries, including a blown-out left knee that limited him to just six regular-season games in 1995–96 with the Avs. He hurt his back in a fight with Detroit's Jamie Pushor in the infamous March 26, 1997, game at Joe Louis Arena, but he played 78 games in 1997–98.

When back and foot injuries surfaced to sideline him early in the 1998–99 season with Detroit, Krupp passed some of his idle time on weekends with some sled-dog racing in low-key events, some of which were in Colorado. When a doctor wrote a letter to the Red Wings saying Krupp's back injury was so severe he should retire, the Red Wings panicked. And the reason why they panicked, which few people knew at the time, was because Detroit chose not to insure his contract and they—not some insurance company—were on the hook for all of it.

Krupp was owed $12.3 million on his deal when the Wings elected to suspend him. A nasty, bitter legal fight over the money dragged on for three years, with the Red Wings going so far as to hire personal investigators to look for incriminating information on him and trying to intimidate family and friends into talking about him.

Amazingly, Krupp returned to play for Detroit for eight games in 2001–02 before getting hurt again—all the while still in a legal fight with the team over the unpaid money from the suspension. Krupp played four games for the Atlanta Thrashers in 2002–03 before the pain from his back proved just too much. He later became a coach for the German national team and, yes, still continued to race sled dogs.

In the first 20 years of the Avs' history, he remained the only player to sign as a free agent with Detroit while last playing for Colorado. But any hard feelings disappeared in the ensuing years. The Avs even gave him a night in his honor, and he has called his three seasons in Denver the favorites of his 15-year career.

70 The Chris Simon / Marc Crawford Blowup and a Big Scoop

Before the Avalanche departed for Vancouver to play Games 3 and 4 of their first-round, 1996 playoff series against the Canucks, the team held a morning practice at the old DU Arena on the University of Denver campus. Avalanche historians should note the Old Barn was where the team practiced its first season in town.

The Avs had just lost Game 2 to the Canucks, with the game-winning goal coming from their "goon" player, Gino Odjick. Not only that, Odjick roughed up more than a couple Avs players with big hits and never had to pay for them physically. The guy whose job it was to address such liberties against Avs players was Chris Simon, a big, wild-haired left-winger who scored 16 goals in the regular season, often playing on a line with Joe Sakic and Scott Young.

Simon also had 250 penalty minutes in the regular season, and was gaining a reputation as perhaps the game's best enforcer who could also play some hockey. But after the loss to the Canucks, Avs coach Marc Crawford was unhappy with Simon and let him know it at the end of practice.

"Are you with us, Chris, or not?" Crawford could be heard saying to Simon, numerous players gathered around him.

Simon became so upset that, as the team dispersed, he fell to his knees and put his hands around his head on the ice. It looked like he might be crying. Teammate Troy Murray tried to console him, but Simon stayed in his prone position for several minutes.

This obviously was big news to us *Denver Post* reporters who were present, a group that included Terry Frei, Mark Kiszla, and me. All of us were slated to board a flight to Vancouver a few hours later.

Nobody, Simon and Crawford included, would talk about the incident much. Crawford dismissed it as not a big deal, and Simon wouldn't comment at all. Needless to say, we reporters thought it was a very big deal. I wrote at length about it for the next day's paper, and Kiszla devoted his whole column to it. The Canucks were the underdog, and it looked as if the Avs might be imploding from within.

Here is probably the biggest reason why we thought it was such a big deal: because nobody from the archrival *Rocky Mountain News* was at the practice. It can't be understated what a bloody cage match it was between the papers at the time. Denver, sadly it would prove later, was one of the last American cities to have two competing, separately owned daily newspapers. It was a genuine newspaper war.

The *News'* reporting contingent of Rick Sadowski, Jim Benton, and columnist Bob Kravitz had already left for Vancouver, taking a morning flight. Shockingly, the *News* didn't send anyone to the practice at all.

This is not to try and brag or embarrass the *News*. It wasn't the reporters' fault—they were just following the orders of the travel agents. Mostly, the reason why I'm telling this part of the story is to illustrate just how different times were back then media-wise.

If the Crawford-Simon incident had occurred any time after, say, 2008, anyone at the practice would have immediately Tweeted news of it, probably with accompanying cell phone video. While cell phones did exist in 1996, they were primitive by today's standards. There was still no way to post news in real time back then, other than maybe being live on TV or the radio. To add to the *Post's* luck on this story, nobody from the local TV or radio stations seemed to notice what happened.

Still, someone would tip off the *News*, Frei, Kiszla, and I were convinced. They would get the story second-hand, maybe; there was no way we would get that big of a scoop. But we all went ahead making as big a story out of it as we could, regardless of what might appear in the next day's *News*.

After getting in to Vancouver and filing all our copy, we bumped into Sadowski, Benton, and Kravitz at the team hotel where everybody was staying, the Westin Bayshore—a lovely place adjoining the huge harbor in the heart of the city. The place always smelled like pinewood, and it had a fantastic, velvety bar-lounge that was usually a who's who of whatever NHL teams and other personnel were in town.

We were all pretty friendly with each other away from our primary occupations of trying to put each other out of business, so we made plans to have a late dinner together. I think it was about 9:00 PM local time when we gathered, 10:00 PM Mountain.

Kiszla, Frei, and I sat in a booth on one side of a table opposite Sadowski, Benton, and Kravitz. Of course, the conversation quickly turned to what we all might have in the paper the next day. We *Post* guys kept our poker faces, though, while Kravitz freely admitted his topic was something entirely different from any Crawford-Simon blowup. It became clear that neither Sadowski nor Benton knew anything about it either.

I distinctly remember Kravitz at some point saying, "So, anything happen at practice today?" Prior to midnight Mountain time, we *Post* guys mumbled something to the effect of "Naw, not that we found. Just another routine practice."

When the clock struck midnight Denver time, however, and we knew it would be too late for them to get anything in the morning paper, we couldn't resist any longer. "Yeah, something might have actually happened at practice today," we said.

I do remember the look on Kravitz's face right then. He was a pro's pro newspaper guy, and he knew instantly that we had something and they didn't, and that it would be bad for his paper the next day. Gradually, as a little more time went by (remember, no cell phones for them to Tweet anything out and no newspaper website for them to post something fast), we told them pretty much the full story. Hey, they asked. It got very quiet on their side of the table, and Kravitz started cursing out whoever had made the travel decisions for the *News* that day. We were aghast that nobody had tipped them off to what had happened, and they were even more so.

Again, this is not to embarrass them all these years later. It's just a story that probably will never be duplicated media-wise ever again. It's basically impossible to keep anything under wraps for long in today's real-time technological world, and if reporters do have a scoop of any kind, they are now trained to just blurt it out as fast as they can somewhere.

As far as Simon and Crawford went, things were never the same between them. Simon did contribute to the Avs winning the series with Vancouver, and he helped the cause greatly with a victory in a fight with legendary Chicago enforcer Bob Probert in the second round.

But Crawford snubbed Simon in the Stanley Cup Finals, never playing him one second. Simon had a bit of a bad ankle, but his skills just weren't deemed necessary by Crawford against Florida. If you look at pictures of the Avs' Stanley Cup celebration on the ice in Florida, Simon can be seen in the background in a tracksuit, a half-hearted smile on his face.

Simon, who made $500,000 in 1995–96, wanted a raise to $1 million, while GM Pierre Lacroix wouldn't go any higher than $625,000. Before the following season, he was traded to the Washington Capitals, along with Curtis Leschyshyn, for Keith Jones and a draft pick that would later turn out to be Scott Parker.

The hard feelings between Simon and the Avs never went away. He told me for one story after his trade that he would "not shake his hand" if he ran into Lacroix in the hallway, and said Crawford essentially lied to him about playing time in the postseason.

By 1998 Simon was back in the Stanley Cup Finals, this time as a top-six forward for the Caps. Crawford by then was out of a job and the Avs were out after the first round of the playoffs.

Kravitz, by the way, got his revenge on me on the basketball court. During the playoffs in 1999 in Dallas, we went to a gym together, along with the *News'* other sports columnist, Mike Littwin. We decided to play H-O-R-S-E, and I thought they would be easy pickings. Being 6'6" and a pretty good player in my day, I thought these two short, old guys were out of their league. I was pretty cocky, and suggested we put a few beers on the games, telling them I preferred Guinness.

While Littwin bowed out of the games early, I could never beat Kravitz. The guy was automatic with his set-shot-style jumpers from around the key. It was nuts. He hit everything. He beat me about 10 straight games. I hate to lose, so I was *really* pissed coming out of that gym. The *Post* bean counters were probably not thrilled either once they saw the "dinner" bills from that trip, with about $40 in beers going into Kravitz's gullet.

71 Lappy

One thing I remember well during Ian "Lappy" Laperriere's first season with the Avalanche (2005–06) was how many fans from his former teams would seek him out. Lappy only played for the New York Rangers for 28 games in 1995–96, but there'd be Rangers fans in his sweater hoping to get it signed. Same for St. Louis, another of his teams. Any stop there, and Lappy would have half a dozen fans hoping to say hi.

And whenever we went to Los Angeles for a game? Forget it, Lappy would be practically besieged by former fans. After getting to know him, it was apparent why he was so popular.

Laperriere was just a tremendous guy, friendly to everyone off the ice. On the ice? He was one tough hombre, someone who would fight anyone bigger than him, someone who always stuck up for his teammates. He was a great trash-talker too. He had this look to him that got under the skin of opponents, driving them to distraction. He had a bent nose, didn't wear a shield, and never whined about anything.

Laperriere came to the Avalanche as a free agent from the Kings, but the first year of his contract was wiped out with the lost season of 2004–05. In 11 previous seasons with the Kings, Blues, and Rangers, Laperriere scored in double figures only twice. In 2005–06 with the Avs, he scored 21 goals and 24 assists. He never scored in double figures again.

Everything just went right for Lappy that first year. He got to play at times on a line with Joe Sakic, which didn't hurt.

As always, Laperriere surpassed 100 penalty minutes. He finished his career with 1,956 PIMs, among the NHL's all-time leaders.

Off the ice, though, Lappy was a beauty. He always had great insight into the game for reporters, and he was always in the locker room well after it opened, win or lose. He always had a soft spot for people in need, especially kids, and while with the Avs he developed a special relationship with a three-year-old local girl named Ellie Rolfs.

At age two, Ellie was diagnosed with Stage IV Widely Diffuse Anaplastic Wilm's Tumor—an aggressive, rare form of pediatric kidney cancer. While in the hospital, Ellie liked to watch Avs games, and Lappy quickly became her favorite player.

A part-time reporter named Kitt Amundson was a work colleague with Ellie's father, and she arranged for Ellie to visit the Avs' locker room one day. She and Lappy bonded instantly, as she did with other players such as Ben Guite and Peter Budaj. Pretty soon, Ellie was a regular at practices, decked out in tons of Avs gear given to her by the team.

Ellie's condition had its ups and downs. But as Lappy never tired of pointing out, she was tougher than anyone in the Avs' dressing room. Eventually, the cancer went into remission.

On the night of October 24, 2015, with the Avs hosting the Columbus Blue Jackets, Ellie was introduced to the crowd. She was 10 years old by then, with long, beautiful blond hair. Suddenly, on the Jumbotron, was Lappy's face. In a recorded video, he saluted Ellie, telling her what an inspiration she was to his life—and Lappy wasn't just saying that.

His career ended prematurely his first year with the Philadelphia Flyers, when he went down to block a shot and took the puck square to the eye and developed a concussion and vision problems. He tried hard to come back but just couldn't make it, and for a while Laperriere dealt with the depression that comes with a sudden end to a job that one loves.

Thinking of how Ellie had toughed it out helped Lappy, and no doubt they will be friends for the rest of their lives. He'll always have many other friends to lean on too.

72 Stanley Cup Supporting Characters

No book on the Avalanche's history would be complete without a chapter on some of the bit players who helped in important ways in the team's first two Stanley Cup wins. There is plenty in this tome on Patrick Roy, Joe Sakic, and Peter Forsberg, but what about guys such as Rene Corbet, Jon Klemm, and Ville Nieminen? Here is the homage to them and others.

Every player on the 1995–96 team made valuable contributions to a championship at some point, including:

- Corbet and Klemm scoring two goals apiece in Game 2 of the Stanley Cup Finals against Florida. Klemm's feat was all the more impressive given his natural position was on defense.

  Corbet was a happy-go-lucky guy, with *luck* being more than just a word. As a player with the Avs, he won $50,000 in a Quebec lottery. He gave it to his parents to put a down payment on a nice house.

- Dave Hannan. Acquired at the trade deadline, he was excellent in the faceoff dots and on the penalty kill.

- Craig Wolanin. Although he fell out of favor with Coach Marc Crawford after a tough Game 3 of the Western Conference Semifinals against Chicago and never played for the team again, he played very well on defense much of the time before that. Wolanin played 75 regular-season games and finished a plus-25—seventh-best on the squad.
- Stephane Fiset. Virtually forgotten from that first Cup team was Fiset's contribution, a 22–6–7 record. He became the seldom-used backup after the Avs got Roy from Montreal, but Fiset helped win a lot of games before that.
- Warren Rychel. Picked up on waivers before the start of the season, Rychel played 52 regular-season games, scoring six goals, and played 12 more in the playoffs. He added another element of toughness that made opponents think twice before taking liberties with the top players.

  Check out the pictures of the 1996 Stanley Cup celebration aftermath; Rychel is in many of them. He still gets kidded about being a camera hog.
- Sylvain Lefebvre and Curtis Leschyshyn. Both veteran defensemen were durable, reliable contributors. They didn't make a lot of noise offensively, but both were smart with the puck in their own end and leaders in the dressing room.

Unsung contributors from the 2001 championship team include:
- Ville "Nemo" Nieminen. Called up from the minors earlier in the season, Nemo wound up scoring 14 goals in 50 regular-season games and was an effective agitator who drew a lot of penalties. When Forsberg was sidelined for the final two rounds of the postseason, Nieminen got more ice time and made the most of it, scoring a big goal in a Game 3 Finals win in New Jersey.

- Martin Skoula. People forget this, but Skoula had some pretty big moments in the Stanley Cup Finals. He scored a goal in Game 3, and assisted on a big goal in Game 6. He was sometimes maligned for a style of play some called too passive, but he had a couple pretty good years with the Avs.
- Dan Hinote. One of the league's better agitators of his time, Hinote was always trash-talking opponents and/or trying to lay big hits on them. He wasn't very big, but Hinote was always willing to drop the gloves. He scored two goals in the playoffs too.

  Hinote was quite popular with the ladies while in Denver. He eventually wound up marrying celebrity Jenny McCarthy's sister.
- Greg "Devo" de Vries. A former castoff from Edmonton and Nashville, Devo played 79 very effective games for the Avs in 2000–01, finishing plus-23. He played a stay-at-home, physical brand of hockey but also chipped in a little offensively too, with five goals.
- Eric "Mess" Messier. A shot-blocker supreme, Mess was a favorite of Coach Bob Hartley. He played on the checking third line with Stephane Yelle and Shjon Podein, after starting his career as a defenseman. He wasn't much offensively, but Messier took care of the puck in the corners and worked like a dog in the defensive end, always willing to put his body in front of an opposing shot attempt.
- Chris "Dinger" Dingman. Dinger played 41 regular-season games, compiling only two points. But he played in 16 postseason contests and contributed four assists, one of them a valuable one in Game 6 of the Finals. It helped set up Adam Foote's goal that got the Avs a 1–0 lead in an eventual 4–0 win.

- Aaron "Millsie" Miller. Millsie alternated between forward and defense a lot his first couple years, but settled in mostly as a reliable D-man for the 2001 team before being traded at the deadline, along with Adam Deadmarsh, to Los Angeles. Miller was a plus-19 in the 56 games he played with the Avs that year.

73 Joe Sakic's 100-Point Year at Age 36

Not since the legendary Gordie Howe had posted 103 points in 1968–69 for the Detroit Red Wings had an NHL player reached the century mark as a player 36 or older. That changed in 2006–07.

Not since 2000–01, when he posted 118 points, had Avs captain Joe Sakic hit triple figures in scoring. As a 36-year-old centerman, Sakic played in all 82 games in 2006–07 and scored 36 goals and 64 assists. He remains the second-oldest player in league history to get 100 points in a season, with Howe still the record holder at age 40.

Sakic entered the final game of the regular season needing three points for 100, and that's what he got in Colorado's 6–3 win over the Calgary Flames. The game meant nothing in the standings, as the Avs had been eliminated from playoff contention in the game before, at home against Nashville (with Peter Forsberg and Paul Kariya playing major roles in the Predators' victory).

But the game meant a lot to Sakic's teammates, who desperately wanted to help get him into the 100-point club for the sixth time in his career. When Sakic did get his third point, on a power-play goal at the 44-second mark of the third period to break a 3–3 tie, he got a prolonged standing ovation from the crowd of 17,551.

Still dominant at 36 years old, Joe Sakic earned 100 points in 2006–07.

One lucky fan also got Sakic's jersey, in what has become an Avs tradition of all players literally giving the shirt off their backs following the last regular-season home game.

Sakic played another two seasons, but the last one was unfortunate. He was already sidelined with a herniated disc when, on December 10, 2008, Sakic suffered severed tendons to a couple fingers after accidentally getting his hand caught in a snowblower. The accident is much more common than you might think; on average, more than 1,000 people in the US every year visit hospital emergency rooms because of similar incidents. Even when snowblowers are turned off, the blades can rotate backward when people try to grab something stuck in them. That's what happened with Sakic too.

He returned to the lineup after that but reinjured his back in the first period of a game in Phoenix and was sidelined the rest of the year. It was an inglorious end to an otherwise brilliant career.

74 Forsberg's Final, Two-Game Return

Matt Duchene couldn't believe it at the time. Years later, he still couldn't.

For two nights in February 2011, Duchene skated on the same line with a boyhood hero, Peter Forsberg.

"I used to play on a line with him on my X-Box, or I'd be him, all the time. Getting to play with him in real life—I mean, it was just surreal for me," Duchene said.

Unfortunately for Duchene and the rest of Avalanche Nation, Forsberg's 2011 comeback was more a cameo than anything. After having sat out from the NHL after the end of the 2008 playoffs,

Forsberg shocked everyone in February by coming out of retirement to sign a contract for the remainder of the 2010–11 season.

Forsberg was 37 by that time, but he really thought he could come back and play again at a high level. His right foot was feeling as good as it had in years, so he owed it to himself, he thought, to give it one more try.

His comeback started on February 11, in Columbus. By February 14, he was retired again, this time for good.

Forsberg played left wing on a line with Duchene and Milan Hejduk against the Blue Jackets, and even though he was minus-2 in a 3–1 loss, Forsberg actually played pretty well.

"Might have been our best player," Coach Joe Sacco said at the time.

After the next night's game in Nashville, however, Forsberg realized he might have made a mistake. While he could still do creative things when he had the puck and a little bit of room, the fact was he couldn't separate himself from others anymore; he couldn't beat anyone with his speed. He was becoming more and more vulnerable to big hits, because he just couldn't move out of the way as quickly.

On Valentine's Day, Forsberg called a press conference at the Pepsi Center to deliver the heartbreaking news: this was it. "If I can't play at the level I think I should, then there's no point," he said. "It's just how it is with me. I thought I could do it, but I realized I can't."

Many fans and media wondered why Forsberg couldn't have suited up for one last game before the home fans later that night, against the Calgary Flames. Why not have one last game before the home folk, so they could properly say good-bye? "Not if I feel like I can't give an honest night's performance," he said. "It wouldn't be fair to myself or the team."

At least Duchene got to play two games with him. "I got the stick from his last game. I just went right up and asked him for it, and he didn't care," Duchene said. "I will definitely always prize that possession."

75 Paul Stastny

He was the son of a franchise icon. He played collegiately in the same city he would first play in as a pro. If anyone seemed a good bet to stay with the Avalanche for his entire career, it was Paul Stastny. But it didn't happen.

Stastny left for the St. Louis Blues as a free agent in 2014, turning down a multiyear offer of $6.6 million per to stay with the Avs for a four-year, $28 million deal for a division rival. Why did it come to a parting over so little money? Because St. Louis is actually the city in which Stastny largely grew up, as his Hall of Fame father, Peter, finished his career there. And because the Avs had two young, starry centers already in Matt Duchene and Nathan MacKinnon.

It was probably a mistake by Avs management that they never traded Stastny at the 2013–14 deadline, when a contract extension was always going to be iffy at best. But it's hard to blame GM Joe Sakic too much over that one.

The Avs were battling for conference and division titles, and trading Stastny for, most likely, only draft picks or prospects would have sent a message that many Avs fans would have had trouble accepting. Sakic was between a rock and a hard place on Stastny's contract, but when the Avs lost in the first round to Minnesota, the decision not to trade him came under second-guessing by another section of the fan base.

Stastny's time with the Avs was great the first few years, not as great in the later ones—although he did have a very good final season under Patrick Roy. Stastny came to the Avs in 2006 as a second-round draft pick after winning two NCAA championships playing at the University of Denver for coach George Gwozdecky.

He was something of a sensation as a rookie, posting 78 points in 82 games, including a stretch in which he notched a point in 20 straight games. He exceeded the 70-point mark in each of his next two full seasons and was rewarded with a rich contract extension in 2008 by GM Francois Giguere. Stastny would receive $33 million over the next five years, with Giguere calling him a "cornerstone player" the team could build around.

But like his team's fortunes for good portions of those five years, Stastny's play declined some. He had an excellent 2009–10 season, posting 79 points, but slipped to 57 and 53 points the next two years, respectively. He wasn't very good in the lockout-shortened 2012–13 season, with 24 points in 40 games and a minus-7.

He reached 60 points in 71 games in 2013–14 and had 10 points in seven playoff games. But his final moments as an Av were of great frustration. He was on the ice for Minnesota's overtime winner, by Nino Niederreiter, right after failing to convert on a two-on-one break-in with Gabe Landeskog.

Sakic made a genuinely good offer to keep Stastny. But not only could he legitimately claim he was "going home" again with the Blues, but St. Louis was in sore need of a top-two center. The Avs thought they already had them. St. Louis won a division title its first year with Stastny, while the Avs missed the playoffs.

76 Forsberg's First Game Against the Avs

It happened on January 14, 2006, a matinee game in Philadelphia between the Flyers and Avalanche. Sylvester Stallone was there, wearing an '06 Flyers sweater with his black, crumpled hat he wore in *Rocky*.

The main attraction otherwise, though, was the first Avalanche game ever featuring Peter Forsberg as an opposing player. And it was a classic.

But first, the night before: Several Avs players, including Joe Sakic, Rob Blake, Alex Tanguay, Brett Clark, Milan Hejduk, Dan Hinote, and John-Michael Liles, met Forsberg at a Philly restaurant for dinner. Forsberg, always generous with his money, picked up the tab for the whole thing.

On game day, though, Foppa nearly stuck the Avs with a bill of goods. Colorado held a 3–1 lead with less than three minutes to play, but I could sense it was far from over. The hunch was right, and of course who led the way for the game going to overtime but Peter Forsberg.

With 2:36 left, Forsberg made a brilliant pass to Mike Knuble for the goal to cut it to 3–2. With 1:12 left, Forsberg tied it up with another brilliant play, coming down the right side and flipping the puck in a small space vacated by goalie Aebischer.

The crowd went wild. All Avs fans were devastated at that moment, seeing their former hero, No. 21, burning them in the clutch. It wasn't long, however, before some smiles appeared on Avs fans' faces again.

Alex Tanguay won the game in overtime, scoring with the Avs on a five-on-three power play. At the 1:47 mark, Philly's Kim

Johnsson slashed Avs winger Marek Svatos. The Avs didn't do much in the first minute of the PP, but with 35 seconds remaining on it, they went another man up when Philly's Mike Rathje was called for tripping Sakic.

It was the correct call. Rathje tripped him all right, but the crowd went nuts, and so did Flyers coach Ken Hitchcock. One of the unwritten rules of hockey is that anything short of disembowelment should not create a five-on-three situation late in a game, and certainly not in overtime. As boos rained down from the Wachovia Center Flyers faithful, Tanguay easily poked a one-timer past Antero Niittymaki.

After the game, Hitchcock ripped the officiating, but he also essentially called Sakic a diver. Sakic embellished to draw the call, Hitchcock said, and when word got back to Sakic on that, the usually mild-mannered captain was livid.

Sakic played on the 2006 Canadian Olympic team in Turin the following month, and Hitchcock was an assistant coach. When the team convened for a mini training camp, Sakic told a PR person he wanted to speak with Hitchcock. Sakic got right in Hitchcock's face, saying, "Don't you ever fucking talk about me like that again. I don't dive."

Hitchcock tried to backpedal some, but Sakic cut him off and turned away. This Canadian team did not win the gold medal, by the way. Who did? Sweden, led by Peter Forsberg.

77 Plane Rides

What is it like to fly on a professional sports team's swanky private plane? As good as you think it is.

As mentioned elsewhere in this book, I spent some of my earlier years covering the Avalanche occasionally flying on the team charter. The team was anxious to make an early good impression on the Denver community. So in a magnanimous gesture, the club often invited the newspaper beat writers to come aboard, for everybody to get to know each other better.

I'm sure the *Denver Post* and *Rocky Mountain News* broke some ethical laws allowing that to happen, as I don't think any money was ever exchanged (despite us always half-heartedly offering to pay). But, oh well, that was still back in the days when teams and the media covering them were on friendlier, more informal terms. Not everything was as hardass and by-the-book then as it is today, and the way it's become is a shame in many ways, because teams have largely shielded themselves from any serious involvement with the press. To me, that only hurts the fans, because they don't get to know the players as much in an open, honest way. Everything today is PR-spun managing of "the brand," which is mostly dishonest and boring.

While flying on the plane itself was the definition of luxury (leather, first-class seats for all, a person waiting on us hand and foot, no security lines, etc.), I came to dread the return flights home. Most of the time, we didn't land until 2:00 or 3:00 in the morning, and then it was another hour or so back to metro Denver from the airport. Not getting to sleep until 5:00 or 6:00 AM would just kill me the rest of the day and foul up my sleep clock for days after. I still don't know how the players are able to do it.

I have some great memories of being on the team charter, though. I remember, for instance, when Marc Crawford, Joel Quenneville, Jacques Cloutier, and Pierre Lacroix were all playing a game called Snarples in their front section. It was a game in which two groups of partners played against each other, and Crawford and Quenneville were paired up.

Apparently, Crawford played the wrong hand or something, causing a loss. Quenneville didn't take it so well. He flung his cards up at the ceiling and started chewing out Crawford. The whole plane could hear it. Lacroix, noticing we could see this, started laughing uncontrollably. In pure hockey fashion, everything was forgotten about a few minutes later.

I remember Lacroix sending me a piece of cake with a flag sticking out of it with "1.99" written on it. The previous day, I had written that the team, after staying at a $300-a-night resort in California, had given a $1.99 night's worth of effort in a loss to Anaheim.

I remember us coming in on approach at the private airfield in Hempstead, New York, in 1995, and the plane suddenly lurching back into the air. Apparently, we almost landed on a runway with another plane coming in the same direction.

I remember the day we took off for Montreal in 1997, for Patrick Roy's first game back against the Canadiens, and Roy was trying to get the clerk's attention at the counter before boarding. "Excuse me, miss. Miss? Can I please get a glass of orange juice?" he said. A few hours later, Roy had dozens of reporters crowding around him for a press conference in a Montreal hotel room.

I remember seeing Jeff Odgers barely got his fork to his mouth from his fight-ravaged right hand following that night's game in which he went toe-to-toe with somebody (and lost).

I remember getting a big plate of food handed to me by the flight attendant after one game. On the plate was a big, red lobster and juicy filet mignon, with some kind of chocolate cake for dessert that was out of this world. I remember thinking, *Yeah, this is the only way to travel.*

Otherwise, I can honestly sum up the experience of being with a team on a plane as not all that exciting. I never made it a habit of talking to players on the record for anything, and the unwritten rule is that they are to be left alone, with most everything we saw being off the record.

But mostly all we saw were players either sleeping, watching a video, or playing cards. That's about it 99 percent of the time. And that was back in the mid- to late 1990s. With smart phones as dominant as they are today, no doubt there is very little interaction on board anymore.

78 Red Rocks

You're in Denver, you've got your Avs tickets, and…well…that's all that matters. But if one wants to see something besides just Avalanche hockey on a trip through the Mile High City, then one must venture southwest to Red Rocks Amphitheatre.

On a nice night, which means most nights in Colorado, you simply won't find a better place to enjoy a concert.

Opened in 1906 and originally called Garden of the Angels, it became known just as Red Rocks starting in 1928 when the City of Denver took over proprietorship. Pietro Satriano and his brass band were the first to play Red Rocks, and thousands of others since, including the Beatles on August 26, 1964.

On June 5, 1983, U2 played a show through a cold, steady drizzle that became an iconic performance. A live album was produced from the show and videos of lead singer Bono shouting

"No more, no more" to the crowd on the song "Sunday, Bloody Sunday" became a staple of MTV and have been credited for breaking the band in America.

Nestled into high, vertical rock, the amphitheatre has perfect, enclosed acoustics and a view as far as the eye can see of the eastern plains beyond the stage.

When not in use for concerts, the steps between rows of seats are a favored place for athletes to train. Many Avalanche players over the years have run the stairs of Red Rocks, with its high altitude offering a world-class workout. When he played for the team, Avs forward Ryan O'Reilly would often head to Red Rocks to run the stairs.

If you try it yourself, you better make sure you have some cardio fitness established. Running those stairs, at altitude, is a beast.

79. The Goose

The most enigmatic player on the Avs I ever covered? That's easy: Alexei "the Goose" Gusarov, a Russian defenseman who never once gave me or any other Denver reporter an on-the-record interview. Except, that is, when he came back to Denver in 2012 as an honoree of the first Stanley Cup team.

It's not that Gusarov was a mean guy, though. He was actually very nice, and very funny. My early years covering the team meant I got to ride the team plane or bus at times, and Gusarov would regularly crack everyone up with jokes in his broken English.

Gusarov just had a natural shyness with the press, probably because of how restricted a culture he came from in the then-Soviet era of the 1960s and '70s. Freedom of speech just wasn't

*Colorado Avalanche defenseman Alexei Gusarov battles for control of the puck
with Calgary Flames center Marty Murray in 1995.*

a communist thing, so Russian émigrés tended to be quiet when coming to North America, with the language barrier another obvious factor.

Gusarov was rail thin, about 6'2" and 180 pounds. But he was a very good skater and knew how to position himself well to avoid big hits against. He was a very smart player, though I'll admit I thought he was awful when I first saw him. I thought he was soft and turnover-prone, and I would occasionally ask questions to coaches that effectively were, "How can you guys possibly keep this guy on the team?"

It was only after learning more of the subtleties of the game that I and other regular Avs watchers started to appreciate Gusarov's style. He made very good passes in his own zone, and made lots of good poke-checks with his stick. With the Avs, he was Adam Foote's defensive partner for five full seasons, and Foote loved playing with him.

"He kept everything so simple. People don't realize how important that is for a defenseman," Foote said. "I learned so much about the game playing with him. He covered up for a lot of my mistakes early on."

Avs fans forget this, but Gusarov actually played against Colorado in the 2001 Western Conference Finals as a member of the St. Louis Blues. He looked so strange in that Blues getup too, I remember. He was one of those players you see in another team's uniform and it just doesn't look right.

Gusarov's most memorable moment as an Av probably was his assist on Joe Sakic's double-overtime game winner against Chicago in Game 4 of the 1996 Western Conference Semifinals. While it looked like a shot, Gusarov actually made a misdirection hard pass from the point in front to Sakic, who tipped it past Ed Belfour. Without that win, the Avs almost certainly wouldn't have won the Stanley Cup, as it would have put them down 3–1 in the series.

The Goose didn't give an interview after that game either.

80 Game 6, 2002, San Jose: Earthquake

It started and ended in the span of about five seconds. Lots of jokes one could make here. But for those five seconds on May 13, 2002—if you happened to be in the press box of San Jose's Compaq Center, at least—we all thought we were going to die.

What happened: With about nine minutes left in the third period of a Game 6 of the Western Conference Semifinals between the Avalanche and Sharks, the building started to shake. For much of the sold-out crowd on hand, that didn't mean a lot. Grounded in cement-foundation seats, the 5.2 magnitude quake did little more than stir the drinks for most of those in the crowd. But for those in the press box, it was a more unsettling scenario.

When the Shark Tank was originally built, they did a magnificent job on everything, except for one thing: they forgot to build a press box. That is, according to all local legend anyway. They just forgot.

So what they did was build a 360-degree catwalk of sorts, supported by wires from the ceiling. A couple other buildings in the NHL—Calgary and Edmonton—have the exact same kind of press box. And actually they are a great viewpoint from which to watch a game. The catwalks are vertically poised just above the front row of the rink, so the view just one level above is great. The action is just right down below you, with an unobstructed view.

On this May night in Northern California, the press box swayed back and forth. The biggest memory I have of the 5.2 quake—which isn't all that big but felt more substantial in a freestanding structure—is of Avs front-office executive Michel Goulet, who was walking right by us, grabbing onto a railing and looking worried. The other side of the overhang, bisected by another walkway, was where the front-office people like Goulet and Pierre Lacroix usually sat. Goulet, the Hall of Fame player with the Quebec Nordiques, admitted to us reporters later he thought he was going to tumble over the railing and down onto the crowd a hundred feet below. "I would have been the story of the night," Goulet joked afterward.

As it turned out, Peter Forsberg was the story of the night. At 2:47 of overtime in a 1–1 game, Forsberg scored to even the series for the Avs at 3–3. In the annals of Sharks history, this is one of their most regretful losses, because they were probably the better team in that series. The Avs came into San Jose down 3–2 and tired, mentally and physically. The Sharks had several great chances to put the game away late in regulation but couldn't solve Patrick Roy.

Given a one-shot-wins-it chance in OT, the Avs just had more killers up front than the Sharks and sent the series back to Denver, where Roy shut out San Jose 1–0. Game 7 was known for two things: Forsberg's lone goal and Teemu Selanne's miss on an open-net shot from about two feet out. Selanne beat Roy on a wraparound move and had nothing but open net to shoot at, but he simply fired wide.

When you look at the replays of the Selanne miss, it's inconceivable that he did. It almost seemed as if the earth tilted a little at the last second in the Avs' favor.

81 Patrick Roy— Skating to the Red Line

Before they moved writers up high like at every other arena, the best press box seats in the NHL used to be at Madison Square Garden. Although we were seated at one corner of the ice, not in the middle, we still were essentially in the front row, right behind one of the goalie nets.

I always envied the Rangers beat writers who got to sit in those seats at least 41 times a year. There's just no comparison, the difference in what you see and learn about a game from being that close as opposed to up in the rafters.

On November 16, 1997, Patrick Roy was just a few feet away from us writers, tending net in the third period of a lopsided game in the Rangers' favor. That's when, to ours, the fans', and everyone else's astonishment, Roy took off out of his net to play the puck as if he were a forward.

To set the scene: The Rangers were up 4–1 with about 3:30 left in the game, and the Avs just didn't have anything that day. The game was over. Bored in his own net, maybe a little frustrated, Roy came way out of his net to play a puck coming his way. Instead of passing it off to a teammate, though, Roy kept skating with it. And skating. And skating.

Roy made a nice deke move past, of all people, Wayne Gretzky, and continued to center ice. Then he made a hilarious spin-o-rama move with the puck, past the red line. He never lost control of it either. He continued to head down to the Rangers' zone, but then referee Paul Devorski blew his whistle.

Turns out goalies can't skate with the puck past the red line. If I had to wager, I'd say about 4 percent of all the media and fans and players knew that was a violation. I had never seen it happen before, and neither had anyone else when we quizzed others after the game.

One of the 4 percent who did know was Rangers TV color analyst John Davidson, who started cracking up over Roy's she-nanigans on the air, all the while saying it would be a penalty if he went past the red line. Roy's little sojourn is on YouTube, and it's a classic moment. Davidson lets out big cackles three or four times watching the replay, while broadcast partner Sam Rosen gets in a couple funny lines as well. "He's out of his mind," Davidson said while laughing uncontrollably.

Roy just shrugged his shoulders after the game, with a "Hey, what'd we have to lose?" attitude. It was classic Roy. He never did anything like that in a blowout game in his favor, though. He knew that would be disrespectful to his opponent.

But when the occasional game got out of hand against the Avs and Roy was still in net, he would do funny little things like that all the time. He'd whip long pass attempts or skate way out of the crease into the corners, sometimes giving a nice little body check to an opponent.

Winning was always No. 1 with Roy. But if that wasn't going to happen, he was damn well going to try to have a little fun at least.

82 Heading to the Mountains?

The rental car is gassed up and there's no hockey for a couple days or more. It's time, Denver visitor, to head west into the mountains. Here are some things to check off the list as the trip progresses:

First, there is Estes Park, a lovely mountain town about 40 miles northwest of Boulder. On the way there, stop in Lyons and play some pinball and other vintage arcade games at the incredible Lyons Classic Pinball. In Estes Park, stay at the Stanley Hotel for a night, but watch out for room 237! That's the room made famous in Stephen King's *The Shining*, which he used as inspiration for the horror novel after a previous stay. In Estes Park, another must-visit is to the Dunraven Inn, where every inch of the walls in the bar area is covered in stapled dollar bills. It's got a great old-school Italian menu, and you might see a bear outside, as I did once during a dinner.

Heading farther west up I-70, one must spend some time in Vail and Breckenridge. Both have world-class ski resorts, and in Vail there is a great old hockey rink called Dobson Arena. You might even see a famous hockey player there.

The Avalanche played a preseason game there on October 3, 1995, against the San Jose Sharks (the day O.J. Simpson was acquitted of murder), and several teams over the years have held training camps there, including the St. Louis Blues, Dallas Stars, and Florida Panthers.

A quick personal story: When the Blues held a short training camp at Dobson Arena after the NHL lockout ended in 1995, I was sent up to do a story on them. I should have been such a happy guy, getting an assignment from the *Post* to go up to the mountains and interview NHL players as a part-time reporter.

Except I was a wreck. A girl I was in something of a relationship with broke up with me the night before. Why she would want to break up with an insecure, needy guy with no full-time job, I still can't understand.

I didn't just wear my heart on my sleeve, I wore it over my socks and shoes and collar and back pockets and anywhere else on my person. I spent most of the Blues' practice session making calls on the pay phone upstairs, leaving long, pathetic messages on her answering machine.

When the Blues came off the ice, I trudged through an interview with Brett Hull as best I could, then into the office of new coach Mike Keenan. Immediately he could tell something was wrong, and he actually asked me about it. "Girl just broke up with me," I said, feeling embarrassed; I was that transparent. "One of those days."

Keenan then proceeded to tell me he was going through a similar thing, only much tougher than my little puppy dog romance. He was going through a divorce, and he was so nice to me in telling me it would be okay, that there'd be another. I was always a Mike Keenan guy after that.

Continuing on your venture into the Colorado mountains: Gotta see Aspen, especially in the fall. Have a drink at the Hotel Jerome and you'll probably see a movie star. Winter Park is another great ski area, and if you really want to keep going, take the long drive to Grand Junction and marvel at the red-rock formations everywhere.

To the south, a visit to Colorado Springs is a must, and to the west of the city, the mountains are just as spectacular or better. Have a drink at the Broadmoor Hotel and marvel at all the great old bottles of champagne and other spirits—many of which go back to the early 1900s—behind encased glass.

The Avs used to hold training camp in the Springs and for years held an annual intrasquad scrimmage at the nearby Air Force Academy.

You can't go wrong when getting in the car and driving in any direction from Denver. Colorado is a majestic place to behold.

83 Tony Granato

Ask anyone in hockey who some of the nicest guys they came across are, and Tony Granato's name often comes up.

A native of Downers Grove, Illinois, Granato starred at the University of Wisconsin but went only 120th overall to the New York Rangers in the 1982 NHL Draft. American-born college players still faced a huge bias in those days from the primarily Canadian establishment.

Granato went on to a successful playing career, scoring 30 or more goals four times with the Rangers and Los Angeles Kings. Especially toward the end of his career, with the Kings and San Jose Sharks, Granato earned the reputation as one of the most media-friendly guys in the league. It's not that Granato would spill every secret of the game to any reporter—he very much abided by the hockey code of "everything stays in the room." But he was, without fail, extremely accommodating to any reporter who asked for an interview.

It was no surprise, therefore, when Granato went right into coaching after his career ended in San Jose in 2001. His natural ami-ability had many believing he might become one of the league's great coaches as people just really, really liked to be around Tony Granato.

But Granato might have started his coaching career a little too fast, at least at the highest level. In 2001 he was still a player with the Sharks. By 2002 he was an assistant coach under Bob Hartley with the Avalanche, and on December 18 of that year he was the head coach of a team just one calendar year removed from winning a Stanley Cup.

When Granato took over for the fired Hartley, the Avs were in a mediocre period, for them. The team was around .500, and there were signs of fatigue among some players over Hartley's ways. For starters, he never seemed to be able to relax, always pushing his players, always barking instructions. Those kinds of coaches usually have a shorter shelf life, even after winning championships. John Tortorella and Mike Keenan are other coaches who come to mind.

Granato was supposed to be the relaxed players' coach. For a while, his methods worked, as the Avs went on to win their NHL record ninth straight division title under Granato in 2002–03. But when the Avs lost to Minnesota in the first round of the playoffs in Patrick Roy's final season, Granato's critics started to become more vocal. They became louder after the 2003–04 season, when, despite the off-season free-agent signings of Paul Kariya and Teemu Selanne, the Avs bowed out in the second round to San Jose. Despite a superstar roster, the Avs never jelled under Granato's leadership. Selanne chafed at his ice time, and Granato seemed too sedate behind the bench for many.

Where was his nasty, snarly side that he often showed as a player? While he was a nice guy to reporters off the ice, Granato had a reputation as one of the nastiest players in the league, never shying away from giving an opponent a good stick to the ribs. Granato, I sensed, felt a little too rushed into being a coach, and it probably wasn't his fault.

But he was very close to former Kings teammate Eric Lacroix, along with Avs GM, and Eric's father, Pierre. Eric was in Avs management by the time Granato was promoted, and there's no question their relationship played a role in his rapid promotion.

The relaxed, free-association Granato as a player seemed replaced by a man cautious of his words as a head coach, which no doubt was propelled by the Avalanche's extremely paranoid world-view of anything said publicly by a club official. You could often sense Granato wanted to open up more to reporters in his time as a head coach, only to be reined in by the Big Brother-ish Avs media-relations presence.

In the summer of 2004, Granato was "reassigned" in the organization, from head coach to assistant coach again, under new hire Joel Quenneville. While the 2004–05 season was wiped out because of a work stoppage, Granato stayed as an assistant under Quenneville through the 2007–08 season, when, after a second-round loss to Detroit, Quenneville was fired.

His replacement? Granato. In one of the few times in pro sports history, a head coach returned for a second time to a team, but the second honeymoon was short. The Avs went 32–45–5 in 2008–09, the worst record since the team moved from Quebec in 1995. Granato wasn't reassigned this time. He was fired on June 3, 2009, replaced by Joe Sacco.

The rehire of Granato never made a lot of sense, as the record showed. He went on to successful stints as an assistant in Pittsburgh and Detroit, and is now a college head coach with the University of Wisconsin.

84 David Aebischer

Your mission, should you choose to accept it: Succeed Patrick Roy as a No. 1 goalie and try to make fans forget about him. Good luck.

This was the impossible mission given David Aebischer in 2003 by the Avalanche. Roy, after two Stanley Cups in eight seasons in Colorado and superb play in every one of them, retired that year after the Avs' seven-game, first-round playoff loss to Minnesota.

Aebischer, the backup the previous three seasons, was given the chance to be the No. 1 guy the following training camp. And the thing is: Aebischer played well in 2003–04. He went 32–19–9, with a very good .924 saves percentage. He outplayed Dallas' Marty

Turco—considered at the time to be one of the best goalies in the league—in a first-round series victory. He played well in the second round against San Jose, but the Avs just couldn't score any goals for him.

But after something of a bad stretch the following season, which was 2005–06 because of the lost year in the NHL, Aebischer was traded to the Montreal Canadiens for goalie Jose Theodore one day before the trade deadline. Aebischer never worked out in Montreal, Theodore never worked out in Colorado, and both saw their careers gradually peter out in the coming years.

Aebischer, a native of Switzerland, was on the last successful voyage of the Swissair jet that crashed one flight later, Swissair Flight 111, on September 2, 1998, which killed all 229 people aboard. The people he walked past at the arrival gate at JFK Airport in New York were the doomed passengers soon to depart. Aebischer was on his way to Denver to begin his second training camp with the Avs.

Two years later, he made the team as the backup to Roy. He was part of the Stanley Cup–winning team of 2001, winning 12 regular-season games for the team. He was a very likable guy, and very smart. He spoke three or four languages with precision, and always offered thoughtful answers to media questions. There were the occasional murmurs that Roy didn't get along with him too well, but whether they were true or not, it wouldn't be that out of the ordinary. There is almost always something of a friction between the starter and the backup, unless the backup is completely resigned to his role and doesn't care about being the No. 1 guy anymore.

That was how veteran Craig Billington, the backup to Roy before Aebischer, always viewed himself, and probably was why he and Roy always had the best relationship of anyone Roy played with in Denver. Roy had a somewhat contentious relationship with Brian Hayward when the two split goaltending duties at times in

Montreal. Roy wanted to play most every game, and he definitely saw himself as the best goalie on any team he ever played on, so anyone trying to encroach on that turf would have issues with him.

Aebischer was blindsided by the trade to Montreal, and never seemed to recover. While he had some good moments with the Canadiens, by 2007 he was released and forced to sign a one-year, $600,000 free-agent contract with Phoenix, where he only played one game. He never played another NHL game after that, spending the next several years playing professionally back home in Switzerland.

85 Which Cup Team Was Better—1996 or 2001?

A stupid question, right? The Avs of 2000–01 were the better of the first two championship teams spread five years apart. The 1995–96 Cup champs had a regular-season record of 47–25–10, while the 2000–01 team went 52–16–10–4.

The 2001 team won the final two rounds of the playoffs *without* Peter Forsberg, who suffered a burst spleen after the Western Conference Semifinals against the Kings. Ray Bourque, Adam Foote, and Rob Blake were the top three on defense for the '01 team.

Why is this chapter even here, and why does its title end in a question mark?

Most people do agree: the 2001 team was better. I mean, come on. Bourque, Blake, Foote, Roy, Sakic, Hejduk, Tanguay, Drury (before Forsberg got hurt).

Yet there are those who think the team that would actually win is the 1996 club.

"I tell you what, that was such a fast team in '96," longtime Avs TV color analyst Peter McNab said. "That team had Forsberg and Sakic five years younger and that much faster. It was a great team, one that probably didn't get as much credit for being great as it should have. Don't forget, that team had a lot of disruption and adversity too, with a new goalie coming in after the first couple months, a high-profile guy. And they beat the team that set a regular-season record for most wins (Detroit, 62) in the playoffs. I'm just sayin': it would be a very interesting matchup."

There's little dispute on this much: the 2001 team had the better defense. Bourque, Foote, and Blake is just better than Krupp, Lefebvre, and Foote. And guys like Chris Drury and Milan Hejduk were better "depth" forwards than guys like Rene Corbet and Mike Keane. Don't forget too: Jon Klemm had to play some forward in the '96 playoffs despite being a defenseman. He played great in that role (two goals in Game 2 of the Finals), but let's face facts: Drury, Hejduk, and Alex Tanguay were better.

I'll go on the record here and say: the 2001 team was best, and would have won a series against the '96 club. That team was not only great but so mentally tough. It had to be to overcome the loss of a Peter Forsberg after the second round.

To my everlasting shame, I picked the St. Louis Blues to beat the Avs in five games of the 2001 Western Conference Finals right after Forsberg went down. I knew that prediction was in dire trouble the next day when I went up to video coach Paul "Fixie" Fixter and asked if this truly was the end for the team (and he was always brutally honest).

"I think we'll be OK," Fixter told me.

Fixie always told the blunt truth, so right then and there, I knew the Avs had a good plan to beat St. Louis without Forsberg, and that happened in five games. The plan, which worked, essentially was: crash and bang Blues defensemen Chris Pronger and Al

MacInnis at every chance, and rough up top forwards such as Pierre Turgeon and Scott Young in front of Patrick Roy.

The plan worked perfectly, as the Blues just didn't seem prepared for the Avs' inner toughness. If not for a Young overtime goal in Game 3, the Avs would have swept St. Louis.

When the series was over, I took a lot of grief from players. "You didn't believe in us," they all said.

No, I didn't. Well, I thought anything was possible, but without Peter Forsberg for the final two rounds? No, sorry, I didn't.

That's what separated that 2001 team from any other. They were great on the ice, and even better mentally off it. But I'd still like to see a real game between the 2001 and 1996 teams. It would be so fun to watch.

86 Disaster Strikes Before Game 1, 2008, in Detroit

I'll never forget going up to longtime NBC hockey analyst and former coach Pierre McGuire right before the 2008 Western Conference Semifinals between the Avs and Detroit Red Wings and asking for his prediction on the series.

"Colorado," McGuire said in his usual direct, excitable manner. "They got this. I think they look like Cup material, actually."

McGuire was someone I'd gotten to know and like a lot over the years. He provided some great source material on Scotty Bowman for my book *Blood Feud*, and he was just fun to talk to all the time. He always had a good story. And he'd call you right back if you needed a quote for a story on deadline. Reporters *love* those guys.

McGuire thought this Avs team matched up perfectly against a Wings team that had home-ice advantage and most other pundits thought would win. The Avs would come into the series with a top-nine group of forwards that included the newly reacquired Peter Forsberg, Joe Sakic, Paul Stastny, Milan Hejduk, Ryan Smyth, Andrew Brunette, Marek Svatos, Wojtek Wolski, and Ian Laperriere. Plenty of top talent there.

Defensively, the club had Adam Foote back, along with good players such as John-Michael Liles and Scott Hannan. In goal, Jose Theodore came into the Detroit series having stolen a couple games in the first round against Minnesota. Things were looking good again for the Avs. Maybe this really was a Cup-caliber team.

Four blowout games later, it was all over for the Avs. It all started going bad in the hours leading up to Game 1 at Joe Louis Arena. In his Detroit hotel room the night before, Theodore started feeling sick. He couldn't keep any food down. He had a temperature in the low 100s. It was okay, he thought; a good night's rest, and he'd be ready to go the next night.

Theodore suited up for Game 1, but he played as well as he still felt: terrible. He allowed four goals on 16 shots before Coach Joel Quenneville pulled him in favor of Peter Budaj. Theodore, in fact, went back to the team hotel to lie in sickly misery some more.

The night of Game 1, I went out to look at the Avs at the pregame skate. There was Sakic, Hejduk, Smyth, Brunette, Svatos, Foote, and...where was Forsberg? Maybe he was just taking his time getting out there, frequently the case. Foppa sometimes liked a dramatic entrance.

Still no Forsberg. Uh-oh, what had happened? Forsberg had been skating well at the end of the previous series against Minnesota, and the team had a few days off in between. Nobody thought there were any problems with his health.

As someone who covered him for so many years, the No. 1 rule with him was to expect the unexpected. Right then I just knew: Forsberg wasn't going to play that night.

True enough. The Avs told the media he had some "lower body" injury, nothing more. Was it one of his wonky ankles? That's what everyone assumed, but the truth was later revealed to be that he had torn groin muscles on both sides of his lower torso.

The sudden loss of Forsberg greatly deflated the team. Everybody felt so good to have him around again, and everyone knew he always played his best against Detroit in the playoffs. He was gone, and the Avs just couldn't overcome it.

Then everything else went wrong. Guys like Wolski and Svatos got hurt, and Hannan could barely skate because of some foot injury. Every game was a blowout. Forsberg tried to play in Game 4, with a weird electric stimulator hooked onto his injured groin, but he just couldn't move well.

What started as so promising ended in a humiliating sweep to the hated Wings. Quenneville would soon be fired, and his assistant, Tony Granato, would take over for the second time.

87 Hit the Pylon, for Good Luck

Patrick Roy was one of the most superstitious players in NHL history. Some of his habits were well-documented, such as talking to goalposts, writing his kids' names on his pads, eating steak and peas before every game, etc.

One time in the 1996 playoffs, when things were occasionally very dicey for the Avs, and Roy was still nervous and wanting to impress on a new team, he was driving to McNichols Arena with

Mike Keane in the passenger seat. Roy accidentally knocked over an orange traffic cone as he was trying to park. When the Avs won their playoff game that night, Roy and Keane noticed the pylon was still down.

"That had to be good luck!" Roy told Keane.

So of course, for the rest of the playoffs, before any home game, Roy and Keane had to drive together and knock over a pylon. And of course, the Avs won the Stanley Cup.

It had to be the pylons.

88 Who Was Better, Forsberg or Sakic?

A great way to stir up any longtime Avs fan is to come right out and ask: If you could only pick one, which center would you keep, Joe Sakic or Peter Forsberg? Or: Who was better?

It's a damned-if-you-do, damned-if-you-don't question all right. Forsberg, even Sakic would admit, had the most pure talent of the two Hall of Fame Avs centers. But Sakic, even Forsberg would admit, was the more durable and consistent player in some ways.

So there is really no correct answer. Forsberg's skill was just breathtaking. He was impossible to knock off the puck, and his sixth sense in anticipating where the puck was going was uncanny. Forsberg's point-per-game average of 1.25 still ranked eighth-best in NHL history entering the 2015–16 season. Sakic averaged 1.19.

Thing is, Sakic played 1,378 games in his NHL career and Forsberg played 708. Both players were winners, though it could be argued Forsberg made his teammates better than Sakic. Forsberg never played on a losing team in his career, while Sakic played on some dreadful Quebec teams early in his career and on a very bad Avs team his final season.

Yet nobody can accuse Sakic of being a selfish or losing player. He won two Stanley Cups and an MVP award in the 2002 Winter Olympics for Canada. Forsberg, too, had great international hockey success, winning two gold medals with Sweden and getting his image on a postage stamp.

So who was better?

"You can't pick one over the other," said Dave Reid, who played with both and later became a respected hockey television analyst. "If I say one, I immediately think, *But wait, I just can't bear the thought of leaving the other guy out.* Forsberg did different things with the puck. He was the better passer, but Sakic's shot was better. Forsberg was probably the better pure skater, but Sakic was anything but slow. They played different games in a way. Forsberg had that power-forward aspect to his game and liked to rough it up. Joe was more of a finesse player. And yet he wasn't soft at all. He could take a hit and went into the corners with anyone. Like I said, you can't pick one over the other really. It's impossible."

A lot of people asked over the years: Was there any rivalry between the two? Did either get jealous of the other or anything like that? The answer is no. Both were private people and tended to hang out only with family or close friends away from the rink. Sakic was married and had kids, while Forsberg was single through his Avs career.

Sakic and Forsberg, therefore, didn't hang out much together off the ice. But both were just nice guys who never got into any trouble and got along with everyone. Both guys only wanted one thing: to win. It didn't matter who had the better stats or ice time among the two, as long as the team won. Sakic was the team captain, so he had to be a little more available to the media, which was just fine with Forsberg, who didn't like questions about

Peter Forsberg's points-per-game average ranks today as eighth best all-time.

ADRIAN DATER

his personal life much. Not that Sakic was a blabbermouth about his private life either. He did have the nickname Quoteless Joe amongst the media, after all.

You can't win in trying to pick between the two players. And you can't lose, either.

89 1998: Four First-Round Picks

It had only happened two other times in NHL history to that point. The 1970 Boston Bruins and 1974 Montreal Canadiens had at least four picks in the first round of the NHL Draft in those years (the '74 Canadiens had five).

In 1998 the Avalanche had four first-round picks, despite being only two years removed from winning a Stanley Cup and winning two straight division titles after that. A combination of their own pick and previous trades gave the Avs picks at numbers 12, 17, 19, and 20. A great job on those picks could have set the Avs up for years. Did they succeed? It's a bit of a mixed bag.

The Avs took Alex Tanguay, Martin Skoula, Robyn Regehr, and Scott Parker. The 2001 Avs championship team had Tanguay, Skoula, and Parker on the roster, so there were tangible benefits from the first-round bounty.

Here's the thing, though: Pierre Lacroix offered all four picks to the Tampa Bay Lightning for the right to draft first. Vincent Lecavalier was the big prize, and despite already having two great centers in Joe Sakic and Peter Forsberg, Lacroix felt he was one of the best prospects in many years and really wanted him.

Tampa Bay GM Phil Esposito never seriously considered Lacroix's offer, however. History has shown that the 1998 draft

244

wasn't a great one. While Lecavalier went on to a fine career, he didn't become the Hall of Fame type most thought would be a given. Many other first-round picks were busts. Anyone remember the names Rico Fata, Bryan Allen, Vitaly Vishnevski, Mark Bell, Mike Rupp, and Nikolai Antropov? They were all picked in the top 10.

The fact that the Avs got four players they got something out of—and in Tanguay's case a genuine star for many years—remains a credit to the Avs' first chief scout, Dave Draper. The one player who never played for the Avs was Regehr, who was traded to Calgary at the trade deadline in 1999 as part of the Theo Fleury deal.

While that deal is often dismissed as a bust—Regehr having gone on to a long, very good career mostly with the Flames—the fact is the Avs got some good out of Fleury. He was a point-per-game player and helped them win two playoff series.

Parker might be the pick the Avs would have done over if they could, but he did his job as an enforcer for several years. He never became the well-rounded player he wanted to be, but he also never was given much of a chance, either. Skoula had a promising start to his career but flamed out soon after the Cup year.

In hindsight it might have been nicer had the Avs gotten a few players who wound up going later, including Simon Gagne, Scott Gomez, and Jonathan Cheechoo. But overall, the summation of the Avs' 1998 draft has to be: it could have been a lot worse.

90 The Biggest Save of 1996

The scene: The Chicago Blackhawks held a two-games-to-one lead on the Avalanche in the 1996 Western Conference Semifinals, and 40 seconds were left in the third period. Joe Murphy, who had been killing the Avs all series, came in on a breakaway on Patrick Roy.

Murphy took a lead pass from teammate Murray Craven and slipped behind the Avs' defense of Alexei Gusarov and Uwe Krupp. Roy had little time to react, because Creighton's pass was one of those long Hail Mary jobs that caught Murphy just as he was streaking over the Avs' blue line.

A goal right there—and Murphy was great on breakaways— and the Blackhawks would have had a 3–2 lead with little time left. That would have been it for the 1996 Avs, I firmly believe. It was a fine team, but coming back from a 3–1 deficit against Ed Belfour and the Blackhawks, who didn't even have Chris Chelios for this Game 4? Not likely at all.

Murphy tried to go five-hole on Roy, but he came in at too narrow of an angle. If he had come in from a wider angle, he probably would have caught Roy moving from side to side and been better able to slip a shot through the five-hole. But he came pretty much straight down the middle, which allowed Roy to move easier when he made a move to his left backhand.

That save rarely gets talked about, but ask Avs players on that 1996 team, and they all remember it. "I thought the game was over right there," teammate Claude Lemieux recalled years later. "Murphy was hot, and here he comes in on a breakaway with time running out. I don't think we would have overcome that, but Patrick just kept us in it. We knew we had to win that game, and losing it would have taken a lot out of us mentally."

Here's another thing nobody remembers about that game: Craven had the game winner on his stick early in the first overtime, after a couple Avs turnovers in their end. If you watch replays of his shot, it looked for sure it would have beaten Roy over the left shoulder. The game would have been over—Hawks win, Hawks win.

One problem: Chicago defenseman Gary Suter, pinching down deep on the play, inexplicably grabbed the net on his way through and pulled it off its moorings. Craven's game winner thus never had a chance to hit the net. There wasn't even much of a collision between Suter and anyone on the Avs. He just pulled the net off the moorings with his right arm for some reason. It was just one of the many fortunate breaks the Avs caught in that most critical of games.

91 Dick Dale Intro

The song that has always ushered the Avalanche onto the ice does not have any singing or any lyrics. It's just a guitar solo by an old Californian named Dick Dale.

Who the hell is Dick Dale? He is a Boston native who, at the time of this writing, is still with us. He is credited not only with the California surf sounds of the 1960s but also with a kind of guitar sound that was incorporated into a new kind of music called heavy metal.

One of Dick Dale's guitar song creations, "Scalped," turned into the introductory music the Avalanche took the ice to for their first 20 years of existence. How do you describe the song in words? You can't do it. You have to listen to it. It's just a hard guitar riff with some melody to it, up and down the scales.

Dale has been given the title of the King of Surf Guitar, and that about explains it. Picture yourself on a beach after a few cocktails, and Dale's guitar sound would register well before lights out.

"Scalped" became as identifiable with the early Avalanche days as Peter Forsberg or Joe Sakic. Play it anytime for old Avs fans and you'll see them tilt their heads back a little and sway to the strings of Dale's guitar.

To this day, it is still played before home games.

92 The Erik Johnson Trade

It came in the wee hours of the morning, Pacific Time. On February 19, 2011, while most of the US was sound asleep, the Avalanche and St. Louis Blues completed a blockbuster trade that sent Kevin Shattenkirk and Chris Stewart to the St. Louis Blues for Erik Johnson and Jay McClement, with draft picks involved.

Two of the Avalanche's most promising young players were suddenly dealt away to a conference rival. Let's just say the trade didn't go over so well with many of the Avs faithful at first. In fact, the iconic former Quebec Nordique, Peter Stastny, whose son Paul was on the team, said the move by GM Greg Sherman would "destroy the team." For a while, the elder Stastny seemed correct.

But in later years, it proved to be hardly a steal for the Blues. By the 2014–15 season Johnson, a former first overall pick of the Blues in 2006, finally started to blossom into the dominant two-way player he'd always been projected to be. In training camp before the 2015–16 campaign, Johnson was rewarded with a seven-year, $42 million contract extension.

Shattenkirk, who was in the midst of a good rookie season with Colorado at the time of the deal, has gone on to be a very good player for the Blues, and played on the US Olympic team. But after a strong initial start, Stewart's play with St. Louis fell off sharply to the point where he was traded to the Buffalo Sabres.

What might have turned the trade into a certified win for the Avs, that first-round pick, has yet to pan out that way. With the 11th overall choice in the 2011 draft, Colorado took defender Duncan Siemens, who had yet to develop into an NHL regular as of the time of this writing five years later.

Johnson's second game with the Avs was a good one at least. It came in St. Louis, and he scored what proved the game-winning goal in the third period. Johnson did struggle some in his first couple years in Denver, though, which only had the skeptics chortling in St. Louis.

Some around the Blues thought Johnson a total bust. The story goes that once Al MacInnis, the Hall of Fame defenseman, moved into Blues management and got a good look at Johnson night-in, night-out, he determined Johnson would never rise to the heights predicted. That supposedly convinced GM Doug Armstrong to shop him around, and many in St. Louis could barely suppress their glee at the haul they got in return.

Then when Peter Stastny chimed in, it made for an extremely awkward situation for Johnson and his new teammate, Paul. The two had been roommates with the 2010 US Olympic team in Vancouver, and now here was a franchise icon saying everything was ruined from a trade he was involved in.

To his credit, Johnson shrugged off the naysayers and kept working hard in the coming years. He won respect from teammates for his no-excuses attitude, and after some initial worries from incoming coach Patrick Roy in 2013 over his game, by 2015 Roy had full faith in the big Minnesota native.

In the 2014 playoffs against Minnesota, Johnson was tremendous. If not for a blown lead late, he would have had the series-winning goal in Game 7. He also made a miraculous, never-give-up save of a rolling puck headed toward a vacated net that gave the Avs another chance at scoring the tying goal, which is what happened, and then Colorado went on to win in OT.

93 Blown Series? Yeah, There Were a Few

For as much success as the Avalanche had in their first 20 years, there are still some blown playoff series that haunt die-hard fans, not to mention those who played on those teams.

The first bad blown series came in 1998, when the Avs had a 3–1 lead on the Edmonton Oilers in the first round. While the Avs of 1997–98 had one of their poorer regular seasons in a while, they were still considered shoo-ins to beat the lowly seeded Oilers. After Joe Sakic won a Game 4 in Edmonton for the 3–1 lead, Game 5 at McNichols Sports Arena was considered a formality.

Except it wasn't. Oilers goalie Curtis Joseph suddenly got red-hot, beating the Avs in Game 5 and shutting out the mighty Avalanche's offensive stars in Games 6 and 7. Edmonton won Game 7 by a 4–0 score at Big Mac. Uwe Krupp seemed to have broken the shutout streak Joseph had going with a shot in the first period. Instead, the puck caromed off both posts behind Joseph. That would have given the Avs a 1–0 lead and maybe things would have been different. Alas, the Avs of 1998 just weren't the cohesive bunch they'd been the previous two years and it would be the final came of Marc Crawford's career as coach of the team.

In 1999 the Avs had a 3–2 lead on Dallas in the Western Conference Finals, with Game 6 at home. Theo Fleury was returning to the lineup after a one-game absence and Dallas had no answer for Peter Forsberg, who had five points in an amazing 7–5 Game 5 win at Reunion Arena.

The Avs got out to an early 1–0 lead on a Claude Lemieux goal and had two open nets to make it a 3–0 game, with Sandis Ozolinsh and Aaron Miller looking at the veritable yawning cage

The Avs might like to have this one back. Unfortunately, Dallas goalie Ed Belfour hung tough during the 2000 Western Conference Finals.

behind Eddie Belfour. But Ozolinsh and Miller somehow missed the tap-ins, and Dallas regrouped to win the game and the series.

In 2000 the Avs had a 2–1 series lead on Dallas in the Western Conference Finals, with Game 4 at home. But Patrick Roy had an off day, Belfour was brilliant, and Dallas again took a series victory in seven games.

The Avs nearly blew two series in 2001, having to go to seven games to beat Los Angeles after a 3–1 lead and blowing Game 5 at home in a 2–2 series. But they won a Stanley Cup instead. In 2002 the Avs again blew late series leads before prevailing in seven against San Jose and L.A., and had a 3–2 lead on Detroit in the Western Conference Finals. Detroit won the final two games by a 9–0 combined score.

In 2003 the Minnesota Wild were down 3–1 to the Avs, with two of the next three slated for the Pepsi Center if necessary. The first-round games did prove to be necessary, and Minnesota came away with a shocking seventh-game win in overtime, on a goal by future Av Andrew Brunette in what was Roy's final career game.

In 2014 the Wild again overcame a late series deficit to beat the Avs in the final two games of the first round. Game 7 was a real heartbreaker for the Avs, who were up by a goal with the clock at less than two minutes. Then Jared Spurgeon deked past a sliding Nathan MacKinnon and beat Semyon Varlamov over the shoulder with the tying goal. Nino Niederreiter won it in OT after Paul Stastny and Gabe Landeskog failed to convert on a two-on-one bid.

Although the 2000 series loss to the Stars did not come after lost sixth and seventh games like what happened in 1999 and 2002, if you ask many longtime Avs people, that was the series that still hurts the most. The Avs were a better team than Dallas that year, outshooting the Stars badly in almost every game. But Belfour got hot late and outplayed Saint Patrick. That's hockey.

94 Jarome Iginla

In the summer of 2014, the Avalanche had just received word from the agent of Paul Stastny, Matt Keator, that he would be leaving to sign a four-year, $28 million free-agent contract with the St. Louis Blues.

Right up to the final hour before the NHL free-agent market opened on July, the Avs believed they might still re-sign Stastny. When it was clear that wouldn't happen, it didn't leave much time to look for a replacement.

The Avs suddenly had a 60-point hole to fill from Stastny's departure, and the pickings appeared somewhat slim. But there was one player who GM Joe Sakic thought could do it.

His name was Jarome Iginla, one of the NHL's best players of the previous two decades, a surefire Hall of Famer who spent most of his career with the Calgary Flames. Iginla had spent the previous season with the Boston Bruins, and Boston wanted to re-sign their leading goal scorer from 2013–14 (30). Trouble was, they had very little cap room.

So despite Iginla being okay to re-sign with the Bruins, they just couldn't make the math work. Iginla's agent, Don Meehan, let word out that his client would be available as a UFA. That morning, I'd gotten a tip that Iginla would be the Avs' plan B should Stastny not come back, and I wrote it on a blog.

A few hours later, a deal was in place: three years, $16 million. Some pundits scoffed at Colorado giving such a lengthy deal to a player who would turn 36 in a few days. Iginla was too old and too much on the downside to deserve a three-year deal, they said.

Those pundits didn't look so smart after year one of the deal. Iginla led the Avs in goals with 29, and despite the team missing the playoffs, he proved he was well worth the money.

He added leadership and professionalism to the Avs' dressing room as well. Iginla was and is one of the classiest guys I ever covered in hockey, which is saying a lot. He never failed to be available to reporters after a game, win or lose. He wouldn't just give rote answers to questions, either. He listened to each question and gave a thoughtful answer, every time. Those are the kinds of guys reporters love.

Iginla will go down as one of the NHL's best right wings of all time. He had a cannon of a shot, especially on one-timers from the left side on the power play. He was tough too. As nice a guy as Iginla was off the ice, he was a fearsome fighter who never backed down from anyone, no matter how big. No, he wouldn't go around fighting each team's big goon, as he knew he was too valuable to his teams to do that. But even the league's toughest fighters knew to stay away from Iginla, whose right hand packed a powerful punch.

He came within one overtime goal of winning a Stanley Cup in 2004 with the Flames, who had the Tampa Bay Lightning down three games to two with Game 6 at the Saddledome, only to lose on a Martin St. Louis goal. The Flames lost another heartbreaker in Game 7 in Tampa Bay.

"Yeah, I have to admit, I still think about it a fair amount," Iginla told me one day. "To get that close to the ultimate goal and not get it, it's tough. That's really what you play the game for, to win the Cup. Everything else that comes with being in the NHL is great, and I've been very blessed in my career, but of course I really want that feeling of lifting up the Cup."

He admitted to choosing the Avs partially over the contract offer, with nobody else offering him a third year. But he wouldn't have taken it, he said, if he didn't feel the Avs at least had a decent chance of going all the way. It didn't work out that first year, but it certainly wasn't his fault.

Iginla liked Denver so much that, early in his second season, he let it be known to Sakic that he would not waive his no-trade clause for any reason—even if it meant going to a top contender. With three young children and two other moves in his previous four years, Iginla put family above all.

The Ryan Smyth– Scott Hannan Signings

In the summer of 2007, the Avalanche was coming off their first nonplayoff season in team history. Despite a 44–31–7 record and 95 points, the Avs barely missed out to the Calgary Flames for the eighth spot in the Western Conference. So something had to be done about that.

This was also the second season since the NHL's drastic lowering of the salary cap from its $39 million figure of 2005–06. The cap for 2006–07 was $44 million, and guys such as Joe Sakic were willing to take markedly lower salaries by that stage to be able to afford some free-agent imports.

Sakic, in fact, played a key role in the recruitment of two expensive new free agents: Ryan Smyth and Scott Hannan.

While they didn't come with the fanfare of the Paul Kariya–Teemu Selanne signings of four years earlier, Smyth and Hannan were two of the biggest free-agent catches of that summer. When they agreed to combined contracts worth nearly $50 million (Smyth, five years at $31.25 million; Hannan, four years at $18 million) the Avalanche was instantly proclaimed a contender again for the Stanley Cup. It didn't quite work out that way.

Sakic used his considerable influence as a respected hockey icon to talk Smyth and Hannan into forgoing other offers to sign with Colorado. The season before, Smyth had been one of the hottest commodities at the NHL trade deadline, with the New York Islanders winning the sweepstakes by parting with two prospects and a first-round draft pick.

The Islanders couldn't agree on a long-term extension for the free-agent Smyth, however, so the Avs jumped in. Despite his lanky frame, Smyth was extremely tough around the front of the net and an expert at screens and deflections. He was a pure hockey guy in the sense that he knew every cliché in the book, peppering his answers with "behind the eight ball" and "one shift at a time," and he also had the bent nose and gap-toothed grin.

Hannan, a defenseman, made his name partially at the expense of the Avs. He had a very good playoff series against them in the San Jose Sharks' second-round, six-game victory in 2004. He particularly frustrated Avs star Peter Forsberg with plenty of hits, some clean and some not. He acquired a reputation as a "nasty" D-man who would transform the Avs' relatively soft defense at the time. Again, it didn't quite work out that way.

Hannan never seemed to play with the same nastiness he showed in that playoff series. He was a relatively dependable and durable D-man, but he just never made the kind of impact the Avs had expected.

Smyth's play with Colorado had its moments but ultimately has to be judged as something of a disappointment. He scored only 14 goals and 37 points in 2007–08, and even was dropped to the third line in the playoffs. He did score 26 goals the following season, but the team was awful. He was traded to Los Angeles for defenseman Kyle Quincey in the summer of 2009.

Hannan was traded to Washington early in the 2010–11 season and played for three more teams after that. Toward the end of Hannan's stay in Denver, he got into a shouting match with team captain Adam Foote in the dressing room of the practice facility. There was some kind of rough moment on the ice between the two in the practice that carried over to the room, which several of us reporters saw. For a second, I thought they might come to blows. But Foote walked away behind closed doors when he realized it might become a very big spectacle.

It's probably too easy of a metaphor to make, but the near-fight kind of symbolized how it went for Hannan and Smyth in Denver. What started out as high hopes for a bright future dissolved into frustration and partings of ways before those big contracts were finished.

96 Andrew Brunette—From Villain to Fan Favorite

He will forever be the answer to the trivia question: who scored the final goal in Patrick Roy's career against him? It happened in overtime of Game 7 of a 2003 first-round series between the Avalanche and Minnesota Wild, when Andrew "Bruno" Brunette put a shot past Roy from in close to complete a stunning Wild comeback from a 3–1 series deficit.

Right before the start of the Stanley Cup Finals between the Mighty Ducks of Anaheim and New Jersey Devils, Roy publicly announced what had been a known, foregone conclusion for a few weeks: he was retiring. The timing of Roy's announcement really ticked off the NHL brass, by the way, and it also cost me a chance to cover that series. I was in New York getting ready to cover Game 1 across the river in Jersey when Roy made the announcement. Typically, the league asks teams not to make any big announcements—trades, signings, retirement announcements, etc.—during the league's marquee event. In pure Roy fashion, though, he refused to play by the rules of convention to the end. I had to suddenly fly back to Denver and cover the press conference and do many follow-up stories.

Anyway, Brunette played another season for the Wild before the lockout-canceled 2004–05 season. The Avs then signed Brunette to a free-agent contract when hockey resumed, and he went on to have three very good seasons in Colorado.

Bruno scored 205 points in 246 games in those three years, never missing a game, and the Avs made the playoffs in two of them. Brunette found a lot of success playing on a line with Joe Sakic, especially in 2006–07 when Sakic scored 100 points at age 36 and Brunette scored 83.

Brunette was virtually impossible to knock off the puck once he had it behind the net or along the boards. If you tried to hit him, he'd just roll off you and go the other way. There were many times when he'd control the puck for 10, 15 seconds at a time down low and wind up with a good scoring chance. He was a very good clutch performer, scoring lots of late third-period goals to tie or win games, and he was excellent on the power play.

The Avs thought he was close to washed-up following a 2007–08 season in which he scored 59 points in 82 games (today, those kinds of numbers get you contracts for $5 million per year), and so they let him go as an unrestricted free agent. It was a dumb decision, as Brunette proved to have plenty left. He went back to the Wild and put up 111 points in the next two seasons, while the Avs sank to 28th place in 2008–09. The Avs missed his veteran presence on and off the ice. He was a very good locker room guy, but not in the rah-rah sense. He could expertly analyze a game, where things turned and what a team's tendencies were, so he was valuable as an extension of the coach in that sense.

I always thought he'd make a good coach after he retired and, sure enough, he did. He became an assistant with the Wild, including a team that beat the Avs in the 2014 playoffs. Roy was the coach of that Avs team, of course, and the Wild won Game 7 on Pepsi Center ice. For the second time in 11 years, Brunette celebrated such a win at Roy's expense.

97 Gabriel Landeskog

He was named the captain of the Avalanche on September 4, 2012, at 19 years and 286 days old. He remains the youngest captain in NHL history, breaking Sidney Crosby's previous record by 11 days.

Drafted second overall in 2011 at 18, Landeskog instantly became part of a core at the heart of a rebuild that had started in earnest in 2009. After a 2010–11 season that saw veteran Milan Hejduk serve as captain, Coach Joe Sacco and GM Greg Sherman—with Hejduk's blessing—felt the passing of the torch to a top younger player would best serve the team.

The move bruised some feelings in the Avs dressing room, particularly those of Ryan O'Reilly, who wanted the role (and some felt he was better suited for it, having two more years of experience than Landeskog).

Landeskog, though, had a lot of leadership qualities. He spoke Swedish, English, and some German. He was a captain of his junior team, the Kitchener Rangers—the first European-born captain in team history. He was always accountable to reporters after any loss, always a plus in my book. Go ahead and laugh, but the players who really care are the ones who stick around and want to dissect what went wrong with the ink-stained wretches, who viewed it as *part of their job.*

Rookie Gabriel Landeskog checks Red Wings defensive wingman Jakub Kindl during a 2011 game.

While he had yet to reach elite-level status as an NHL player, he had many good moments on the ice in his first few seasons. He played a tough, at times dirty, game—all the while with the ability to coalesce into a pure skill game. In Patrick Roy's first year as coach, 2013–14, Landeskog scored 26 goals and 65 points in 81 games, and followed that up with a 23-goal, 59-point season.

The one fair question to ask: did Landeskog sign too big a contract extension before he'd really proven himself, thereby leading to, maybe, a little complacency? In August 2013 Landeskog signed a seven-year, $39 million extension. His points-per-game production went down in 2014–15 and 2015–16, in both of which the Avs failed to make the playoffs. Fair or not, those are the kinds of tough questions captains have to be asked when their teams don't win.

To Landeskog's credit, he never dodged them.

"You always have to have the attitude that you can be better," Landeskog said in 2014. "And I know that I can and need to be better, while I still have the ability."

98 Travel Tips for You!

Okay, I can't write this book without passing on some of the knowledge I gained from 20 years of constant travel. I looked it up: In the 20 years I covered the Avalanche, I flew more than one million air miles, the majority of them with United, but lots more with Frontier and Southwest. I flew on every other airline you can name for my era, including Northwest, American, Delta, AMA, USAir, Air Canada, Alaska, WestJet, and several rinky-dink airlines you've never heard of and hopefully never will.

I had more than 1,400 single hotel room nights in that time. That's close to four full years of my life, or 20 percent of the time I worked covering the team. The funny thing is, I think I only took one airplane flight in my life until I was 23.

Here is a veteran traveler's advice for you, whether you're a first-time traveler or a real road warrior:

1. Always, but always, be nice to the gate attendant in an airport

This is nonnegotiable. You have to be nice to the gate attendant, or anyone else who has a direct say in how you may be traveling on an airplane within the next 24 hours. Gate agents—and I know because I asked a friend who was one once—have discretionary powers to either give you that last seat on the airplane that will get you out of Muskogee or keep you camped out in the airport bar for the next, oh, 16 hours or so.

Gate agents, either those at the check-in desk before you drop off your luggage or those right at the gate for your flight, can and will screw with your day if they don't like you. Now, when I say "be nice" to them, I don't mean always be "too nice." If you look and act like a pushover to gate attendants, they will think you're weak and put you where you don't want to be. It's just a fact.

You have to be, as I'll call it, "politely firm." If you have a big-time flight status with a particular airline, then that is an invaluable card to play when there's only one seat left and you want to get out of town on a standby. If you're a frequent flier, and you mention something like, "Whew, man, I always love how you guys take care of me in situations like this. I hope this won't be an exception," you will put the gate agent a bit on the defensive and make him/her want to accommodate you. If you just run up to the gate, though, and yell out, "Do you know who I am? I have 51,421 flight miles on this airline this year!"

and demand special treatment—when, really, we both know you're not that big of a big shot—then you probably will be put in the back of the next flight out. Have fun hanging out in the Yankee Candle store in the concourse until then.

But let's say you're just an average flier. No big status to brag about. You have to up your game a little, then. You have to be very personable, try to get to know this agent as much as you can, try to establish as much in common as you can before he/she makes the decision whether to give you what you want or not. If you find that, "Hey, I'm from New England too!" or "Wow, I looove [insert agent's favorite pro or college team here]," then you will have built rapport with this person. Once they think you're anywhere near their hometown and/or love their particular team, then they are going to think you're *one of them.* You'll be amazed at how many doors suddenly open up to you when this happens.

I guarantee I probably talked my way onto 20 or 30 flights that otherwise seemed hopeless a few minutes before. I might have been told, "No, there's no way you can get on this flight" by an agent on the phone, but once I got to the airport and tried again with another agent, really doing my best polite/firm/hey-you're-from-Kansas-too! story, I suddenly found myself with a ticket to board. Where karma really is in full effect is at airports. You do something nice for the airline agents, and they will want to do something nice for you.

2. Don't ever buy insurance on a rental car

Your personal auto insurance, not to mention your credit card probably, will cover any damages on a rental. You'd be surprised at how many people get suckered into buying the $17.99-a-day insurance, though. This is the rental agent's big sales opportunity, and they will make a nice commission on every unneeded insurance package they sell.

Don't be a dummy. Decline all the insurance, and don't believe their little song-and-dance about potential horror stories if you don't.

3. **When checking into a hotel, always ask for an upgrade**
   You don't have to be pushy about it. Like airline gate agents, the front-desk clerk at a hotel is someone you need to develop a strong rapport with. But my experience has shown you can be a little tougher on hotel clerks and reasonably expect results.

   There are going to be a million little things that will go wrong during a hotel stay. You might request a low floor and get something at the very top. You might request a wake-up call at 6:00 AM (before cell phone alarm clocks, this was a crucial part of a hotel's service) and it doesn't come. You might have heat that won't shut off or AC that keeps the room at 15 degrees on a cold winter night.

   Whenever these things happen, you're going to want to have a good relationship with the front-desk clerks. If you do, 99.9 percent of the things you complain about will be instantly upgraded or taken off your bill. But even if you're not BFFs, you need to complain. Something always goes wrong at a hotel, and they don't want the hassle of dealing with this while there are 10 people waiting to either check out or check in.

   When checking in, always politely ask if there's a room upgrade. If you have frequent travel status, this often is done for you without asking. But not always. Always ask. The one-bedroom at the end of the hall might suddenly turn into a spacious suite. It happened that way for me at least two dozen times over the years.

4. **Miscellaneous**
   Don't buy a GPS system from the rental car agent. Even the most rudimentary cell phones now have GPS you can access for

free.... Be careful with room service. It used to be that you could leave an honest tip for a delivery person after you'd ordered your cheeseburger and fries. But then hotels started adding on a delivery fee, usually $2.50, and also a 15 to 20 percent gratuity fee. So was your tip already covered by that 15 to 20 percent? Of course not. The bill to sign almost always includes an "additional gratuity" or just plain "tip" line item. If you give more money there, you have essentially tipped the hotel three times for your burger and fries up a few flights on an elevator. If you pay the extra tip, you are a sucker. If you don't, you feel like a cheapskate. Hey, it's not your money you're spending, right? Either way, you can't win. The smarter play is to get some good Chinese takeout from some place nearby and rid yourself of room service altogether.... Always—*always*—sign up for the frequent driver plan with a rental agency. I've stood in lines for more than an hour before waiting to rent a car, when a simple fill-out of a form would have put me in the no-wait lane.... Never get behind a couple with a baby in a stroller in the airport security line. Just don't.... Do not ever check a bag on a flight. You can pack a lot of stuff into a regular bag. You will lose an hour of your life every time you check a bag as you stand around waiting for it after your flight.... Park in the economy lot and walk. I probably saved the *Post* a few thousand dollars over the years parking in the economy lot. Did I ever get any thanks for that? Ha ha.... Do not ever use the hotel parking service. You want to blow $35 a night having to wait for your car to be brought up from a sleepy valet guy, then have to tip him too? Have fun. I'd rather have a nice meal out with that money, and there's probably a free lot somewhere a block or two away.... Ask the front desk clerk at a hotel if there are any spare phone cords. Maybe fib a little saying you lost one. Chances are you'll get a perfectly good iPhone charger, which will come in handy when you actually do lose your next one.

99 Favorite Places In 20 Years of Constant Travel

Some of this book has included travel tips and other observations from the road. This chapter is for the hybrid hockey fan who also travels a lot. You won't be disappointed with some of the following recommendations based on my experience:

- If in Montreal, go to Gibby's in the Old Town section, order the surf and turf and have the *chocolat souchard* cake, if it's on the menu. Pierre Lacroix recommended the dessert to me on our first trip there, preseason 1995, and I will forever be grateful.

- If in North Carolina for a Hurricanes game, make the three-hour drive to Mount Airy, and maybe spend the night in Andy Griffith's boyhood home, which is now a bed-and-breakfast. The main street of Mount Airy is essentially untouched from Andy's youth, and it's why he based the fictional town of Mayberry on it for his classic TV show. Stop in at Snappy Lunch (the diner in the TV show) and order the pork chop sandwich. You will thank me.

  During the 2002 Cup Finals between Detroit and Carolina, I spent a night in Mount Airy and even got my hair cut by one of the two original barbers at "Floyd's" barbershop. His name was Russell Hiatt. As a huge fan of *The Andy Griffith Show*, I absolutely thrilled to hearing his stories of cutting Andy's hair, as he cut mine. I wound up writing a big story about what life was like in the town during a Stanley Cup Final, and it's one of my favorites of my career. I even went to a bluegrass music festival that night and watched many seriously good bands play to boot-scootin' locals. It's one of my most indelible memories.

- In Boston, have the clam chowder at Union Oyster House and see the Old North Church, where Paul Revere passed on his way to warning the Americans of the British coming.
- In Philadelphia, stop in at City Tavern. Some guys named George Washington, John Adams, and Thomas Jefferson used to gather there for drinks after a hard day forming the United States of America. The Jefferson and Washington original recipe ales (they made their own, and the recipes are truly original) are strong and stout. Take a cab back to the hotel.
- If in Nashville for a Predators game, drive to the suburban town of Franklin. It's got an old-school main street and a great place called the Carnton Plantation, where a big Civil War battle was fought. There is a fascinating, spooky Confederate graveyard there, and late one night I actually walked around in it, shining a flashlight from my cell phone on the headstones.
- In Los Angeles, make the 30-minute drive to Manhattan Beach. Most of the Kings players, and many former NHL players such as Chris Drury, have places there. Eat at Mama D's, an Italian joint. Prepare to wait in line. Order the linguini and white clam sauce. Walk down the steep street from there to the pier and breathe in every millimeter of the magnificent Pacific.
- In San Jose, do a few things:
  1. Drive to San Francisco. Eat at Scoma's on the water. Old-school waiters in tuxedos will pamper your every whim. Bring your wallet.
    Definitely, tour Alcatraz.
  2. Back in San Jose, drive to the Stanford campus in Palo Alto and just walk around. Gaze at the original Rodin sculpture *The Thinker* and ponder life along with that muscled nude man who looks like he's sitting on the can.
  3. If still stuck in San Jose, go to Original Joe's, around since the 1950s or so, and eat anything from their charcoal-fired grills, in full view of everyone. The waitstaff is in tuxedos

here too. Anytime you can eat in a place with people dressed in tuxedos, you have to give it the benefit of the doubt.

- If in Columbus, Ohio, take in a Jackets game and then head to Tip-Top Kitchen & Cocktails and order the pot roast sandwich. Man, you'll thank me for this one. Oh God, I can taste one now.

- Dallas? You should tour the Sixth Floor Museum, even if visiting a museum based on the assassination of one of our most popular presidents sounds a little bit of a drag.

- Chicago? Stop in at the Lodge near Rush Street. Sing "Sweet Caroline" with the rest of the drunken locals at closing time. Walk up and down Michigan Avenue a few times. Order a "cheezborger" at the Billy Goat Tavern.

- Vancouver? You must walk around Stanley Park for free. Watch Beluga whales swim around. Walk down to the harbor under the Lions Gate Bridge. Experience this and your blood pressure will drop 20 points. Drive to Whistler Blackcomb ski resort if you can, rain, snow, or sleet.

- Phoenix? Dinner at the Camelback Inn—fantastic view of the southwest skyline. Stop in Santa Fe, New Mexico, if you can, on the way back. You'll get sucked in to the café-infused scene in no time.

- Toronto? Stay in the section near the old Maple Leaf Gardens. Lots of youth and energy there. As you spread out more toward the suburbs, it gets boring very fast. The bar at the Westin Harbour Castle probably should be sectioned off for the Hockey Hall of Fame, though. So many hockey deals went down in this space. And so many other great hockey conversations, including the one I can't remember anymore between me, Ray Bourque, and *Lawrence Eagle-Tribune* Hockey Hall of Fame writer Russ Conway on the night Bourque was inducted in 2004.

100 The First Championship Parade

A parade through the streets of Denver by a championship professional sports team was something that had never happened until June 12, 1996. Technically, Colorado had a previous pro sports champion, as the Colorado Foxes of the now-defunct American Professional Soccer League won league titles in 1992 and 1993. (I was the beat writer for those teams, covering home games only, and the team's public relations director, Chris Spaulding, was my best friend and former high school classmate—Mascoma Valley Regional, Canaan, New Hampshire, 1983. We moved to Denver a few months apart in 1991, living in the Tamarac Apartments where, little did I know at the time, future Avs GM Greg Sherman and future Cleveland Cavaliers and Los Angeles Lakers head coach Mike Brown shared an apartment together.)

But the parade celebration of those teams winning it all consisted of the drive by the players from the airport to their homes in anonymity.

The parade given by the city to honor the Avalanche in 1996 had a massive crowd. Official attendance totals have varied, but most safe estimates put the number at about 350,000. The parade remains a warm memory for anyone who lived in Colorado at the time and cared anything about the Avs.

The parade route spanned one and a half miles and 15 city blocks. Players rode on the tops of 11 fire trucks. Sakic was on the last of the 11 trucks, with the Stanley Cup.

"Almost as much as winning the thing itself, I think that parade is what I'll most remember from that time," Sakic recalled. "It was awesome. I'd never been in anything like that, and just seeing all the fans and people of Denver like that, it was really fun. We were used to living in Colorado by that time, but I think that's the moment when a lot of us felt like Denver came into our hearts more."

The crowning moment came at Civic Center Park, on the steps of City Hall Plaza, where Sakic came out of artificial fog lifting the Stanley Cup over his head. Ascent Entertainment CEO Charlie Lyons was patched into a phone call with US Vice President Al Gore, and Lyons held the phone out to the crowd to give Gore the roar of his life. President Bill Clinton also was patched through to the team in a phone call, in which Crawford wished him good luck in the next election of 1998.

"Well, I hope to get a sweep like you did," Clinton said.

The Avs' second championship parade, in 2001, had a smaller turnout (an estimated 250,000) but was another grand affair, with Ray Bourque drawing thunderous cheers lifting the Cup for the first time after 22 years in the NHL.

The Denver Broncos filled the streets with parade-goers for two straight years (1998 and 1999) after winning Super Bowls. The '98 parade was the biggest of all, at an estimated 650,000.

But the Avs will always have bragging rights over the Broncos and every other team that played professionally in Denver. When it came to championship rings and big parades and the greatest sports memories, the Avs were the first.

Acknowledgments

This book was a lot of fun for me to write, as I hope it was for you to read. The people and players in these pages are the real story, but having been there for all of it, I couldn't help but write in a more personal style.

The Colorado Avalanche will always mean a lot to the hockey fans of Denver and their many other fans around the world. That goes for me too. I was their beat writer for the *Denver Post* from 1995 to 2014. In 1991 I was living in my parents' basement in Concord, New Hampshire, working as a proofreader for the local paper there. I decided to chuck all that and move to Denver, basically on a wing and a prayer. No job was waiting for me. I had little money, no car, and knew only one person—a good friend named Chris, who coincidentally moved to Denver.

Four years later, I was sitting on the Avalanche's private plane, looking down on cities like Montreal and Toronto and knowing I'd soon be sitting in the press boxes of the old Montreal Forum and Maple Leaf Gardens.

What a team I got to cover right off the bat too. Many sportswriters spend their whole careers without getting to write about a champion team. That's okay—the good writers do it for the love of the craft, for the chance to just tell stories about people. But don't let any sportswriter kid you—it's more fun to cover a winner, and those early Avs teams did a lot of winning.

Two Stanley Cups and six trips to the conference finals in the first seven years in town is what the Avs accomplished. Not too shabby. This book talks a lot about those winning times.

I want to thank a bunch of people, people who have stuck with me through the good times—and the bad—of my life, people without whom this book probably wouldn't have happened.

First and foremost: my beautiful wife, Heidi, and fantastic son, Tommy. Thanks to Joe Sakic for writing the foreword to this book and for all the help he gave me, personally and professionally. Thanks to the editors of Triumph Books for making the book happen.

Thanks to the following people as well, for their help to me with the book and with life in general: Jean Martineau, John Henderson, Allen Daniel, Kieran Nicholson, Jim Ludvik, Bill Speros, Sean Jensen, Bob and Jen Danisewich, Josh Kroenke, Brian O'Reilly, Bruce Morgan, Sharon Heberlein, Caroline Kenney, Terry Frei, Scott Campbell, Clint Malarchuk, Darrell Rubin, Ryan Boulding, A.J. Haefele, Brendan McNicholas, Scotty Bowman, Will Brink, Noah Dater, Marc Crawford, Claude Lemieux, Matt Duchene, Rick Sadowski, Pat Graham, Bob McKenzie, Elliotte Friedman, Mike Brophy, Kevin Paul Dupont, Dan Petty, Derek Kessinger, Sandy and Lonnie Phillips, Jim Nill, Erik Johnson, Gabe Landeskog, Lisa Merton, Ian Laperriere, Sylvia Garcia, Steve Harms, Dario Ronzone, Peter Forsberg, Roger Forsberg, Dave Reid, Ray Bourque, Pierre Lacroix, Charlie Lyons, Brian Kitts, Lou Personett, Marc Moser, Michael Farber, John Rolfe, Eric Yates, Ben Chodos, Buddy Oakes, Greg Wyshynski, Josh Cooper, Michael Russo, Steve Harms, Erin Durst, Craig Morton, Steven Winkler, Melissa Kretzmann, and my mother, father, and stepfather.

—Adrian Dater
December 2015